Katz *on* Dogs

Katz *on* Dogs

A COMMONSENSE GUIDE TO
Training and Living with Dogs

JON KATZ

RANDOM HOUSE TRADE PAPERBACKS
NEW YORK

2006 Random House Trade Paperback Edition

Copyright © 2005 by Jon Katz

Published in the United States by Random House Trade Paperbacks, an imprint of
The Random House Publishing Group, a division of Random House, Inc., New York.

RANDOM HOUSE TRADE PAPERBACKS and colophon are trademarks of
Random House, Inc.

Originally published in hardcover in the United States by Villard Books, an imprint of
The Random House Publishing Group, a division of Random House, Inc., in 2005.

Photographs by Peter Hanks

LIBRARY OF CONGRESS CATALOGING-IN-PUBLICATION DATA
Katz, Jon.
Katz on dogs: a commonsense guide to training and living with dogs / Jon Katz.
p. cm.
Includes bibliographical references
ISBN 0-8129-7434-4
1. Dogs—Training. 2. Dogs. I. Title.
SF431.K38 2005   636.7'0887—dc22   2005046209

Printed in the United States of America

www.atrandom.com

2 4 6 8 9 7 5 3 1

Book design by Susan Turner

For Orson,
who rescued me

Animals are a symbol of the rehumanization of society to the extent that they are allowed to function as members of the animal world, rather than as four-footed humans whose very nature is denied, and are permitted to bring their owners into that world of life, impulse, and love.

—BORIS LEVINSON,
Pets and Human Development

CONTENTS

I T'S 6:30 ON A STICKY, LATE-SUMMER MORNING AT BEDLAM FARM IN upstate New York. The sun will soon dry the wet grass and thin the mist drifting along the mountain rim before me. Although the flies and mosquitoes are still ferocious, the first golden leaves have appeared, a sweet hint of fall.

My dogs and I are deep along a shady forest trail near the farm, the two border collies exploding into the woods after chipmunks, squirrels, anything that moves—as always, finding work to do. In contrast, an energetic little puppy is chugging gamely along with a stick in her mouth, happy to stay close by my side. Although I've only had her a short time, I love her dearly. I think we needed each other—or, to be more precise, I needed her.

Clementine, a ten-week-old fat and happy yellow Labrador, has been on the farm for three weeks. It's going well. I've never picked a dog more carefully or thoughtfully. She is an appealing, almost irresistible opportunity to try out what I've learned, mixing research, experience, and my own evolving ideas about training.

Our simple stroll looks mundane, one of the many millions of walks countless dogs and humans take in America every day. But it's more than that; for me, it's a milestone, a benchmark, another length tacked on to a deepening journey into a life with dogs.

It signifies the painstaking progress I've made with one complex, troubled border collie who a couple of years ago couldn't walk even a few yards alongside me, and a second whose intensity could easily have made her impossible to live with as a pet. The puppy, seemingly so uncomplicated and eager to please, is actually my neediest dog. Newly arrived, fresh from the litter, she's in urgent need of direction, socialization, affection, and leadership in her still-strange environment with me, my family, my farm, and my other dogs. In these few weeks, much of her future and our relationship will be determined. We've struck a contract: I will show her how to live in the world; she will give back much more.

So it took a long time—years, really—for this peaceful woodland walk to happen. One only has to look at any park and see sheepdogs obsessed with Frisbees, frantic, out-of-control Labs, plus poorly trained rescue and shelter adoptees to know how enormous a struggle it is to live well with a dog, how easy it is to mess up these extraordinary creatures.

IF HAVING A DOG IS REWARDING ALMOST BEYOND WORDS SOMETIMES, IT can also be daunting, confusing, overwhelming. Dog lovers face countless decisions.

What kind of dog should I have? There are so many breeds and kinds. Can people work and have dogs? How often and for how long can they be left alone? Is it heartless to put a dog in a kennel? Should she come along on vacation? Will she miss us? Will she get lonely? *Do* dogs get lonely? Is it okay to have only one dog, or should he have company? But if he does, how can we handle a multi-dog household?

Which training method is best? How to housebreak and socialize? Are choke chains and shock collars okay? Are crates cruel? Do I need to play alpha dog and show her who's boss? Or should I be so positive that I never raise my voice? How can I exercise her in a lawsuit-crazy world where dogs are banned from almost every public place? How can I walk her instead of having her walk me? Does she need extracurricular activities?

What's normal, natural behavior for a dog, and what's aberrant? Should he have a vegan diet? Or an organic one? See ordinary vets or holistic and other alternative practitioners?

How can I teach him to be appropriate with people and other dogs? How do we know if he's aggressive? What if he bites somebody? Is it cruel to find a new home for a dog that isn't happy and is driving me crazy?

What are our dogs thinking, anyway? Are they really members of our family, children with fur? Can they really love and understand us, read our minds, know our moods? What is at the heart of this profoundly rich, ancient connection, the human-canine bond, perhaps the closest we humans will ever forge with another species?

What problems from our own lives do we bring to our relationships with dogs? Can we train and understand dogs without understanding ourselves?

How can we manage the dog love many of us feel—a powerful social and cultural force—yet keep our human lives in balance?

And, as we love dogs in more complicated ways and find separating from them increasingly difficult, one of the most fraught questions will inevitably arise: When should their lives end? Often that, too, is our decision to make.

These are some of the questions I want to address in this book.

To me, our late-summer walk represented a lot of research, a lot of talking and reading and thinking about and living through these issues. It also represented a lot of work—on sweaty days and freezing ones, through sunburn and bug bites, with patience, concentration, and observation—so much that it sometimes staggers me to think about it. I often screwed up, and still do regularly, and so do my dogs, but we never quit on each other.

I've had dogs around my whole life. When I was in fourth grade, I waited outside a school entrance on a bitter winter morning because a puppy was being given away to the first kid in line. I won and I lost: I got to take the dog home, but Lucky soon died from distemper. Next came Sam, the willful basset hound who pushed me out of bed on chilly nights, and King, my brother's German shepherd who rampaged through the neighborhood and brought home swatches from mailmen's pants. We never thought to deal with his attacks, nor did anybody suggest we should.

In that not-so-distant time, dogs lived on the periphery of family life, not at the center. They came and went, tormented milkmen and postal workers, scattered garbage, had riotous sexual encounters, never knew a leash, rarely saw a vet. They wandered great distances and sometimes came back, sometimes not. Today, many people would consider such treatment abusive.

Still, in my troubled family, dogs were very important to me; their memories still comfort and haunt. Students of the human-dog relationship have long understood that dogs are outlets for our affection, reflections of our own emotions, and these are among the reasons we treat them so uniquely in a society where detachment is commonplace. Dogs were a vital source of love and stability for me when I was young, and they still are. I've always felt a sense of gratitude and debt toward them.

I crossed from being a dog owner to a true dog lover in my forties, when I left corporate life to become a writer. I'd had a genial, allergy-ridden golden retriever named Clarence, bought from a pet store as a surprise for my baby daughter—a classically dumb way to acquire a dog.

Clarence, whose life ended after eight years due to severe kidney disease, was plagued by behavioral and health problems. Not that I had to deal with many of them: I went to work before dawn and returned late, and our relationship consisted mostly of weekend walks and some ear-scratching at night.

Everything changed when I began working at home and found a respected Labrador breeder in northern New Jersey. Two faithful yellow Labs, named Julius and Stanley, accompanied me lovingly and faithfully through that transition and into middle age. They were family dogs, but primarily my dogs; I took care of them and walked them. My first writing dogs, one or the other was lying at my feet beneath the desk for every word I wrote, just as my dogs are doing right now.

My dog life later entered a new phase when a Texas breeder sent me Orson (formerly named Devon), a frenetic, bothersome border collie who was in deep trouble and at first seemed untrainable, at least by me. From the moment I saw him, I loved this dog so much that I knew I had to learn more to help and keep him—and I did. No other dog had demanded so much from me, or changed me so profoundly. What I saw, heard, and discovered was fascinating. How little I knew about dogs—and, despite the great American love affair with canines, how few people, books, or theories could really help—was stunning.

My daughter has joked that if anyone ever writes my biography—which she considers extremely unlikely—it ought to be called *One Thing Leads to Another.*

Consider: Orson led me to write a book called *A Dog Year,* which steered my career in new directions. I used to be a mystery novelist, a media critic, a technology writer. Now I write, think, and talk about dogs—in books, in a column on Slate.com, in magazines, on a public radio show out of Albany.

Orson and a second border collie, Homer, brought me to sheepherding and introduced me to trainers, behaviorists, and dog lovers. Orson and Homer also led me to a farm in upstate New York, where I acquired a third, badly needed, border collie, Rose. Her strong herding lines and ferocious work ethic challenged and enriched me, and emboldened me to acquire sheep. It seemed a small step to add a couple of donkeys, plus a rooster and a few hens.

Working with Rose on the farm through a brutal winter was transformative. I grasped more fully the power of the bond between humans and dogs and our rich history of helping one another. I was living it.

Finally, things led to Clementine, Rose's biological opposite, as genial and accepting a creature as exists in the dog world. The border collies have intense concentration; Clem is easygoing. They are relentlessly busy; she relishes lying around, dozing by me as the collies rush from window to window, checking on traffic, sheep, clouds.

Along the way, I've acquired hundreds of studies and shelves of books on dog behavior and human attachment; had thousands of encounters and friendships with vets, trainers, breeders, rescue and shelter workers; met more dog owners and lovers than I can count. I've exchanged e-mail with dog people all over the country and—as translations of my books proliferate—all over the world. I've encountered readers on book tours, on the street, and at parks. Stories are the currency of dog lovers, who relish exchanging tales and pictures and memories of dogs come and gone. Few of these people would consider themselves trainers or behaviorists, yet they teach me a great deal every day.

Dogs occupy a major part of my life now, but I am eager to keep them from taking it over entirely or warping my perspective. My dogs are not my children, and I would hate for my daughter to ever think they are. I don't want my wife to believe my dogs understand me better than she does. I adore my dogs but they are not substitutes for humans. They function best in my life when they lead me toward, not away from, other people.

I remind myself continually that they are comparatively simple animals, really. Dogs think and feel in a primitive and sensory language we know little about; it is not our language and we can't communicate in it.

They don't speak to us, at least not in our terms, though we attribute all sorts of thoughts and motives to them. They have alien minds.

To forget or deny that dogs are animals is to fundamentally misunderstand them, and our relationships. It puts them in an unresolvable bind. We love them more and more, and increasingly bring them into our homes and emotional lives. Yet almost all their natural behaviors— running free, hunting prey, having sex, rolling in gross stuff, chewing whatever they come across, peeing wherever they feel like it—are either illegal or repellent. Dogs are the most loved and abused of creatures. Nearly seventy million of them are under the care of humans, but another ten million languish in shelters, most doomed.

People spend enormous sums to buy exotic purebred or designer breeds, while tens of thousands of other animal lovers have set up an elaborate nationwide system to rescue, transport, and "re-home" unwanted or mistreated dogs. Both types of dog people sometimes seem to know little about the species they're so involved with.

Something is seriously wrong with the process by which we acclimate our dogs. How many well-trained dogs do you know? Dogs jump on people, destroy furniture, bark obsessively, fail to respond to even the most elemental commands. They bite hundreds of thousands of Americans each year, including nearly five million adults who report bites to the police and more than 400,000 children who then require hospital visits.

Because dogs are too often acquired in the most thoughtless and impulsive ways, millions of owners abandon or effectively euthanize their dogs, shocked, angry, or disappointed that the pets in their lives rarely resemble the ones seen cavorting in dog-food commercials.

Bookstore shelves are stacked with training manuals and "idiot's guides," yet according to veterinary association statistics, only about 3 to 5 percent of Americans train their dogs at all. And those who do often quit along the way, and for understandable reasons. They are frustrated and confused.

When it comes to teaching and guiding our dogs, the overwhelming majority of us do a poor job. We blame them, yet they are blameless—and helpless. There is much talk in the dog universe these days about treating dogs in more egalitarian ways, more like humans. But can any relationship really be equal when one party is totally dependent on the other for its food and shelter, its literal survival? The responsibility and obligation is ours, not theirs. We need to ask more of ourselves.

Writing about dogs these past few years, I've become increasingly conscious of dog lovers' desperate, nearly poignant, search for help; for gurus and advisors, methods and guidelines, even psychics and channelers. They want to do better but often seem stumped.

A neighbor—a smart and decent man—proudly told me he housebreaks his dogs by tethering them for hours near their urine or feces. How about another idea? I suggested. Try feeding them in a crate, waiting fifteen or twenty minutes, then letting them outside and praising them when they go. He seemed shocked by the idea, but quickly embraced it.

Sometimes this disconnect isn't so funny. A merchant down the road kicks his mutt when a customer comes into the store, an attempt to teach the dog to stop jumping on people. How about tossing a liver treat over his shoulder instead when customers enter, I suggested, and saying "Off"? It took the proprietor ten minutes to impart this new notion successfully. "Great idea," he said. "Kicking was the way my dad always did it."

Both these men were intelligent, loved their dogs, and generally treated them well, but even smart people are often not so smart about dogs.

In fairness, who can blame them? I've been vaguely dissatisfied for years with what often seems the complicated, rigid, and generalized nature of training methods.

A kind of tyranny surrounds training. Experts and authorities tell dog lovers what they must always (or never) do. People struggle to comprehend these commandments, and so many come to feel foolish or frustrated or ineffective that they give up. They are busy and distracted, and their dogs seem unresponsive, uninterested, or just plain disobedient.

Sometimes the gap between what they want to accomplish and what they're actually teaching is almost comic. Trainer and author Patricia McConnell has written that when people yell "Be quiet" or "Shut up" at their barking dogs, the dogs think they are just joining in the fun, and bark all the more. How can we love dogs so much and settle for so little?

Sometimes these problems stem from poor breeding, or litter behaviors, or abuse; sometimes from owners' laziness or neglect. But even highly motivated dog owners often can't get the help they seek from manuals, classes, and the conventional wisdom passed around parks and vets' offices. One training study conducted by a veterinary pharmaceutical company found that of people who do attempt to train their dogs, more than 90 percent fail to meet their initial goals.

So many people have asked if I can recommend a helpful book or approach that I decided to try to write one myself: call it a Rational Theory of Dog Training.

Having brought Clementine to my forty-three-acre farm, a de facto laboratory for dog life and training, I wanted to come up with a brew of existing training methods, modified by my own instincts, observations, trials, and errors. For me, every new dog is an opportunity to do better. Training is the means, not the end.

I ought to make it clear that I'm not writing a book because I know everything about dogs. Quite the opposite—over thirty years, I've made almost all the mistakes you can in getting, training, and living with a dog. That's what gives me an acute sense of the need for a more rational, realistic, flexible, and useful approach.

I bought Clarence from a puppy mill. I loved him, and tried not to notice that he growled at children, suffered health problems, and died too young. I took in one stray found by friends of friends and never trained her at all. I got two show-quality Labradors who turned out to be overbred, and they, too, died quite young. I've given up a dog I loved because I screwed up his training so badly.

I've read dozens of training books, yet until recently I've trained my dogs in haphazard and random ways. I've yelled as I watched them chew up the house, eat furniture, and jump through windows. I've lost my temper, tossed sticks and choke chains. Over time, I came to realize my ignorance about what makes these beloved but misunderstood creatures tick.

When I took in my first and most disturbed border collie, I knew I had to learn more if I was going to keep him. Orson marked the real beginning of the reading, experimenting, and observing that led to a radically better relationship with my dogs and brought me to the point where I dare to share my failures and successes. But it was my fumbles, not my triumphs, that led me to undertake this book.

And my fumbles made me doubly determined to do well by Clementine.

TRAINING METHODS FAIL, I BELIEVE, IF THEY DON'T TAKE INTO ACCOUNT the owner's psyche as well as the dog's, and the particular environment in which both parties live. There's something almost sacred about the private space between a dog and its owner, something intimate. Dogs see us in our most unguarded moments. They see traits and actions we shield from other humans. It seems impossible to understand what a dog will need without knowing something of this relationship.

The person who trains his dog well isn't really seeking only to induce a creature to sit or lie down. Training isn't just about power or control; it's a dialogue between two species. The dog lover is literally forging his relationship with the animal, showing his dog how to live in the world.

When tiny Clementine first crawled onto my shoulder and licked my chin, I decided I had to work harder so that this dog's life would be easier, and my rewards greater. I had to listen to myself as well as to the authorities.

Training, I came to believe, is individual, idiosyncratic. Nobody can tell me how to train Clementine without knowing something about me, my family, and my animal-thronged environment.

I am a difficult man, impatient and distracted and easily frustrated. I make countless mistakes. I'm preoccupied and can barely remember to turn off the stove before I destroy a teakettle. Meanwhile, Clementine is curious, alert, and responsive.

But I am learning. These dogs have taught me much, as have other people's stories.

I believe strongly in the effectiveness of positive training, also known as "auto-training" or "positive capture": giving the dog a chance to succeed, then rewarding him, rather than yelling at his mistakes. It works for killer whales, why not dogs? We don't need to be pulling, shouting at, and shocking our dogs so much. Yet I am not an entirely positive person. I often lose my temper, speak to my dogs grumpily or impatiently, communicate my wishes poorly or imprecisely, and then get angry. If I'm having a bad day, the dogs are the first to know. I am continuously working on this, but I suspect these shortcomings will always be with me, just as other people will have their own handicaps.

Since I've communicated with so many people about their dogs in recent years, I asked dog owners in different parts of the country to train their dogs along with me—to talk through individual approaches to behavioral or other training problems and experiment together to see what works.

Tag, in Kentucky, was among those who enlisted. Her hunting dog wouldn't come, so she was about to head for her third obedience class.

"You're smart and you're creative, and you and your husband know that dog better than anybody," I urged her. "Sit down with your husband and come up with two or three things you absolutely know will get that dog to come to you."

Tag and her husband, Bob, remembered their dog—also named Bob—loved nothing more than searching for Bob when he ran around the corner of their house and hid in the shrubbery. "He always comes flying when Bob does that," she told me. Fine, I said. Have Bob run around the corner with some frozen meatballs. When the dog comes rocketing around, yell happily "Good come!" and toss some meatballs around. In two days Bob was coming to Bob 100 percent of the time. And why wouldn't he?

The dog was trained without even knowing it. There was little chance of failure, and the word "come" now had the best possible connotations—successful hunting and food, a far pleasanter association than screaming at a dog to come (so that the dog wants to do anything but). The best thing about Tag's strategy was that it came from her, not from me or anyone else. She did know her dog better than anyone.

So instead of feeling that she had failed at training her dog, she felt successful and confident, eager to move to the next level. Both Bobs were having a good time, too.

My volunteers agreed to compile lists of questions and training problems and to keep track of how they did with them. The results were fascinating and helpful. Some attempts succeeded and some didn't, but we learned something from each experiment. I am grateful to these people and their dogs. Their stories—successes and failures—are interspersed throughout the book. In some cases, the names and information about these volunteers have been changed at their request.

Although the concept of the abused dog has gained considerable attention in recent years, in many ways dogs in America are being treated better than dogs ever have been in terms of food, shelter, medical care, and affection. Most people want to do well by their dogs. They just need help and encouragement.

Before Clem arrived, I'd tried reading or rereading dozens of books by reputable trainers and dog observers. I can enthusiastically recommend many (and include a list later in the book), and even those I struggled with provided some insights or helpful advice.

Yet while each book or article had something to impart, none fully covered the nature of my life with Clem or Orson or Homer or Rose. As good as many of these books are, none really showed me how to train my dogs in a personal, rather than generic, sense. That was up to me.

I wrote this book in part because I believe we have a moral obligation to understand the species with which we have undertaken this extraordinary partnership.

This is not a detailed training manual. There are already plenty of those. Besides, I don't have all the answers for everybody. Primarily, I want to argue for an *approach* to living with dogs, a philosophy. Nowhere is that more critical than when it comes to training. The true motivation to train a dog well will never come from a book, but I believe I do have some ideas and experiences that might be of use.

If I were thinking of buying a book about dogs, I would wonder about the author's credentials. And when it comes to dog books, it's an especially valid question. There are so many books, and it's nearly impossible for readers to figure out who is qualified, or even what qualifications mean in this context.

Outside of academe and medicine, there are no universally accepted definitions or regulations that permit someone to claim expertise in dog behavior and training. I am knowledgeable mostly because I say I am.

After taking courses and working with herding and other dog trainers for several years, I joined the APDT (Association of Pet Dog Trainers). But almost anyone with interest and experience could do the same.

So why should anybody listen to me? I came to dog writing relatively late in life; my first ten books were novels and nonfiction books about other things.

But my journey into dogs and dog-human relationships has been both deep and intense for the past six years. I have intensively trained some difficult dogs and witnessed the training of scores of other people's. I've studied and practiced herding, interviewed and talked with hundreds of trainers, behaviorists, breeders, and vets, plus thousands of dog owners and lovers of dogs. I've attended a half dozen veterinary conventions and spoken at several others. I've read countless books, journals, and studies on the domestic dog.

I've spoken about dogs and human-animal attachment to a number of groups, including the American Psychiatric Association. My columns, articles, and radio shows, which generate lots of comment and exchanges with readers and listeners, have put me in contact with many thousands more. I now live with three working dogs on an active farm and am directly involved in the choosing, rescue, and training of many more. There is a lot of practical advice in this book.

When I began training dogs, I not only enjoyed it but found that I'd learned a great deal that I wanted to pass along. Still, I consider myself a writer about dogs more than a trainer of them.

I am no canine guru, and have no desire to be one. One of the points of this book isn't that I have all the answers but that I don't, and that nobody really does. Training doctrines can be awfully rigid. I believe that nobody can prescribe for you how to choose, train, and live well with a dog, but I feel certain I can help explain why it's wise to give such matters your thoughtful attention.

Those who claim omniscience about dogs and living with dogs are often failing their followers, which is why so few dogs are chosen wisely and trained at all, let alone successfully.

In this book, I try to pass along not only what I have experienced, and what I've seen and learned from others, but a way of thinking about dogs and our lives together. I mean to be not all-knowing, but useful. There's a big difference.

IN 1975, PIONEER BEHAVIORIST BORIS LEVINSON, AUTHOR OF *PET-Oriented Child Psychotherapy* and *Pets and Human Development,* wrote a *Forecast for the Year 2000* that has proved awfully prescient.

"Suffering from even greater feelings of alienation than those which are already attacking our emotional health, future man will be compelled to turn to nature and the animal world to recapture some sense of unity with a world that otherwise will seem chaotic and meaningless," Levinson predicted. "Animals will become junior partners and friends, effecting a revolutionary transformation of man's attitudes."

It's almost a job description of the powerful new role dogs are playing in many of our lives.

My hope is that this book can help people of good faith—and I meet many dog lovers who would do anything humanly possible to help their dogs—to do better.

We don't have to have dogs that chew up our houses. We shouldn't have to automatically medicate dogs for anxiety and depression and other human-like neuroses. We should not have to yell, kick, scold, or shock them into coming when called or otherwise living peaceably with us. We shouldn't have dogs biting millions of children and adults, or threatening other dogs and animals; such behavior endangers all dogs and our lives with them.

We shouldn't have to condemn millions of them to death because of our simplistic, ill-informed, and impossibly high expectations. We can live a life with dogs that's meaningful, loving, and as free as possible of anger, brutality, disappointment, failure, and frustration.

AFTER OUR MORNING WALK, THE DOGS AND I MAKE OUR EARLY FARM rounds, one of my favorite times of day. Each dog has a distinct role.

Rose races up the hill to find the sheep and bring them down. Orson and Clem stay outside the pasture gate. We fill the water tubs, put out the feed buckets for the sheep, count the herd, toss out pellets for the hens. I go into the barn to scoop some oats for the donkeys. Orson, as always, is a silent shadow, ever by my side; Clem searches for revolting things to eat.

I learned early on that we are always in training, even if we aren't explicitly having a training session, so I praise Orson for coming to me, applaud Rose for staying close, cheer Clem when she *isn't* eating donkey poop. One day—it might be years away—Orson will come instantly, Rose will walk right by my side, and Clementine will go twenty-four consecutive hours without throwing up. I have faith.

Working with these dogs has made me more patient, though I have quite a way to go. Meanwhile I clang the gate to the pasture shut, the signal for the dogs to gather, and we head into the house.

Each dog goes to his or her own bowl and waits for me to set down the food, a civilized approach I am enormously proud to have achieved. If anybody moves or lunges to the bowl, it goes back up onto the counter until he or she is still. Then we head back upstairs for a brief quiet period together before I shower and put on nonmuddy clothes and we plunge into our busy lives, together and separately.

Knowing the routine, by the time I walk upstairs the border collies are already curled at the foot of the bed. I help Clem up—she's still too small to make the jump—and after effusive greetings to Rose and Orson, whom she has not seen for at least a minute, she curls into a ball and plops down too.

For fifteen minutes—before a computer gets turned on, the phone rings, or anybody stops by—we lie in a silent, affectionate heap. If my wife, Paula, is at the farm (she commutes from the city), she's part of the heap. We stroke the dogs and get licks in return. Sometimes we all doze off again for a few minutes.

Like our walks, this pause seems a simple matter, hardly worthy of mention. But it means something. All three of my dogs arrived knowing how to do many things—run, bark, eat, chew, squabble, chase. None of them knew how to do nothing, how to remain calm and at ease. To stay and wait. In some ways, that may be the most valuable thing I'll ever teach them.

If a dog can be calm, he can hear you and pay attention. He can be called away from the street or from other dogs. He can wait while you work, and respect your time reading, watching TV, or being with friends or family. If a dog can be still, he can enjoy the peace we all seek, and spare himself scolding and punishment. If a dog can be your unobtrusive companion, he can learn to live harmoniously with other dogs and with his single greatest challenge: difficult, impatient, unknowing, and irrational humans. This will make him secure, and safer. He will be less likely to harm other animals or people. And less likely to be abandoned, abused, or returned by the people he coexists with.

And then we will all be happier.

JON KATZ
Hebron, N.Y.
September 2004

Katz *on* Dogs

WHY DO I WANT A DOG?

IT'S THE QUESTION PROSPECTIVE DOG OWNERS SHOULD ASK FIRST, perhaps the most important in anyone's life with a dog:

Why?

The most critical decisions about our lives with dogs are often made before we bring one home. Acquiring a dog in America is disturbingly simple. You can trawl online, find a breeder, or take one of the puppies some kid is offering outside the supermarket (I wouldn't advise it). You might come across a stray while out walking or driving.

Some people seek dogs for rock-hard practical reasons: security, hunting, therapy, search-and-rescue. But most of us, say psychologists and behaviorists, have more complicated emotional and psychological motives.

The more trouble humans have connecting with one another, the more they turn to dogs (and other pets) to fill some of the gaps. We seem to need to love and be loved in ways that are uncomplicated, pure, and dependable.

Contemporary America is, in many ways, a fragmented, detached society. Our extended families have moved away; we often don't know our neighbors; many of us hole up at night, staring at one kind of screen or another. Divorce is commonplace. Work has become unstable, uncertain for many, often unpleasant. Many people seem to find it easier to live and interact with dogs than with one another, and so the bonds between humans and dogs grow steadily stronger.

Yet this development in the relationship of these two species is onesided. Many dogs are well served by humans' deepening attachment, but the dogs can't make similar choices. It's human need that has spawned the great canine love affair.

Humans have decided to bring dogs into the center of their lives. For all the fussing about animal rights, dogs have none. They don't get to make consumer decisions. They're dependent on us for everything they need to survive. They can't talk back; they have no say about their environments or futures.

Although dogs have helped and worked with humans for thousands of years, it's only in recent decades that they've come to be seen as something other than (perhaps more than) animals. Pet-keeping was popular among the wealthy and powerful in medieval times, notes animal ethicist James Serpell in the book *Animals and Human Society: Changing Perspectives,* but it didn't acquire widespread respectability until the late seventeenth century, a time of growing enthusiasm for science and natural history and increased concern for animals' welfare.

Since then, our attachment to dogs has intensified significantly. We humans have never been closer to another species. We spend tens of billions of dollars on their care, feeding, and amusement; give them human names; talk to them as if they can understand us; believe we know what they are telling us in return.

This emotionalism often entangles dogs in our needs and wants. It is commonplace now, though it would have been shocking even a gen-

eration ago, to hear people say—without apology or embarrassment—
that they love their dogs more than they love most people, that they see
their dogs as members of their family, that they confide their most intimate problems and secrets to their dogs, who are more loyal and understanding than parents, spouses, lovers, or friends. Spending a few days
in a vet's office as part of my research for a book, I was amazed to hear
one woman after another urge, "Look, Doctor, I can live without my
husband, but you've got to save this dog!" Yet vets tell me they hear it
all the time.

And not just from women. Behavioral research shows that women
love dogs in part because they seem emotionally supportive yet complex, able to understand their owners in a profound though wordless
way. Meanwhile, men love dogs because they are perfect pals, happy to
go places and do things, but unable to hold or demand conversations.

Like it or not, our dogs' upbringings reflect our own. We tend to
treat our dogs the way we were treated, or the way we wish we'd been.
Either way, our own pasts profoundly shape our attitudes about dogs
and the ways we train and communicate with them.

This is usually an unconscious process. Few owners bring much
self-awareness to their canine relationships or reflect on their own families when they scream at their dogs to come, or coo at them as if they
understood. One school nurse I know grabbed her dog by the ears
every night when she came home, yelling, "Do you love me? Am I your
sweet mommy?" She wondered why the dog tried to run off during
walks.

So the motives for getting a dog become important, if you are worried about its welfare and want a good relationship. Is your answer to
the why-a-dog question that it's easier to seek companionship from a
dependent animal than from a person? Do you want a dog because of
subliminal messages from TV and movies? Are you more drawn to rescuing creatures than to training and living with them?

Do we discipline in ways we were disciplined, ask for the levels of
obedience and perfection demanded of us, criticize them in the voices
and words we heard? Are we reenacting old family dramas, trying to
heal traumas? Can we honestly say that we or somebody else in our

household is willing to take emotional responsibility for a dog, not only loving but training and caring for it?

A WOMAN NAMED SUSAN TOLD ME SHE WANTED A DOG BECAUSE SHE FELT unsafe in a gritty, impoverished neighborhood in Elizabeth, New Jersey. So she got an English mastiff so enormous that her landlord soon made her give him away, then a German shepherd named Thunder. The dog does effectively protect the house, charging the front door when strangers come by. But since Susan, who works as a New Jersey Transit conductor, concedes she is a poor trainer with little interest in working with the dog, she has to lock Thunder in the basement when friends or relatives visit. She's come home to find countless pieces of shredded mail; the dog understandably sees envelopes coming through the door slot as a menace. She's also had to replace scratched doors and broken windows.

By now, Thunder weighs ninety pounds and pulls Susan all over the sidewalk when she takes him out. The neighbors and their children are terrified of him, though he's never actually bitten or harmed anyone. The dog doesn't seem aggressive so much as conscientious; he is doing the job he was hired to do, a victim of his own effectiveness. But Susan, who says she loves Thunder, concedes that she never really wanted a dog for its own sake. She probably should have taken a self-defense course or called a security-alarm company instead. "It would be cheaper in the long run, and easier."

Understanding the reasons we want a dog is central to choosing the right ones, training them properly, living with them happily. The more we understand about ourselves, the better choices we are likely to make for both species.

When you think about it, you probably know plenty of people who complain that their dogs are too active or too sedentary, too interested in chasing squirrels or too distracted to come when called, too protective of the house or so nonthreatening they'd help carry out the valuables. Though the dog usually gets the blame, as often as not the owner made an unfortunate or ill-considered choice. Consequently, the dog is under pressure to be something other than what it is, while the humans have their hands full. With a little thought and research, the lives of dogs and their people can be a lot easier and more satisfying. But that does require some understanding of one's own psychology and emotions, some thought about where we are in our own lives and how our dogs fit in.

Jim, a hunter who lives near me in upstate New York, keeps three beagles in a large kennel 360 days a year. They emerge for a few morning hours on the other five days to track game. They spend a lot of time waiting, but when their time comes, they shoot out of the kennel and into the woods. "They are great dogs," says Jim, who hasn't even named them.

Does he like having them? I asked him once. "When they do their jobs I do," was his response. I feel reflexively sorry for the dogs when I drive by, especially when I consider my own dogs' pampered lives, but Jim's dogs, while they're loud, don't seem to know they are deprived.

Not all dogs could live that way. But Jim's beagles demonstrate the startling adaptability of dogs. They're there to hunt, period. Jim has a wife and four children to whom he's devoted, and he's busy with his construction firm; he doesn't need dogs to be his hobby or his confidants.

Once a day, he heads out to the kennel with a bucket of meat and leftovers and tosses the contents into the kennel. At Christmas, he adds a bucket of biscuits. They get all their shots, and see a vet if they're ailing. The beagles have never been inside his home. He speaks of them proudly and fondly, but they're tools, like a drill or a new rifle, not little people, not even really pets in the contemporary sense.

Yet the dogs seem content and healthy. Jim knows precisely why he wants them. They understand the simple rules and, since dogs lack human awareness of the passage of time, don't know how long they go between hunts. It may not be the way many of us would wish to have dogs, but his clarity about the kinds of dogs he wants and why seems to work well for everyone involved.

Then there's Andrea, an artist who lives on a fifty-acre farm in Vermont. For various complex reasons, she's given up on the idea of men, marriage, a family; instead, she sought out a collie rescue group. She, too, understood exactly why she wanted a dog, and the bond she's formed with hers appears to make them both happy.

"I have not been fortunate with relationships, at least not yet," she says. "But Whisper and I adore each other. I have so much fun with her, and she gives me so much comfort and love. I hope she's a bridge to another relationship, but if she isn't, I'll be okay."

It isn't for me to say—and in truth I can't really decide—whether Andrea made a wise or healthy choice. But she thought about her motives, about how a dog would fit into her life, and she made a considered decision.

"Because my kid's been begging for one" is, on the other hand, usually a suspect reason to acquire a pet. It's a common refrain, but dogs bought as Christmas surprises for demanding children often have a rough time of it. Promises get made and forgotten; interest in the newcomer peaks, then wanes.

Not always. A twelve-year-old neighbor of mine asked for a golden retriever last year for Christmas and his parents agreed, on the condition that Jeremy take responsibility for it. Perhaps they had confidence that he actually would because he'd already proved his commitment by feeding his fish and cleaning out hamster cages.

In any event, Jeremy does take care of Clancy. He walks him before and after school, feeds him, brushes him, takes him to training classes every Saturday. Each day after school, Jeremy and Clancy train together. The dog has learned to come when called, to sit, stay, and lie down on command. People in rural areas familiar with 4-H programs know how healthy it can be for children to take responsibility for animals. People in child- and dog-crazed suburbs—where the rule often seems to be, the smaller the yard, the bigger the dog—know how unusual it is. For Jeremy, getting a dog does seem like a positive thing; he kept his word, or perhaps his parents took the unusual step of insisting that he keep it. Either way, I've encountered few kids like him. Parents, beware: somebody in a household has to take primary responsibility for a dog, and if the kids don't, Mom or Dad has to step in.

Parents often give their kids things they think are good for them—cell phones, computers, dogs—without much thought about how these things will be used or treated after the purchase.

So why *do* you want a dog?

If the answer, in part, stems from a complex emotional history (as is certainly the case with me), make sure you understand and think through just what it is you are asking of a pet.

DESPITE OUR HABIT OF ANTHROPOMORPHIZING DOGS, THEY DON'T understand what we're thinking and can't possibly grasp the nuances of the emotional roles we sometimes ask them to fill. They can't even behave amiably—by our definitions—if not properly chosen, exercised, and trained. Since our expectations are usually much too high, we become easily disappointed or angry. There's substantial evidence that we're *creating* problem dogs—biters, chewers, barkers, neurotics in need of antidepressants. This happens partly because so many people get the wrong dogs at the wrong times for the wrong reasons.

There's a moral component to taking on a dog. Though they aren't capable of higher-level thought processes, dogs certainly have emotions. They experience pain and loss, fear and affection. This has given them and other animals some moral standing among people of conscience. It may not make them the equivalent of children, but it does obligate us to think about how we treat them. But every dog isn't *for* everyone. I don't accept the growing, politically driven notion that every dog is equally deserving of rescue, that all dogs are essentially alike in their adaptability to our tense, crowded, litigious human environment.

I don't find that to be true. Dogs are ferociously idiosyncratic, varying wildly depending on breed, genetics, litter experience, treatment, and environment. Some are genial and calm, bred for temperament, and some are violent, bred and trained to hunt or fight. Few of us have the training skills or time to alter all of those behaviors. The wrong choice of dog can prove a nightmare for you, your family, and your community; the right one, a joy.

Some dogs need to work, some don't; some will hide from thunder while others won't even notice it; some hate people in hats and others chase bikes. You can't always know these oddities in advance; all the more reason to proceed with caution.

THE BEDLAM FARM CHECKLIST FOR
PROSPECTIVE DOG OWNERS

■ *Get the dog you want.* The abuse of animals in general, and dogs in particular, has led lots of owners to the conviction that the only moral option is to save a dog from a pound, where he faces euthanasia. It can be a wonderful experience to rescue a dog (my rescued border collie Orson is lying beneath my desk), but, like dog ownership itself, it's not for everybody. It can also be a wonderful experience to find a great dog from a good breeder. I have two of those, as well: one herds sheep and runs my farm, and the newest, Clem, suffuses my home and life with sweet companionship. I smile almost every time I look at her.

Nobody can dictate what kind of dog you ought to get, certainly not I. You've got to take care of it, so find one that you're likely to love.

But do your homework.

Even with forethought, it remains something of a crapshoot. Dogs bought in pet stores likely come from puppy mills—high-volume breeding operations where inbreeding creates and perpetuates health and temperament problems. According to studies cited by editor James Serpell and his colleague J. A. Jagoe in *The Domestic Dog,* dogs obtained from pet stores are much more likely to exhibit social fears and dominance-type aggression than dogs from breeders or shelters.

Many rescue and shelter dogs have behavioral problems, through no fault of their own. They've been abused, traumatized, or repeatedly re-homed, to the point that, according to the University of Pennsylvania School of Veterinary Medicine, they're much more likely to have problems like compulsive chewing, aggression, barking, overeating, and what humans call "separation anxiety," than purebreds from quality breeders.

Responsible rescue groups and shelter workers not only acknowledge this but make sure adopters understand it, so that the dogs don't bounce back or, worse, suffer mistreatment or injure others. But I've encountered some rescue workers—suffused with passion for and dedication to needy dogs—who are too eager to move violent or troubled dogs into mainstream homes.

And even dogs from conscientious breeders are shaped by their mothers and siblings, so that some are damaged, fearful, and cowering, while others learn to feel safe and trusting. Plenty of unscrupulous or greedy breeders mass-produce dogs for cosmetic or commercial reasons, without regard to health or temperament history. Since the dog universe is almost completely unmonitored and unregulated by overwhelmed, underfunded local governments, people who want dogs are truly on their own. That's why it's a good idea to ask breeders and rescue groups for references, so you can see how their other dogs have worked out.

It's dicey to make dog selection a moral or political act. Know that if you choose a rescue dog, he or she may need particular patience and skill. Most dogs can be trained or retrained, even at older ages, but if you're not willing or able to make the consistent commitment of time and work, a different sort of dog may suit you better. Getting a purebred dog when there are so many needy dogs in shelters is still, to my mind, a perfectly valid option, and sometimes the better one.

■ *Impulsiveness is your worst enemy when it comes to bringing a dog into your home.* Take your time. Don't decide on a dog because you saw one you liked on a TV show or walking down the street. Or to surprise your kids, or your empty-nesting parents, or because you heard a breed is smart. Border collies are smart, but they do unspeakably stupid things, like trying to herd garbage trucks. A smart dog isn't necessarily a great pet, anyway. I was neither amused nor philosophical when Orson figured out how to open the refrigerator and remove an entire chicken.

■ *Lower your expectations.* The pups frolicking on lawns in dog-food commercials are beautiful, but odds are you will acquire a real dog. Real puppies have accidents during housebreaking training, mistake carpets for lawns, chew things you treasure. Real dogs roll in deer scat and then hop onto the couch. They need shots and medications; they get sick.

Real dogs may never get much of a chance to bound alongside you through the park. Because so many dogs are so badly trained, they make non–dog lovers increasingly uneasy. Cops all over the country write tickets for people who walk dogs unleashed. Dog owners get sued for their pets' bites, even for menacing behavior. Insurance companies increasingly check to see which breed of dog you have, and cancel policies if they don't approve. Some animal-rights groups believe dogs should be given greater legal status, almost equal with humans'. Some don't believe humans should be allowed to "own" a dog at all. But the Rational Theory of Dog Training emphasizes the responsibilities of ownership.

■ *And these responsibilities can seem unremitting.* Dogs need to go out even when it's pouring and freezing. They need attention, affection, stimulation, and exercise, even when you're tired, busy, or not in the mood. Their needs don't abate when you want a weekend off or if you stay late at the office.

Informed dog lovers expect these problems and navigate them with humor and patience. In return, they get much love, fun, and companionship. There are conflicts and rewards in any relationship, human or canine. I believe in taking a long view when it comes to dogs. You need to see beyond the moment, especially when you are on the floor at three A.M. dabbing at the carpet with Nature's Miracle, trying to remove the odor.

The long view only comes with understanding the nature of these animals, and accepting that even with great effort they won't always mesh with ours.

■ *Beware the abuse excuse.* Just a decade ago, dogs were still "adopted," not "rescued," an even more emotionally charged notion. More dog owners than I can count now introduce or describe their dogs with the phrase: "She was probably abused." When I ask how they know, the evidence is often circumstantial, at best.

Be cautious if the desire to save a dog from abuse is the primary reason you want one. There are lots of ways to express humanity and empathy, for people or animals, but this particular animal is moving into your home. If you misread your own purposes or make erroneous assumptions, both of you will be coping with the aftermath for years.

Steven R. Lindsay, in his seminal two-volume *Handbook of Applied Dog Behavior and Training,* explores assumptions made about abuse in the acquisition of dogs.

Fear of human contact and other avoidance behaviors can sometimes be traced to previous mistreatment, Lindsay acknowledges. But shelter workers are quick to invoke that explanation when they talk to prospective adopters, without knowing whether it's true. "Undoubtedly, physical and emotional abuse occurs and may be a significant cause of fear," Lindsay writes. "However, it probably occurs far less often than one might expect from the frequency of such reports."

Since dogs can't correct us, or complain about their

parents, it's simple to assume that they're victims of human cruelty, an idea that also often fits our own emotional needs and histories. But genetics, inbreeding, and conditions in a litter, among other factors, can also profoundly shape a dog. Most of the time, we will never really know—a reality that may prove less satisfying than a rescue fantasy. Would you love this dog as much if you knew that she was fearful because she was insufficiently socialized as a puppy?

■ *Be skeptical of yourself and expect skepticism in the people you're getting a dog from.* Good breeders and conscientious rescue and shelter workers will be wary of your wish for a dog, even to the point of obnoxiousness. They'll ask about your schedule, yard, fence, kids, dog-owning experience—and they should. In fact, if they don't, take it as a warning sign that you might be seeking a dog in the wrong place. So many people know so little about dogs when they get one or have such unrealistic expectations that millions of dogs are mistreated, returned, or abandoned each year. The people who distribute them have seen a lot, too much sometimes. You don't want a dog from someone eager to give or sell you one without asking some tough questions.

■ *Know yourself.* People tend to blame dogs when problems arise, but they are almost always our fault. Either we made a dumb choice (bringing a huskie to a condo in Boca Raton), or we don't really have the time and personality for training a dog, or we took refuge in fantasies.

Most likely, you're getting a dog because you need or want something to love, or another thing to love, or because you'd like to replace things you love that are gone. There's nothing wrong or troubling about that, but it does a dog no service to repress or deny it by insisting, "I got a dog for the kids" or "I just got it to keep burglars away."

And does that desire to love outweigh other characteristics? Are you patient? Do you have a high tolerance for noise, disorder, and tumult? Do you prize clean rugs and furniture? Or sleeping late on Sundays? Do you anger easily? Getting a dog is a big, expensive, life-altering decision that affects you for years.

■ *Dogs are not human, remember.* They don't think in human words or terms. They can't tell stories, follow narratives, read our minds (although they do sense our moods). They are not "children with fur," or children at all. We may love them to death, but that doesn't mean they're like us.

In fact, most dog owners love them because they're *not* like us. To deny them their dogness is a disservice to both species. To forget that they are animals, driven largely by instinctual desires for each other and for food, sex, and attention, is to alter the reality of their natures, and to endanger them.

■ *Dogs aren't therapists, either.* Your relationship with the dog will likely be affected and shaped by your own family history and emotional past, but the dog's ability to heal old traumas or fill voids is limited. People will tell you that their dogs understand their innermost thoughts and know their deepest secrets, but don't dump your emotional baggage on an animal. If you need help with problems, major or minor, get it. If your dog understands you better than your husband or wife, give the dog a bone, then go see a marriage counselor, or at the very least have some discussions with your spouse. Don't ask your dog to make you happy or treat your depression. Your dog's thoughts probably center on when you're going to get off your butt and feed him.

■ *Dogs are increasingly being seen as sagacious spirits and prescient souls.* The Rational Theory doesn't buy it. The simpler your relationship with a dog, the better, because dogs are simple. They love rules, routine and clarity, leadership, intriguing smells, other dogs, and, of course, food and the people who provide it. One of the cornerstones of the Rational Theory: Your dog is crazy about you, but he can also learn to love almost anyone else holding a hamburger.

■ *A bedrock notion of my approach to living with dogs is that we need to be realistic, flexible, and creative, harder on people but easier on dogs.* Expect a lot of yourself in terms of patience, determination, and consistency. As you are, the dog will follow suit. Try not to think in terms of "good" and "bad" dogs. These are human notions that do not apply to animals. There are, instead, dogs that understand how to live in the world and dogs that don't. Occasionally, dogs are inherently violent, genetically damaged, or mistreated beyond repair. Happily, they're rare.

A CAUTIONARY TALE

ACQUIRING A DOG IS A FAR MORE SEMINAL EVENT IN A PERSON'S OR family's life than the purchase of a plasma-screen TV or an SUV. Yet people will spend weeks or months test-driving cars, researching models and prices on the Net, gawking in parking lots. Then they'll buy a dog—a living thing who will be with them for years, often at great expense—having done no research, and with nothing ready but a bag of dog food. Dog and owner both pay for this, one way or another.

Hence my trepidation about Kyle, a TV producer who called to tell me he'd decided to adopt a border collie from an upstate shelter to share a one-bedroom Brooklyn apartment with him and his wife. "They're the smartest dogs, I hear. And this one is beautiful. I don't want to see him put down. I believe in helping dogs."

It was an admirable impulse but a poor choice, for man and dog. Millions of dogs fill our shelters, and it would be wonderful to adopt all of them. But a border collie isn't likely to thrive in a cramped, urban environment. I worried that Kyle was more interested in feeling righteous than in choosing the right dog.

A bad decision, I cautioned him. Border collies need a lot of work and exercise. They often go mad, almost literally, when they have nothing to do or are confined in a tiny space. And both Kyle and his wife worked long hours in Manhattan.

"Oh, we have a way with dogs," he said airily. "We'll work it out." He didn't want to hear any objections. He'd heard that border collies were smart, so he wanted one, an impulse outweighing the best interests of both parties, a common story to anyone who spends time with dogs. The shelter, however, had the good sense to refuse to give him the dog.

Two days later, he was back on the phone. "There's a pit bull here in the Brooklyn shelter. They say he has problems with kids and dogs, but he might be okay with training. I bet I can turn him around. I bet he's not a bad dog." Another troubling choice. Pit bulls are not bad dogs, of course, but they're dangerous if treated poorly or in the wrong hands. Did Kyle really have the time and skill to work with a pit bull with a history of aggression? I asked. His neighborhood was full of kids and dogs. While he was filling out the paperwork, the dog bit a shelter volunteer and was deemed too dangerous for adoption.

"Why do you want a dog?" I finally asked Kyle, noting his confusion and impulsiveness.

"I just like dogs," he said.

Soon he was clicking around Petfinder.org, a nationwide online clearinghouse for rescue groups, where he learned of a Boston terrier available in North Carolina. The local rescue group, which operated out of a basement in a private residence and about which Kyle knew nothing, had only had the dog for a couple of days, but he seemed "nice and friendly and housebroken," the website declared.

That was enough for Kyle, who rushed to the rescue, driving through the night to meet the dog and a member of the rescue group about halfway, in Norfolk, Virginia. This time he didn't ask for my advice, and I didn't offer any.

I heard from him a month later. The dog barked for hours when left alone and wasn't, in fact, housebroken, traits that didn't endear him to Kyle's apartment-house neighbors. He was friendly enough with people, but not with other dogs, so he was soon barred from the local dog run. He had to be walked wearing a muzzle. "He's got problems," Kyle acknowledged.

It was hard to imagine a happy ending. The last I heard, Kyle had confined the terrier to a corner of the kitchen, and had just bought a citronella spray collar, a device that sprayed what is, to dogs, a noxious scent whenever he barked. What happened thereafter, I don't know. It's usually good news when a dog is rescued, but this was the canine equivalent of Russian roulette.

I've made errors of judgment myself, and I've tried to learn from them. The three dogs in my current household all came from breeders, Rose and Orson from Wildblue Border Collies in Falcon, Colorado, and Clementine from Hillside Labradors in Pawlet, Vermont. Breeders Deanne Veselka and Pam Leslie spent countless hours talking with me, helping me choose dogs.

When it came to Rose, I already knew I was buying a farm with enough acreage for a flock of sheep, so I wanted a dog with working lines, one I could train to herd on my own, away from the oppressive dos and don'ts of the herding and training worlds. I wanted to make my own mistakes, experience my own triumphs, work free of scrutiny and second-guessing. I wanted to trust my dog, give her the chance to do her work by following her instincts.

I wanted a partner to help me move animals around and run a farm. She didn't need to be cuddly or terribly social. I didn't picture her snuggling on the sofa with me, although she sometimes does. I imagined her as my primary working dog.

This suits Rose's serious, businesslike demeanor. She's not all that interested in creatures without fleece, but she's always ready to work, whether that means herding sheep or chasing water from the garden hose. Understanding her role and her nature has made our mutual tasks clear and her training easier. Rose is the only one of my dogs who works with sheep.

It's different with Orson, my elder border collie, who is and will al-

HOLD THEM

ways be my soulmate. He wants little more than to stay by my side, and except when Rose and I are working, I'm always happy to have him there. Orson is a handful, complex and excitable. I have worked with him for years, and will likely work with him for many more, but we're pretty close to the outer limits of how far we can go with our training. He bears the emotional scars of a tense and fearful early life.

Still, he's made remarkable progress. He seems at ease, clear about his role in my life and on the farm, confident of the rules. Sometimes, for brief periods, he will sit on the farmhouse's front lawn by himself, gazing out over the valley and its patchwork of cornfields and pasture. He does not see me peering out the window at him, smiling.

After Orson and Rose, I found myself wanting—perhaps needing—a calmer, easier dog. I pictured a dog for whom two or three leisurely walks a day would constitute plenty of exercise, a writing companion who'd happily curl up under my desk rather than feel the need to monitor every passing bird, chipmunk, or truck from the window. Conscious of coming from a troubled family marked by turmoil and discord, I wanted more affection. Training a dog gently and well is a powerful experience for me, a truly healing one.

Developing a clear notion about why I wanted each dog made it much easier to find him or her and greatly increased the odds that our lives together would be mutually rewarding. Knowing the breeders and the breed well also helped. Orson was a rescue whose training forced me to be a better human being. Rose was my working associate, my right hand on the farm. Clem was a loving lie-around dog who, as working dogs do, quickly sensed her true role and was happy to fill it. At nine weeks, she crawled onto my lap and dozed through an entire Yankees game. Then I went outside to herd sheep with Rose. Next morning, when I settled into my office to write, Orson was wrapped around the chair leg. I am a lucky man.

The lessons learned from years with dogs are beginning to take hold. I know why I want dogs now, and I know what sorts of dogs can provide what I need. I try to do the same for them.

Everyone has to make individual decisions about these things. I want dogs in part because they force me to step outside myself. I wouldn't write about dogs or have a farm if not for Orson, or sheep if not for Rose. Clem speaks to a very personal need to give and get affection. Knowing that helps us live together happily.

When Orson came to me, I was shocked at how little I really knew about dogs. Now I know a bit more, and I've come to believe that the more we think about why we want them, the more likely we are to get the dogs we want.

WHEN YOU'VE FIGURED OUT WHY YOU WANT A DOG, IT'S TIME for Round Two: choosing the perfect one.

The rule about Americans and dogs seems to be that we love them more and more all the time, and know less about them than ever. For dogs, that's a dangerous situation.

We are busy people with acquisitive natures, little patience, fickle tastes, manipulated consumer instincts, lots of distractions, and scant free time. We are often sold things on the basis of convenience. We're used to guarantees and refunds. If we don't like a toaster, we return it. Things we acquire are supposed to work out; if they don't, we replace them. More bad news for dogs, and one of the primary reasons millions languish in shelters. The greatest danger they face is us, and our ignorance.

In contemporary cultural depictions—TV shows, Disney movies, soft-focus dog-food ads—dogs offer lots of personality and demand very little. They are unfailingly genial, happy, loyal, and intelligent. You can't smell dogs in movies or commercials. They not only don't pee on your new carpet, they don't seem to eliminate at all. All they want to do is bound along, preferably in slow motion. Unlike my dogs, they never dash off after chipmunks, sneak food out of children's strollers, or vomit. When they appear in your spotless kitchen for their miracle chow, they never dribble any onto the floor.

Disney dogs love you so devotedly that, should you both become lost in the Arctic, they will trudge hundreds of miles through the snow, facing grueling and dangerous challenges, risking all to bring help. They have a knack for locating missing children. They can probably perform CPR, too. (My own dogs, dropped off in the wilderness, would find the nearest deli.)

When you talk to these dream dogs, they tilt their heads in that adorable way of perfect dogs, fully grasping your meaning, then quickly doing whatever you want. You never see such a pet in the act of being trained, apparently because none of them need it: they come fully equipped. If you are blue, they intuit it and bring you a bone or toy, dropping their heads in your lap and gazing at you soulfully until you smile and feel better. No wonder everybody wants one.

The sad news is that they don't exist offscreen. If studios made movies about the lives of real dogs, we probably wouldn't own nearly so many. Our culture celebrates the ideal of the tidy, low-maintenance (yet heroic) canine. I haven't read a novel about a dog who has diarrhea, though I could probably write one.

One of my crew herded a blind patron's guide dog right out of a bookstore and under a truck in the mall parking lot. Another has actually thrown herself onto the blades of a snowplow.

Various of my dogs have jumped through (closed) windows, wandered off for heart-stopping hours, and eaten every kind of clothing. The thought of having my carpets tested for organic life-forms is unsettling. Paula and I are expert at picking dog hair out of clothes, bed linens, even our teeth.

And from the tales I hear from people I've met and from my e-mail correspondents, I'd say my dogs nevertheless score on the higher end of the dog behavioral scale.

The problem with finding the perfect dog is that there's no such thing.

But there are dogs that will suit you or won't, that will fit more easily into your life or will cause major disruptions. If there's no perfect dog, let's shoot for something realistic: the least imperfect dog, the one that will maximize your pleasure in his companionship and minimize the associated problems, hereafter known as the Right Dog for You.

SHELTER VERSUS BREEDER

WERE IT UP TO ME, I'D REMOVE THE POLITICS FROM THE EQUATION. GO for a dog, not a politically correct, or morally justifiable, dog. It's a phony distinction. Both purebred and rescue dogs need good homes. I've seen trial and agility dogs in as much trouble with hellish owners as shelter dogs. Some people find it strange to buy a dog when so many are available for free and in danger of being euthanized, and I think they're correct in many ways, but this approach is too simplistic.

I'd consider both options, ruling out neither. The director of a rescue group I know well supplied the following example, followed by another from my own recent experience.

CASE STUDY: *Sheila and Crackers*   SHEILA D'ALESSANDRO, AN accountant at a giant firm in Manhattan, did it right.

She lives in Bloomfield, a working-class New Jersey suburb about fifteen miles west of New York City. Bloomfield feels congested, its houses and apartments built cheek by jowl, its streets clogged with traffic, its bustling downtown surrounded by highways. The town was built in the twenties and thirties and, like most suburbs, not with thousands of dogs in mind. A town ordinance against excessive barking can result in a costly citation. In its parks, laws forbid dogs to be walked off-leash.

So dog lovers meet in secret early-morning groups to let their dogs run; the police usually look the other way if no one complains. Invariably, though, somebody eventually *does* complain and the groups dissolve. Enough people in town have been bitten or, in rougher neighborhoods, where drug dealers operate, been menaced by aggressive dogs, that the police come and write tickets. Like many towns in America, Bloomfield is not an easy place for man or dog.

Yet Sheila grew up with dogs and wanted one ever since she graduated from college. But she either had roommates or lived in tiny apartments until, a couple of years ago, she and her husband bought a small house—a two-story Colonial with a narrow backyard. Even then, she hesitated. She catches a 6:40 A.M. train into the city and returns on the 6:15. Once or twice a week—more often during tax season—she works later. "I was worried about getting a dog under those conditions," she says. "I didn't think it would be humane."

Then her husband died of bone cancer at a shockingly young age. She was devastated and, as the months passed, isolated. "I wasn't in any shape to start dating again, but it was hard to be alone. I began to think more and more about a dog," she recalls. Sheila kept seeing photos of appealing-looking dogs in the local weekly, ads placed by the town shelter. "I believe strongly in rescuing rather than buying dogs," she says. "But I also wanted to be careful, to be fair to me and the dog, and to my neighbors, too."

Several of her friends had dogs, and visiting them was often unpleasant. The dogs lunged eagerly at whoever walked through the door, begged for food during dinners, barked for hours. "I didn't want a situation like that."

So, perhaps because of her financial training, Sheila pursued the adoption idea with organization and precision. After visiting several Humane Society websites and dog-lover mailing lists, she drew up a research plan and a reading list.

She decided to tour area shelters, a different one each Saturday. Online, she scoured breeder and rescue sites like Petfinder.org to "see just what was out there." She was stunned at the range of dogs up for adoption in every corner of the country.

She dropped by several nearby obedience classes to see how other people's dogs were doing, how much was involved in training. The visits were sobering. "I saw a lot of people trying, but not succeeding. Their dogs were all over the place, barking, jumping, fighting with other dogs. Nobody had much time to talk one-on-one with the trainer. Some people told me they were probably going to quit, or that this was the third or fourth class they'd taken." The humans felt frustrated or discouraged, and few of their dogs could come, sit, stay, or even pay attention. "It made me realize, 'Whoa, you better take this seriously. It might be more complicated than you think.'"

Sheila didn't have a lot of spare time. Her days were long and her commute arduous, and she often brought work home. "But I decided to make the time, so that if I got a dog, I would know what to do, how to avoid mistakes."

She estimates she also talked or visited with half a dozen vets or their assistants. "They were amazingly helpful," she found. "They all made time to talk with me and said it was much better to ask questions *before* you get a dog, not after."

It wasn't long into her research that Sheila decided she wouldn't get a dog, any dog, for at least six months, no matter what she saw or who called. She knew she'd be seeing and hearing about a lot of needy, appealing pets. "But I didn't want to make a decision that way," she says. "This was important. I'm a single woman working in the city. I saw pretty quickly that this could be a nightmare as well as a happy story, and I'd had enough nightmares."

In all this, she is unusual. Few dog owners I've met feel, as Sheila did, that they can and should control the process, rather than act on impulse.

The trap was believing that every dog she saw was going to die unless she brought it home. "It might or might not be true," she says, "but my odds of finding the right dog for me in my circumstance depended on being careful, doing the work."

People did call—the vet's offices passed on information about dogs they knew who needed homes, and so did neighbors, relatives, shelter workers. A woman even showed up at Sheila's door with a puppy, and her mother called with news of a friend's litter. "Once people knew I was looking for a dog, everybody seemed to have one in mind. There are so many; it's hard to say no all the time." If she ever did it again, Sheila decided, she wouldn't tell anyone about her plans; she'd conduct her research in secret.

ONCE SHE HAD A GRASP OF THE POTENTIAL PROBLEMS, SHE REALIZED SHE needed to know more about types and breeds. "If you can figure out what the breedlines are, what the mix is, you can get a better sense of what you might be getting, even from a shelter."

Sheila also considered her environment. Most of her neighbors had kids. Her mother was in her sixties and had a bad hip. Her sister, to whom she was close, had two small children, one just a toddler.

Taking the long view—seeing beyond the quick thrill of an instant rescue or the joy of bringing home a gorgeous pup—she realized that as a single, working woman with close family ties, living in a populous neighborhood, she had people other than herself to think about. Unlike many dog owners, Sheila thought about them.

"With my life, I would need help, someplace the dog could stay when I was away or terribly busy, people who could help me care for him." The environment dictated choice of breed as well. Sheila wasn't in a position to rescue one of the pit bull or rottweiler mixes that filled local shelters. The training and retraining required would be too consuming. "I know they aren't bad or mean dogs naturally, but I just didn't want a dog people would be afraid of. I wanted a dog people want to come up to and pet, one I could trust. I had my nieces and nephews to think about—we all spend most Sundays together. My mom isn't so strong; I don't want her having to deal with a dog that will drag her around the neighborhood if she tries to walk it. When I have friends over, I don't want them rolling their eyes about my out-of-control dog."

Out of this process, she developed a list of characteristics. She still wanted a shelter dog. She didn't feel it was necessary to own a purebred, and she felt confident there were enough adoptable dogs to choose from, especially with the Internet as a backup. Besides, she felt better saving a dog than buying one.

She wanted an older dog, too. She couldn't be home enough to train a puppy properly, she feared. "The smarter thing was to get a dog that was already trained," already neutered and housebroken, past most of the chewing and teething phase, settled—yet still in its prime with years of healthy life ahead. A dog between the ages of two and four, she figured.

And not a large one. "I don't have any place for a dog to run. And I don't care what anybody says, these big retrievers need to run—I learned that from reading and talking to vets, and from watching them go nuts at obedience class. Some dogs are okay with less exercise, but mine has to handle being inside much of the day." That, she realized, ruled out some of the most popular breeds—Labs, golden retrievers, beagles.

Her dog had to have an easygoing temperament. Sheila decided she would temperament-test her dog, a service offered by some vets and animal-welfare groups and trainers for free, or for a reasonable charge. To gauge a dog's disposition and response to stress, trainers or vets check its reactions to children and other dogs and to strange situations like being suddenly poked or pulled, or having its food interfered with.

"Getting a rescue dog means you don't really know its history," she reasoned. "A lot of these dogs are abused, or at least people say they've been abused, and that can cause training problems. If you're careful, you can check out the temperament and not bring a dog home that you love but that is gonna terrorize your neighbor's kids. I want other people to love my dog, too."

The picture of her life with a dog was growing clear. The remaining step, before setting out in search of this fellow, was to develop a support system. Sheila located a neighborhood dog walker who'd be available to take the dog out during the day, when she was in the city, and again at night if she was working late. Her sister agreed to provide doggie day care now and then, assuming the dog was trustworthy around her kids. So did her mother, and a neighbor two doors down.

Meanwhile, Sheila made a list of the things she would need: a crate for training and safety, a toddler gate to fence off parts of the house until she and the dog got to know each other, and, depending on the dog's age and nature, beds, chew toys, and nutritious food. A local vet agreed to see and evaluate the dog when it was time. Finally, she felt ready.

Save the Pets, Inc., spearheaded by a woman named Betty Jean Scirro, had impressed Sheila as she searched online for local rescue groups. Two vets she'd talked with spoke highly of it.

Scirro had been rescuing animals for decades, scouring shelters in New York and New Jersey, and posting a list of previous adopters on her website so prospective owners could check out the organization. Sheila called two or three satisfied customers, who all raved about Betty Jean and the other volunteers at Save the Pets, about the dogs, about the way the group followed up with training and health advice. The group spent weeks "fostering" the dogs they brought from shelters in temporary homes, to socialize them and make sure of their personalities.

So Sheila called Betty Jean, who, two nights later, came over to drop off the group's detailed questionnaire, meet Sheila, and check out her house.

Scirro is legendary in rescue circles for her experience and dedication, and for her instincts about matching dogs with people. About five hundred dogs a year are adopted through Save the Pets, and very few come back.

Betty Jean asked a lot of questions: work schedule, physical surroundings, training commitment. Sheila's hours and commute and her small yard ruled out many of the dogs she rescued, but she was impressed with the knowledge Sheila had accumulated.

The battle-hardened, skeptical Betty Jean—who turns down at least half the people who come to her seeking dogs—took particular note of Sheila's circuit of obedience classes, vets' offices, and shelters. "Usually people call you, try to get a dog, then do their homework later—if you're lucky. Sheila was doing it the right way."

She'd had too much experience with people who cooed at the cute puppies but knew nothing about dogs and seemed unaware they required training, veterinary care, or exercise. Those were the ones who would call three days or three weeks later to return the cute puppy. Sheila already understood, before Betty Jean told her, that her living and work situation ruled out many dogs. She understood that crates and kennels could be beneficial, not cruel. She'd lined up reliable backup. "She gave me the numbers of her mother, sister, dog walker, friends, and neighbors so that I could see for myself that she had a support system," Betty Jean reported. "I called a couple of them and they all told me that she'd been researching this for months, that she was mature, responsible, and prepared.

"And she was very committed to training—you never hear about that. She'd read a lot about it. I wish she didn't work in the city. I wish there was someone home more of the time. But she seemed willing to compensate, to be patient and wait for the right dog, and that's the difference right there. I knew she would do well by a dog, and that I could find one for her. Sheila knew she shouldn't have just *any* dog, but that didn't mean she couldn't have a dog."

Sheila's ability to see fairly precisely what kind of dog she wanted—small, older, easygoing—also made things easier. "That way, when I go into shelters I can look for the dog she wants," Betty Jean said. "I'll recognize him or her right away. It improves the odds of a good match."

Even so, it took her more than a month to find Crackers, a curly-coated cockapoo (mostly), in a Long Island shelter. His owner had suffered a stroke and was no longer able to care for him. He was about three, had been lovingly treated by his former owner and her children and grandchildren (all of whom had dogs themselves and couldn't take in Crackers, who was a bit delicate after being hit by a car in his youth). He loved to walk, but he didn't go very far. The injury had made him even quieter than he was by nature.

Betty Jean learned that Crackers, who was housebroken, was often left alone but never did any damage. He was friendly to children and dogs and had learned to come, sit, and stay. He might need some "freshening up" on his commands, Betty Jean thought, but he was alert and responsive. He wouldn't be unhappy lolling around Sheila's house waiting for the dog walker, especially in contrast to the crate he'd occupied for several weeks. Older dogs, especially those with injuries, are much tougher to place than puppies.

Betty Jean brought the dog from Long Island to a foster home, where one of Save the Pets' volunteers observed him for a week as he encountered kids and other dogs.

Crackers, under his curly black mop, was a little skinny—perhaps his appetite had slackened with his dislocation. He wasn't the most beautiful dog, but he had lots of personality, a permanent mischievous twinkle in his eyes. And he was calm, responsive, affectionate—just as ordered. Sheila took a few days off from work to get him settled.

She had a crate all ready, full of rawhide chews and toys. At first, Sheila fed him in the crate and left him there when she went out, so there were no unpleasant surprises, or opportunities for him to develop bad habits.

She left him alone at home for a few minutes at first, then for an hour, then a few hours. He met her mother, sister, dog walker, neighbors, and friends, all of whom brought treats and toys and pronounced him a sweetheart. Having done her homework, Sheila knew that dogs basically live by food, attention, and a few rules; Crackers got all three.

Since he had a safe place from which to study and adjust to his new environment, Sheila didn't worry about coming home to accidents or garbage strewn about her house. When she saw how well behaved he was, though, she gradually began leaving the crate door open. Still, most of the time when she came home, he was sleeping inside it. At night, despite her pledge to be hardheaded about training, Crackers quickly ended up in bed right next to her.

Her vet pronounced Crackers a happy and healthy dog. His injured leg would never completely heal, and there might be some arthritis later on, but mostly, the vet said, Crackers would compensate. "I felt bad for him," Sheila said, "but good for us."

It was a happy match for both species: Sheila had an easygoing pal who fit her lifestyle; Crackers was saved from almost certain death. But as Betty Jean had observed, "Matches like this are not accidents. People work pretty hard at them."

Once he was acclimated, Crackers began to get around. He spent afternoons with Sheila's mother (who was crazy about him) once or twice a week, visited her sister once a week, and strolled once or twice a day (depending on Sheila's schedule) with the neighborhood dog walker.

"I am wild about this guy," Sheila says now. "He's always happy to see me, but he's at ease when I leave, too. He gets along beautifully with everyone. He has fit right in. On weekends, we go to parks and sometimes drive to the beach. But he doesn't go far. I think it's his bad leg. His favorite thing? Cuddling with me while I talk on the phone or watch TV. How perfect is that?"

CLEMENTINE

I NEVER WORKED MORE DILIGENTLY AT ACQUIRING A NEW DOG THAN I DID with Clementine. I wanted to apply all the things I'd been hearing, reading, and learning, to start from the beginning and see how I'd do with a puppy. I wanted to learn from my previous mistakes.

Everybody has different needs and interests when it comes to dogs. Over the years, I've adopted unwanted dogs and I've also purchased purebreds. Lately, I've grown partial to finding great breeders and buying the established European working breeds, for several reasons. First, I like to do things with my dogs—herding, hiking, swimming. Tending and hunting dogs, such as border collies, Labs, retrievers, rottweilers, and deerhounds, have been bred for centuries to work with humans.

Second, I have a complex emotional history with my own family and sometimes worry that by rescuing a dog I will entangle an animal in the lingering consequences of my own past. That's not always beneficial to a dog, and not really what I'm looking for at this stage of my life.

And stages of life are critical when it comes to choosing a dog. In my late fifties, I want dogs that will keep me active but not overwhelm me. I help rescue and re-home dogs several times a year, mostly border collies. But for me, I want dogs that are trainable, whose known genetic and behavioral histories make that likely. I want to be present and involved in every phase of my new dog's life, to be a partner in shaping a dog, rather than inheriting a dog somebody else has shaped. None of this argues for or against rescuing dogs in general; it just reflects where I am in life. In ten or fifteen years, moreover, I might well be less active. I am a large man with a bad ankle; I now wear a cumbersome foot brace.

So while I hope I will end my life on this farm, looking ahead—something I believe in when it comes to getting a dog—a dog that's easy around people, one that grows calmer over the years, makes sense.

To me, the first step is ruling out the dogs that don't fit. I am fond of terriers, for example, but find them more excitable than the dog I'm looking for. Hounds like bassets and beagles are tough to train, not because they're ill-tempered but because they pay so much attention to smells and are so independent-minded. And, fairly or not, I don't want a breed people typically feel afraid of, which eliminates some of the bigger and more rambunctious breeds. Because I travel a lot and am often around strangers and kids, I have to make sure all my dogs have even dispositions.

By now so much is known about breeds and temperament that it's puzzling that people don't bother to find out more about them.

Studies cited in James Serpell's *The Domestic Dog* report "significant" behavioral differences among breeds. So many Labrador owners complain to me about their dogs being stubborn and willful. Yet Serpell and other researchers have found Labs to be one of the easiest breeds to train, among the most affectionate and least excitable.

Breeds vary significantly in such characteristics as excitability, general activity, and playfulness. They're more or less responsive to obedience training and housebreaking, more or less prone to barking. They exhibit varying degrees of dominance over their owners, as well as varying degrees of territorial defense, of aggression toward other dogs, and of destructiveness.

I considered those factors as I clicked around the American Kennel Club website and read through a number of breed research books. Labs could be excitable, but because they are responsive to training, they could be taught calmness. They were active, but I had a farm with room to roam. They were affectionate with kids, a critical point for me. They barked when strangers approached, didn't generally treat other dogs aggressively, and accepted human dominance. They were easy to housebreak, especially once encouraged to go outside, because they were scent-driven. Unless given plenty of chewbones and treats, they could eat up a house. But I planned to crate a puppy most of the time for the first month or so, and I also planned to blanket the house with rawhide and toys. The Rational Theory posits that if a dog has plenty of his own things readily available to chew, he's less likely get into the habit of eating yours.

As I pored through my research, the characteristics followed a certain logic. Many of the hunting, retrieving, and working breeds—Labradors, golden retrievers, rottweilers, Great Danes—were calm, bright, and trainable. Hounds and flushing dogs—beagles, Afghans, poodles, Dalmatians—were less mellow, prone to following their noses and setting their own agendas. So-called lap dogs (Chihuahuas, shih tzus, Lhasa apsos, Pekingese) were more excitable and territorial, and the energetic terriers (schnauzers, Scotties, Boston terriers) barked a lot and were among the most challenging to train.

It makes sense. Dogs bred for guarding and patrolling are generally more menacing. Dogs bred to sit by hunters for hours waiting for birds to fall out of the sky are more attuned to humans. Dogs bred as indoor personal companions often grow very attached to their owners, thus very protective. They also tend to need less exercise.

It's all important stuff to know, and fairly easy to find out. I told myself that if I got the wrong dog, I had nobody to blame but myself.

A Lab seemed suited to me, a healthy counterpoint to my edgy border collies. I like the holistic approach to having dogs, looking at the big picture. I had one dog—Rose—who needed hours of intense work each day. A dog who'd spend hours a day lying around seemed a good balance.

Besides, I knew a fair amount about the breed. I still often miss my two sweet yellow Labs, Julius and Stanley, fine companions who both died during the same trying year. Pound for pound, a well-bred, well-trained Labrador is among the very best pets in the world.

Like all dogs, they can also present problems. Overbred, as many popular breeds are, they now appear, sadly, on lists of the most frequent biters. Many suffer from hip dysplasia and other health problems. If poorly trained—and we know how few Americans train their dogs at all—they can become frenetic and obnoxious. I've seen them drag sizable adults down suburban sidewalks. Garbage trawlers, they're happy to eat almost anything, digestible or not. Vets tell of finding the most unlikely things, from rubber balls to aluminum cans, in Labs' stomachs. Large dogs, they're prone to become overweight, especially if they don't get sufficient exercise. They like to roll in unappetizing stuff. They shed.

On the plus side, they can be playful, loving, at ease in unfamiliar situations. Unlike border collies, they come with an off switch. After they reach two or three years old, they seem to settle down, to weave themselves into your life in a way few dogs can.

It all comes down to being handled properly. Labs can grow up to be calm and responsive dogs, eager to walk and play, happy to lie for hours by your side. Poorly trained, they're among the sad stories of the dog world, out of control, confined to basements and backyards. Labs rarely get the exercise, training, or work they need, hence their growing reputation for being unruly and obnoxious slobs. Becoming one of the breeds of choice for the upper middle class has done them no favors.

So, a Lab. And a female, I thought, might ease the pack politics. Orson is a very dominant dog, but he likes female dogs, and is peaceable as long as he isn't annoyed or challenged. The most high-strung and complicated dog I've ever owned, or am likely to, Orson doesn't take to male dogs, enthusiastic dogs, dogs that bark and race around, or anyone who bothers his food or gets in his face. I had to consider these traits when adding another dog. He had the most to lose, which meant he had the most potential to cause trouble; a female might make fewer waves.

I wasn't worried about Rose; she was the most single-minded, focused, and professional dog I'd had. As long as she had sheep to push around, she was both busy and happy—which, in her case, were synonymous.

A female yellow Lab would add the right flavoring to our canine mix—a dash of sweet, a pinch of calm, different kinds of activities, like hiking and exploring streams, which aren't easy with border collies.

I searched for a good breeder for months. Pam Leslie's Hillside Labradors in nearby Pawlet, Vermont, kept coming up in conversation. I'd seen some of her dogs around—whenever I saw a Lab I liked, I stopped and asked where it came from—and was amazed at how beautiful they were. Her dogs were well known among dog lovers, vets, and trainers, and they'd won daunting lists of awards and ribbons.

Like many good breeders, Pam keeps a fluid waiting list: she gives her dogs to people and homes because she likes or approves of them, not simply because it's their turn.

I called and made an appointment to visit, and a few days later made the thirty-minute drive to Pawlet. A half-dozen gorgeous black and yellow Labs were romping and running in a two-or-three-acre run behind a clean, well-tended kennel. If Pam took as good care of her dogs as the building they lived in, this could work.

She'd been breeding Labs for decades, and I could tell she'd seen a lot of prospective dog owners come and go. Applicants had to pass muster if they were going to leave with one of her dogs. When she asked me why I wanted a dog, and I told her about my situation, she had the "convince me" demeanor common to good breeders and shelter people.

She raised some concerns of her own. Multiple-dog households could be difficult, she pointed out. Was I prepared to train a Lab? She was particularly worried about how a puppy would deal with two energetic border collies. Had I considered that? How would I keep the Lab from developing leg and shoulder troubles from racing to keep up with dogs that were so much faster? I *hadn't* considered that, I confessed, but I would.

Pam brought me into her kennels, which were large, well-lit, and odorless. One great-looking dog after another came out to greet me, all of them curious, alert, friendly. I'd love any of these dogs, I thought.

The female named Sarah was particularly lovely, with a pale gold coat, enormous dark eyes, and a dignified mien. She took a biscuit from me, graciously, and I sat down on the floor to scratch her ears.

"I'd take this one home in a minute," I said, even though Sarah wasn't a puppy.

"You and a lot of others," Pam retorted, listing a few of the dog's titles. "But the good news is that Sarah's expecting a litter. If you are patient, we can talk about it."

We did talk about it, for weeks. Encouraged by Pam, I drove over regularly to spend time with Sarah. I met the sire, a big, easygoing fellow on loan from another breeder. I was impressed by almost everything I saw. Sarah was warm without being obnoxious, approaching slowly and calmly. She had a bright attentiveness, but also a poised reserve that I liked. I could see why she was a prizewinner.

Pam and I also connected. She liked the way I behaved with Sarah. She met my border collies, who watched the proceedings suspiciously from my truck.

If the right female yellow emerged from the upcoming litter, she would consider me, Pam said. I was grateful to have made the cut. Pam had devoted much of her life to improving Labradors, breeding for the best reasons and in the best sense of the term, and she had clearly succeeded. I didn't see many dogs like hers, and I see quite a few.

Moreover, the puppies would live in wood-chip-lined enclosures that opened to the outdoors, so it would be easy for them to begin housebreaking themselves. Pam kept her puppy areas scrupulously clean, so the pups would want to be clean as well. Usually, they left the kennel almost completely housebroken.

Her blunt philosophy was that she'd provide the best dogs possible, but the people who bought them needed to take over from there. People sometimes called with the oddest questions and complaints. "One man called me up and said, 'Can you guarantee me that this dog will hunt?' I said, 'Can you guarantee me that you can *teach* this dog to hunt?' " Pam had worked hard on her breedlines, but once the puppy was born and weaned, the responsibility became mine.

Three months later, Pam called and said Sarah had given birth. Did I want to come see?

Did I?

But I warned myself: remember that all puppies are adorable. That doesn't mean one of these dogs is the right dog for you. Study them, pay attention to what each one is like. Be prepared to walk away and try again next time.

Behaviorists had cautioned me about puppies that bounded up and jumped all over you. People often say they pick a puppy from a litter "because I could see how much he loved me" or "because the dog chose me." I don't buy it. This was my choice, not the dog's. The most excited puppies often become the most hyper dogs. The shy ones may be fearful.

I was looking for a "middle" dog, one that noticed me, showed curiosity and affection without boisterousness, neither charged at me nor skulked away—a dog that observed me, then made a choice to investigate further.

I saw the puppies the day after they were born—they looked a lot like hairless rodents—and about once a week thereafter. I knew from my reading that they wouldn't develop distinct personality traits until the fifth or sixth week, but I checked them out anyway as they grew, calling to them, feeding and handling them. At first, they all seemed alike. But after a few weeks, I saw two blacks—a male and a female—that I liked; they seemed independent, curious, and sociable. The yellow female didn't appear to pay much attention to me for the first month or so. I couldn't get a read on her.

Pam, of course, spotted physical traits and personalities earlier than I could. My visits often became lunches that turned into extended yaks about dogs, their training and behavior. Pam had a breeder's detached eye for lines, color, and energy. But she also had ideas about training that would prove invaluable.

By the sixth week, I had a name in mind for a new dog. Clementine seemed to fit a Lab female, particularly the sweet-natured one I had in mind. I'd shown up early for my weekly lunch with Pam and her associate, Heather Waite. Pam regaled us with stories of competitions, demanding customers, dogs loved and lost, the staples of a breeder's life. We all talked about my training ideas.

Sarah was often away from the pups when I was there. They were being weaned and had started eating solid food. I volunteered to feed them their pan of mush.

That day, the yellow female emerged from the squirming mass as her own distinct personality. The pups were crawling out to the ramp that led to the yard when her head popped up in the doorway. She looked at the food, then at me, and sat down while her siblings charged the pan. After checking me out for a moment, her tail began to wag and she joined the fray. She was, after all, a Lab. I had been to the kennel half a dozen times since she was born, but this was the first time she seemed to recognize me from previous visits.

She calmly nosed her way to the bowl, scarfed down her share, then turned and sat looking at me quizzically. I brought her into the whelping room, where Pam and Heather were talking, and set her on my lap.

A few days later, she came bouncing in from outside when she heard my voice, squirming in greeting, tail waggling. As before, she sat down, sized me up, and apparently approved of what she saw. I thought I saw the makings of a glorious dog. She was affectionate and alert, and I liked her slight distance. Like her mother, she had calm dignity.

When I picked her up, she licked my chin. And when I set her down in my lap, she crawled up my chest and curled on my shoulder, falling asleep on that precarious perch, as comfortable and trusting as if we'd known each other for years.

At that moment, there was something palpable, a communication between us. I could feel her rapid heartbeat through my shirt. "Well, I guess she's your dog now," Pam offered dryly. I thought so, too.

SEVERAL DAYS LATER, WE DROVE HOME, CLEM ASLEEP ON THE FRONT SEAT next to me. I was ready. I had a crate for her downstairs by the door, another next to the desk in my study, and one upstairs in the bedroom.

In our separate ways, for our different reasons, both Sheila and I had taken pains to find the Right Dog for Us. Now the real work would begin.

THE RELATIONSHIP BETWEEN HUMANS AND DOGS HAS ALWAYS BEEN confusing, controversial, and complicated. Thousands of years old, it's a story of love, fealty, and service, yes, but also of cruelty, misunderstanding, and difficult interactions between two species that are radically different, yet deeply enmeshed.

Training is the language between dogs and people, the tangible glue that connects the two. Your choices and decisions about training, more than any other factor, will shape your life with a dog and a dog's life in your world. The training sets the tone for dogs' interactions with the rest of the world, and gives it importance beyond our own homes and families. I'll talk more about specific training tips in a subsequent chapter; for now, let's consider *why* training is so crucial.

Those of us who love dogs need to consider the rest of the population, something we occasionally fail to do. Its non–dog owners are increasingly unhappy. When they go for walks, they are often menaced or annoyed by poorly trained or aggressive dogs. Canine feces soil their gardens, lawns, and parks. Parents with small children, elderly friends out for a stroll, clusters of teenagers—none of them can tell whether a dog bounding toward them is friendly (many are not) or hostile.

Increasingly, therefore, dogs are being banned from public places, and it's sometimes hard to blame the people banning them. Dog owners, however loving, can be lazy, ignorant, or irresponsible. We want our dogs to be good citizens, but they're not born knowing how to deal with unfamiliar people, streets and buildings, urban and suburban tumult. We have to show them.

So training is not only a personal but increasingly a civic issue, concerned with whether dogs can ever walk off-leash, with a growing number of dog attacks, with politicized advocacy groups that want to keep even dangerous dogs alive. Training is our moral obligation, not only to our dogs and the members of our human families, but to our neighbors and communities.

Evidence of dog training dates back nearly 14,000 years. The ancient Egyptians and Romans used dogs for hunting, warring, and companionship. Farmers and herders have used highly skilled working dogs for centuries. Yet dog training has always seesawed between cruelty and affection, bullying and teaching, need and recreation.

Ideas about training seem to lurch ahead at odd intervals. In the eighteenth century the British invented notions of animal rights and raised the subject of cruelty to dogs and other creatures, sparking advances in our comprehension and treatment of animals. Every war spurs further advances—especially the two world wars and Vietnam—as armies train dogs for such tasks as search-and-rescue scouting, security, even combat.

Famed psychologist B. F. Skinner's work with animals led to "operant conditioning training"—the study of conditioned and reinforced behaviors in both animals and people—which dominates many progressive training approaches today.

In the 1970s, the monks of New Skete (an Orthodox Catholic community in upstate New York) produced a series of still-popular books that introduced the idea of dog training as an almost spiritual form of interspecies communication.

The rise of competitive trials—like obedience and agility contests and American Kennel Club shows—made training more sophisticated and helped dog training evolve into a respected, full-time profession. Animal behavior became a science, spawning a rash of new theories and methods.

In contemporary America, dog training has grown to be a huge and booming business, with thousands of books, pamphlets and guides for "dummies," instructional videos and DVDs, classes, seminars, camps. . . . I await the first degree-granting canine college any day.

But partly as a consequence, mainstream dog owners—those who own dogs but don't work with them for a living or take them to shows and trials—can feel overwhelmed by gurus and experts and their theories. Training in the United States involves no uniform licensing or certification, so dog owners and lovers are almost rolling the dice when they sign up with a trainer or obedience instructor. Some are great, some aren't.

PROS AND AMATEURS: CAN I DO THIS MYSELF?

ONE OF THE TRICKIER DECISIONS A DOG OWNER MAKES IS WHETHER TO homeschool a dog—train it yourself—or to hire a professional for individual sessions, or to sign up for one of the many obedience classes and programs that trainers offer. Each choice is okay, but they're very different.

In general, it's easier to train a dog than to retrain one, easier to get it right the first time than to try rectifying mistakes and misfires. Some dogs are resilient and forgiving, others sensitive and easily rattled. Some come with histories you may not know or understand. Some trainers take what I call an indiscriminate approach to dogs—"I can train any dog to do anything." I'm not so sure.

You can damage your relationship with a dog if you choose the wrong dog, bring him into the wrong environment, misread his nature, choose the wrong training approach for you, or simply don't care. I'm surprised at how many people announce, defiantly, "I'm not spending a couple of hundred bucks on dog training!" They're thinking about living with an animal in close quarters with their families for a decade or longer. Often, they've already spent more than a couple of hundred dollars on a purebred dog and his accessories. For the price of taking the kids to a major-league ball game, you can radically improve the odds of having a pleasant life with your nondestructive dog.

Over the years, I've trained my own dogs using a variety of these methods. For Orson, who was already two when he arrived and had lots of behavioral difficulties, I went to a trainer and sheep farmer in Pennsylvania once or twice a week for two years. She and I never really managed to make Orson a competent herder, but she taught me enough to help turn a maniacal misfit into a (mostly) genial companion. I homeschooled Rose here on Bedlam Farm, teaching her (and being taught by

TRAINING CLEM WITH DONKEYS

her) how sheepherding works. I talked to many trainers about Clementine but ultimately felt I'd learned enough from my other dogs to train her confidently and knowledgeably.

In my decades with dogs, I've probably tried everything, including not training a dog much at all (I was young and dumb). I attended obedience classes with a previous dog, but it's not the right choice for me. Too many people, too many dogs, not enough individual attention, too short a period. Nevertheless, I understand that lifestyle and budgetary considerations make classes the best approach for many. Large classes seem to function best to socialize puppies—no small thing—and pass along fundamental notions about obedience and commands. Besides, as with twelve-step or Weight Watchers programs, having a group to report to every week fosters support and accountability and supplies a chance to measure progress. You might be more inclined to actually do the training if you have to show up with King on Tuesday nights and the instructor and your classmates can see what you've accomplished, or haven't.

If you prefer to work with your dog on your own, remember you are forming your relationship with this creature. Be extremely careful about frightening and scolding a puppy or making training sessions unpleasant and tense, problems that fall into the category of stuff-that's-hard-to-undo-later. Very young dogs—eight to twelve weeks old—have short attention spans, lack long-term memory and problem-solving skills, and are easily bored and distracted. Often they simply cannot yet do spit-spot comes, sits, and stays.

Basic obedience training can be undertaken at almost any time in a dog's life, but dogs, like kids, vary in attention span, maturity, and the ability to grasp commands and skills. So build a trusting and loving relationship with your dog—lots of treats and toys and fun—before you begin formal training. If you take care to do the one, the other will follow much more easily.

Have clear and measurable goals. First, sit. Then lie down. Then stay. If each takes a month, fine. Be patient. If the dog messes up, try again later. If the dog is distracted or bored, quit and come back to the

STAY (NO STREET)

process in an hour or two. I find late mornings a good time to train. I like to take the kibble I serve for breakfast and use it as a reward for basic obedience instead. Dogs are hungry and alert in the morning, which helps the process.

If, instead, you hire a one-on-one trainer, you can go to her or she can come to your home. The latter would be my choice since she (or he) can see you in your own environment and get a sense of your family, the neighbors and their dogs, the streets, and the outdoor spaces the dog will have to negotiate. A trainer will spot things you might not think of—where in the home to place a crate, what furniture needs protection, where fencing might help, what outdoor distractions to be conscious of.

Make sure you are comfortable with the trainer, though. Go over any concerns you have, and if you trust him, listen to him. People feel so helpless about dog training that they often assume any trainer knows much more than they do. But a good trainer will help *you* train your dog, not take over or bully you in the process. He shouldn't force any method that makes you ill at ease or doesn't seem sensible. If you don't like and trust a method, it's a good bet you won't convince your dog to adopt it, either. Trust your instincts. You know your dog. If he seems frightened or uncomfortable, stop and try something else.

On the other hand—with dogs, it seems there is *always* an other hand—a professional trainer isn't likely to see your little Bootsie as the sweet and childlike entity you might think of her as being. A trainer can be firmer than you would be, and still be very good. Talk and think it through in advance.

I'd avoid trainers who are quick to recommend methods like choke chains and shock collars. Sometimes aversive stimuli are necessary, depending on safety considerations and the severity of a dog's problems. But a good trainer almost invariably challenges you to look at your own behavior—your body language, temper, and way of communicating—and generally tries positive training methods first.

If the trainer takes too rough a stance, ask for an explanation. You might want to ask about a gentler, more positive approach. If he makes you feel stupid or helpless, find another trainer. The approach may or may not be wrong, but it probably isn't going to work.

Because serious training and socialization take time, patience, and consistency, I'm suspicious of anybody who claims you can train your dog in a few weeks. A trainer can get you off to a strong start, but if you're committed, you'll be at this for months and years.

It does seem logical that if you're not a professional dog person, haven't been around a lot of dogs, or haven't tried this before, good professional help can save time and steer you in the right direction. But I believe training a dog is something many people can do themselves. And it's rewarding beyond measure.

ANIMAL IGNORANCE

FEW DOG OWNERS KNOW MUCH ABOUT DOGS. THAT WAS CERTAINLY MY situation before I adopted a demented border collie. My subsequent choice, however, was simple: either learn how to train this hooligan or get rid of him. The latter was never an option, really, so I began learning the things I should have learned many dogs ago.

Orson provided a crash graduate course in canine studies. Training him also took me to the Raspberry Ridge Sheep Farm in Bangor, Pennsylvania, where trainer Carolyn Wilki enriched my life and taught me a great amount about dogs in a short time.

It's been shocking, though, to realize how poorly prepared I was to live well with dogs. I yelled at them, threw choke chains at them, attributed numerous wrongheaded and misguided motives to their behavior, didn't use treats or crates or any of the training tools that now seem indispensable. I trained sporadically and quit far too early; I mismanaged everything from feeding to the most elemental commands. Now that dogs are also my work, I'm even more amazed at how much misinformation circulates.

In a dog run in New York, I see people hysterically screaming and grabbing to break up minor dog squabbles. I meet people all the time who obsess over exotic diets, reject veterinary care as unnecessary and malign, relate what a channeler has divined about Rover, yet I rarely meet a dog who's even moderately well trained, who comes reliably when called, lies down when asked, stays off people when requested. Instead, I meet innumerable dogs who drive their humans crazy. People tell me, often apologetically, that their dogs misbehave because they are too abused to train, too stubborn and manipulative to listen. They're likely to be wrong about that, but such beliefs help explain why so few owners train their dogs at all.

Curiously, there's no real connection between loving a dog and knowing anything much about the species—like the fact that the best human response to most dogfights is to turn and walk away. Or that yelling at a dog almost invariably reinforces the very behavior you want to end. Or that adult dogs don't really need play groups and play dates. Or that it's okay to have a dog and still have a job. Yet people do, indisputably, love their dogs.

Rule One of my theory of dog training: If you're like me, you probably know rather little about dogs when you start out, so own up to it.

Wipe the slate clean; purge your mind of advice and stories from well-meaning friends, neighbors, and your uncle Harry twenty-five years ago. Their dogs are not your dogs, their experiences not necessarily of value to you. Each dog and each owner is different. What matters is what works for you and the dog you live with.

TRAINING THEORIES

TRYING TO FIGURE OUT WHICH TRAINING METHOD WILL WORK WHEN several of the most commonly used seem nearly contradictory is a tough call.

Perhaps the most traditional and familiar training approaches teach that dogs are pack animals and that to train them well we must show them their place in the social hierarchy: namely, below us, in submission to us. Pack-training theories hold that dogs in their natural state establish hierarchies, through instinct or force. When they breed, play, or hunt, the pack leader sets the rules. When a dog joins your household, therefore, you must become the chief dog (the alpha) so that the new member of the pack will submit and obey.

This approach, while it often brings results, is by its nature coercive (some trainers would say aversive). It imposes your will on a dog, often by intimidation, sometimes by force, to persuade him that you're in charge.

In discipline, write the New Skete monks in *The Art of Raising a Puppy*, the owner puts the dog in a subordinate position and plays the alpha in much the way the leader of a wolf pack does. The monks urge dog owners to communicate decisively and authoritatively, to say "no" clearly and quietly, as if you were throwing a "verbal beanbag" at the dog.

A second method of pack discipline, the monks suggest, is a cuff on the chin—reserved only for serious offenses, and only after a good relationship has been established between dog and human. With the dog in a sitting position, "your fingers meet the underside of the dog's mouth in an upward motion. . . . Eye contact is very important in discipline," write the monks. "Wolves disciplining each other make eye contact. Never hit a dog from above. Your fingers should be closed together, your hand open."

I trust the New Skete monks to pull this off successfully, but I don't trust too many other dog owners, myself included. My border collie Rose is hypersensitive to all sounds and gestures. A "verbal beanbag"— a simple, clear "no"—does the job. For Clem, on the other hand, a gentle cuff under the chin would probably go almost unnoticed, or prompt a spate of wagging and licking.

I respect pack theorists, especially those as experienced and thoughtful as the monks of New Skete, but this isn't the method for me.

I know of trainers who lie atop dominant dogs until they stop struggling, to force them to submit. Others escalate to shock collars, choke chains, sharply corrective verbal commands, even sticks or training rods.

In the hands of professionals, I've seen this kind of coercive training work quickly, especially with dominant dogs who need a lot of persuasion to accept human authority. More often, though, pack training is misused by people who confuse dominance with aggression, who think that if you scream at the dog or knock him around, he will obey.

"Showing the dog who's boss" also leads, I have observed, to rough treatment of puppies and new dogs, especially by men, who often take the notion too far. Perhaps they've experienced too many bosses in their own lives and work.

A different training approach originates with animal behaviorists, who try to teach us to read a dog's body language—head and tail postures, and various other gestures—to communicate.

One example: a human will greet another human, especially in America, by moving directly toward him. We teach our kids to extend their hands and greet strangers by looking them in the eye.

In the dog universe, however, this is rude and aggressive. Among themselves, dogs generally avoid eye contact and head-on approaches when meeting other dogs. (When they don't, beware.) They use smell, rather than sight, to get acquainted. People love it when dogs lick their faces, but even then, if you notice, a dog will usually approach your face from the side. Dogs generally don't like to be hugged and squeezed, either, and rarely appreciate that form of affection as much as humans.

Well-meaning dog lovers often communicate the opposite of what they mean to. Just as the best way to teach a dog to be quiet is to ignore his barking and reinforce his silence, one of the worst ways to get a dog to come is to pull on his leash, looking directly into his face. In fact, this is a great way to get a dog to stand still.

"All dogs are brilliant at perceiving the slightest movement that we make, and they assume that each tiny motion has meaning," writes Dr. Patricia McConnell, an animal behaviorist and the author of *The Other End of the Leash: Why We Do What We Do Around Dogs*. But we don't incorporate this knowledge into our interactions; in fact, she writes, "we are often oblivious to how we're moving around our dogs." The random signals we radiate merely confuse them.

It's amazing how skillfully certain trainers can interpret dogs' motions and positions, so unusual an ability that we call people who do it well "dog whisperers" and invest them with an almost spiritual mystique. It's not something that I'm particularly good at, however.

When I remind myself, I can read some of my dogs' behavior. When their noses go to the ground, they've spotted something they might chase. When their bodies stiffen, they're expecting trouble. Panting, squinting, or cowering are symptoms of anxiety. Watching for such signals is both fascinating and helpful—if you know when your dog is about to bolt, it's much easier to teach him not to. Watching a dog's body language can also tell you if a child is upsetting him, or if another dog wants to play or wage war.

But while reading a dog's behavior is obviously helpful for good training, I don't think it's a natural skill for humans. We live in our own worlds, absorbed by the details of everyday life—kids, work, warbling cell phones—and few of us have the ability or focus to read dogs' behavior consistently or reliably. We're rarely conscious of how we're holding our own heads, hands, or shoulders; studying those traits in our dogs is an alien behavior.

So the training realm in which I generally feel most at home is positive reinforcement, an offshoot of Skinner's work. This theory, increasingly influential, argues that desirable behaviors ought to be reinforced through praise, food, and attention, while unwanted behaviors are to be ignored—not reinforced—or eliminated by creating controlled environments. Positive trainers reject long-standing anthropomorphic misconceptions about dogs' motives. Dogs don't obey us out of a desire to please, they contend, but because appropriate behavior gets reinforced.

Modern trainers generally agree that there's no such thing as a "good" or "bad" dog, a "nice" or "mean" dog. All dogs are animals. All will bite under certain circumstances, all are affected not primarily by human-like emotions but by more biological factors: breeding, genetics, litter experiences, training, and interactions with humans.

Though I'm most comfortable with these broad principles, no theory is always good for everyone. I like repeating behaviors that are rewarding and successful, avoiding those that aren't. I agree, too, with the conviction that your dog already knows just about everything you want to teach him. He can come, sit down, stay, and so forth. Your job is to put words to these actions when he does them.

But broad principles crumble fast when a neighborhood kid comes charging up your lawn, the monster mutt next door has gotten out of his kennel, or your dog is streaking after a cat across the street. At such moments, all but the most disciplined trainers throw positive reinforcement out the window and start screaming or praying. Certainly I do. It's okay—chalk it up as one of life's growth experiences.

My experience has been that any of these approaches can succeed and any can fail, depending on the disposition, temperament, and environment of dog and owner. Platitudes and absolutist theories tend to give way under the force of our individual environments. To live well with a dog requires looking at and within yourself.

I live on a farm where my border collies have sheep out the back door and my young Lab has woods and streams to roam, sniff, and swim in. There are no small children within a quarter of a mile, but there are abundant deer, wild dogs, snakes, coyotes, and rabid raccoons.

It makes no sense to train my dogs the way I would if we were all still living in northern New Jersey. What works for me and my dogs on

Bedlam Farm might not apply in suburban Sacramento. A busy commuter with a family in a crowded community needs a different training regimen from mine.

Because trainers and owners tend to embrace one theory or another, the notion of a correct or incorrect way to train a dog has become endemic. Some positive trainers consider it nearly abusive to ever yell at a dog. I probably yell at my dogs two or three times a day, depending on what drama is unfolding at the moment. On walks, where I tend to lose myself in thought, I might look up suddenly to see the border collies rocketing off after some unseen woodland critter. I yell. They come.

Yet almost all my formal training is entirely positive, my instructions reinforced with praise and treats and much whooping enthusiasm. My dogs come running when I call because they usually get something nice in return.

I also accept some elements of pack, or dominance, training, though. I have to be the leader—not the boss—of my dogs. I find the hierarchy within this little universe fluid and evolutionary, not as clear as many books and theories suggest. Orson is a powerful and dominant dog, for instance. The younger border collie, Rose, defers to him most of the time, but will run him off the bed in a flash if she feels crowded. And near sheep, she will run him into the barn if he interferes with her work. Clementine is by far the most congenial and easygoing creature on the farm, but even she can turn into Cujo if one of the others gets designs on her basted rawhide bone. Still, I notice that when I raise my voice, even the border collies freeze and lock their eyes onto mine, awaiting instructions; that's gotten us out of many a hairy situation.

Getting dogs to submit is not so difficult, I've found. After all, I control access to outdoors, food and treats, and toys, all the desirable things. I can dominate my dogs through rules and leadership.

I love psychologist and author Stanley Coren's wise edict: Never give a dog anything for free. Before we go anywhere, before they get any treat, the dogs must lie down, sit, come, or stay, an organic form of training woven into our daily walks, meals, and routines. I see it as a toll; I charge my dogs for everything. Lie down outside the door, get a treat, then tear around. Lie down at the road, get a treat, then dash across on command. If Rose wants access to sheep, she has to lie down at the gate; if Clem wants her breakfast, she has to stay for a minute or so.

We take several daily walks where they can get in touch with their inner pups and horse around, but when things get too exciting, everybody is summoned to me, and we go through a series of calming exercises: lie down, get treats; stay, get more treats.

The point isn't to have spit-and-polish dogs who obey with military precision; I certainly don't. It's to establish leadership and promote respectful submission by using the things they like to do as reinforcement for things I want them to do. I set the rules and they follow most of them and are rewarded, with minimal scolding, no shocking or whacking. So far, we're living together quite contentedly.

So I've come to believe in customized, personalized, mostly positive, homegrown training. Among my few rules: Know yourself. Know the dog. Set clear, simple goals that are likely to succeed. (If you hold a piece of a frankfurter, back away, and say "Come," the dog will come; when he does, praise him. If you do this every day for a couple of months, you will have astounding recall. There are no guarantees in the dog world, but this is as close to one as you can get.) Finally, have realistic expectations, because it may take months or years to train your dog properly. And be flexible. If one method doesn't work, try another.

This means seeing through, and moving past, certain misunderstandings, excuses, and blame. For instance:

"My dog isn't listening to me." Dogs have astounding hearing. They listen very carefully to their owners, in truth, providing their owners make sense to them. Often we haven't learned how to do that. So our confused dogs think their names are "Susie-come-here-right-now!" or "Harvey-what-did-I-tell-you-about-jumping-up?" Few people have gone to the trouble of establishing basic name recognition and eye contact before moving on to grounding exercises and obedience commands. If our dogs—who have phenomenal hearing—aren't listening, it's because of what we're saying or the tone and volume with which we're saying it.

"My dog is like a kid, rebellious, independent, and mischievous." Of course, children are very different from dogs, in almost every biologi-

cal, emotional, and instinctive way. For both species' sakes, dogs shouldn't be viewed or treated like kids. The smartest dog, remember, isn't as bright as an ordinary three-year-old, so it's no service to dogs to humanize them.

"My dog can't be trained. He'll never change. There's nothing I can do." True, some badly damaged dogs can't be helped. But barring genetic damage or the most severe kinds of trauma, virtually all dogs can be trained or retrained, their unwanted behaviors modified, if not eliminated. We can change their names, if that makes sense for easier training. With common sense and hard work, we can usually deal with even seemingly intractable behaviors—barking, aggression, chewing. We can try different training methods, use food or toys or confinement. If we can't make progress toward better behavior, one trainer or another probably has some answers.

"He was terribly abused." Maybe, but maybe not. Researchers believe that while much abuse does, sadly, occur, its extent is overstated, especially among people who need to see their dogs as piteous and needy. Dogs can't tell us whether they've been abused or not, so it's easy to assume that that explains their—or our—problems.

But even if they have been mistreated, that's not an excuse for aggression or other compulsive or obnoxious behaviors. Dogs with such habits need training even more urgently than more placid types; in many ways, their lives may depend on it. Abuse is a serious problem for dogs in America, but lack of training is arguably an even bigger one, for dogs, their owners, and everybody else.

COMMON SENSE

Sam, one of my New Jersey volunteers, presented me with the vexing problem of a two-year-old West Highland terrier named Pundit. The dog had never learned to come; in fact, he was prone to running away when Sam called. With a busy street nearby, this was dangerous, Sam realized.

"How do you try to get Pundit to come?" I asked.

"I yell, 'Come, come!' and when he doesn't I get frightened and pissed off and start running after him to try to grab him."

"And what does the dog do?" I asked.

"He runs away."

Sam, no dummy, runs a successful corporation; he's educated, bright, very savvy. Yet he was actually teaching Pundit to bolt. Pundit, after all, wasn't stupid either. What would any of us do if somebody ten times our size came charging after us, screaming?

Take advantage of the dog's behavior and instincts, I suggested. Take some hot-dog slices or meatballs from the refrigerator, then back away from the dog. When outside, actually run away. Say "Come." When the dog follows, as he invariably will, scatter some meatballs on the ground and praise him for coming.

Sam called back a week later. "That was brilliant," he said. Much as I appreciated the compliment, tossing meatballs to a dog doesn't approach brilliance. At best, it's common sense, a handy commodity.

Like my other volunteers, Sam had bought armloads of training books and attended several obedience classes. But through his life with his dog, he already knew a fair amount about what could induce his Pundit to come, once he thought about it. He could transcend conventional wisdoms about authority and obedience. In fact, "obedience" is a lousy word to describe training, which is mostly about communicating.

Pundit, like most dogs, is a simple creature who will respond to food, praise, and attention more readily than to bellowing or charging. For some bits of meat and kind words, he was quite happy to come to Sam, and the anxiety and tension in the relationship eased.

On, then, to Sam's next concern. He owned a lovely ten-acre property and wanted Pundit to have the run of it. "I feel bad that I have all this land and he doesn't get to use it because I can't trust him. So we never let him off-leash outside. It's a shame."

I disagreed. Westies are small dogs popular with apartment-dwellers, not hunting or herding dogs. Why would a single little Westie need ten acres to roam?

It's often risky to give dogs too much freedom. On Sam's ten acres,

Pundit could encounter rabid raccoons or feral cats, or human tres-
passers, or traffic on the adjacent road.

Here was a man with ten acres whose dog couldn't use any of them
because his owner had a fantasy about his being able to run free. Why
not a wooden or invisible electric fence around just one of those acres,
or half an acre? "Aren't electric fences cruel?" Sam asked.

Some dog lovers think so. Others worry that a dog will bust through
the shock and not come back. But when these systems are properly installed and introduced, they can provide real and long-lasting benefits—like safety for the dog and others—after some minimal initial
discomfort. They aren't nearly as cruel as a dog's getting hit by a car, or
being denied time outdoors at all. Most of the dog owners I know who
use these fences and have trained their dogs properly around them are
happy with the results.

Sam had an invisible fence installed around one acre outside the rear
entrance. Pundit got a mild jolt, then never approached the fence again.
But he got to go outside half a dozen times a day, running around, hid-
ing bones, chasing balls. Later on, Sam got another Westie, and the pair
had a lively time, playing with each other and with their humans, getting
exercise, and easing their owner's mortification.

THE QUITTING POINT

WORKING WITH VOLUNTEERS, E-MAILING DOG LOVERS, TALKING WITH
thousands of owners and behaviorists and breeders and trainers in recent years, I've noticed a pattern so pronounced as to seem nearly universal: the Quitting Point.

This is the point in training a dog when people just stop. They've
tried some training, had some mixed results, and then drop the process
altogether.

There are all sorts of reasons. People have wildly unrealistic expectations of what dogs can learn, and how quickly, so they're easily de-
flated by reality. Or they find their enthusiasm for pets waning on

bitter-cold mornings or broiling afternoons, or when their kids break their solemn promises to share the load and hop back on their skateboards. In our busy and disposable society, people get distracted or drawn by new passions; dogs, like everything else, compete with lots of things for attention. Besides, we all know that dogs can be destructive, annoying, and genuinely obnoxious. Hence, the Quitting Point.

Jiminy, a mixed-breed shelter dog, was adopted by Nancy, a medical technician working in an office in Philadelphia. Nancy dutifully took him to several obedience classes, where the instructor showed her how to make Jiminy come by tying a long lead to his collar, yelling "Come," then jerking sharply, pulling him toward her.

He also suggested tossing choke chains or soda cans filled with coins over Jiminy's head. The idea was that the clatter would frighten him into running toward her, so that she could praise him when he did. Nancy was bothered because Jiminy seemed more wary after that exercise, but her instructor told her that was respect, not fear. She was the "alpha," he said, and the dog would thus obey.

Neither Nancy nor Jiminy really enjoyed the experience, but somewhat to my surprise, it worked most of the time, especially when the dog thought something was about to be thrown behind him. So that was it, Nancy decided. Jiminy eliminated outdoors and came when she called, more or less, and that was enough. She was a working woman; she had plenty on her mind. Training classes weren't much fun, so why put Jiminy and herself through more angst?

Since she asked, I confessed my disappointment, which I always feel when somebody like this tells me they've made that decision so early in the game. Training a dog isn't just about a few commands, I argued, but about building a relationship with the dog, and about the dog's relationship to everything else. Nancy could go farther if she chose, do more.

You could argue this one either way. On the one hand, you could celebrate the fact that a caring but busy person had adopted a dog headed for death, giving him a good home, and that both dog and owner seemed content. On the other hand, I wondered why she'd halt the progress they'd made. I asked Nancy to think about her friends and their dogs, about which ones had the kind of relationship she wanted with Jiminy. I reminded her that she was at a critical point; in many ways, their relationship was being determined right now.

Why not try an experiment? I urged. Her assignment (it's one I've given many of my volunteers, since they know their animals best) was to think of several things that would cause Jiminy to come to her voluntarily. It wasn't hard to come up with a few: his favorite squeaky toy, which always brought him running; liver treats, which he adored; the scraping sound of his food bowl being picked up off the kitchen floor.

That made three reliable ways of recalling the dog. Nancy, who just needed a bit of a shove, now saw that training need not be a complex, formal undertaking, but something that could easily be incorporated into her everyday life with Jiminy. Soon, using these attractions and praising him when he responded, she had Jiminy coming to her happily, and nearly all the time. She moved on to some grounding and bonding exercises as well, and to what I call "organic training"—casually working on Jiminy's "lie downs," "sits," and "stays" with a bowl of kibble while she watched TV in the evening.

Over weeks and months Jiminy made better eye contact, saw coming to her as purely rewarding and safe, and training as fun and successful, a source of treats, toys, and attention. Nancy rarely had much reason to scold or yell at the dog, nor to startle or throw things at him.

Over the months, they advanced until Jiminy could heel reliably, sit down when they reached street corners, and walk off-leash in state parks and at the beach.

Instead of coexisting with a nervous dog who wasn't too much of a hassle, Nancy saw their relationship blossom into one of those great human-canine bonds. "There's such a difference between having a dog who isn't doing any harm, and having a dog who's keyed in to you, who trusts and loves you and likes doing things with you," she reported six months down the line. "I'm thinking of getting a therapy certificate and visiting some nursing homes. We're having a blast. I'm so glad I stuck with it."

When people don't stick with it, perhaps it's because they lack time and patience, but often I think it's because they just can't see beyond the Quitting Point to the potential rewards. If training results merely in a dog that will lie down on command, is that worth months of effort? Lots of people conclude that it isn't.

Like Bill, who got a border collie from an online rescue group. Border collies—like Labs, German shepherds, and golden retrievers—are becoming something of a sad story in the dog world. Increasingly popular, thanks to TV commercials, movies like *Babe,* and cable coverage of herding and agility trials, they attract owners who don't understand how much work and exercise they need, or how neurotic they can get without it.

Bill was a busy Chicago lawyer, drawn to a border collie because he'd heard they were intelligent and he wanted "the smartest dog there was." Bill hadn't been allowed a dog when he was a boy, so he'd fantasized about owning one much of his life. "I had this idea in my head of a dog that was my buddy, my pal, that I could bring everywhere and do things with." It's a notion many of us grew up with.

But Bill was astonished at the manic energy of his new dog, Stripe, and at the dog's intense need to work. To get Stripe off his back and assuage his guilt, he began tossing a Frisbee or a ball day and night—outside in the yard, on walks, even in the house. He'd intended to train the dog to do other things, but once the Frisbee-chasing began, he quit.

"Stripe was getting lots of exercise, and it fit into my schedule, which is very busy," he explained. "So I stopped." He conceded he had a "neat" dog, but not the companion he'd always envisioned. Stripe was a bit of a pest, one-dimensional and obsessive.

One could argue that in this case both owner and dog were reasonably satisfied, but dogs are neither happy nor sad in a human sense. Stripe didn't know he could be out chasing sheep or geese; like most dogs, he was adaptable and made do with what he had.

So he'd become a Frisbee addict, bringing a toy to people and then chasing it whenever possible, to the exclusion of almost everything else. That had become work and play, the structure of his life, the basis of his relationship with Bill. And Bill found himself sitting in his living room tossing a ball down the hallway while reading briefs or watching TV.

"It turned out I didn't really have time for more," Bill said; and it seemed he couldn't really see a payoff, either.

Many dogs are worse off than Stripe, who got exercise and attention, food and health care. But it seemed a shame that Bill had gotten such a dog, then taken matters no farther than he did. If he was too busy to train Stripe, perhaps he didn't need a border collie. But if he had worked with Stripe, invested some time, perhaps he *could* have had that dog he had always wanted. I understand busy modern lives and distractions, but I also believe that dogs present a moral obligation, and that Bill had failed in his obligation to Stripe.

The Quitting Point generates all sorts of rationalizations. Owners are genuinely too busy, or they feel dumb and frustrated because their books and classes don't result in much obedience. Perhaps they're told to remain purely positive with their commands, but they lose their tempers. Or they're trying to dominate the dog, but he blows them off. They attribute all sorts of human emotions to the dog, handy excuses: the dog is angry, jealous, devious, rebellious.

Or sometimes the Quitting Point arises not from failure but from limited success. The initial training works; the dog comes, sits, and stays. Like Jiminy, he gets along pretty well, causes little trouble.

So people quit.

Everybody's lives are different, filled with responsibilities, pressures, obligations, challenges, realities. Those people you see at trials and dog runs whistling and hand-signaling their instantly, almost robotically responsive dogs may be doing terrific training work, but that isn't for everybody. It isn't for me.

Yet to quit training is an important decision, a major choice in the evolution of your life with your dog. Often it limits the nature of your relationship, the possibilities of communication and understanding between human and animal. People who have experienced this connection know it can bring satisfaction, even joy.

So while the Quitting Point is understandable, and sometimes unavoidable, it comes too soon for many dogs and the people who own them.

Well-trained dogs are often the best loved. They have the strongest relationships with the people who own them. They can move more freely about the world. They're the least likely to harm people or animals, or damage homes and property. They make us better people by forcing us to honor our contracts with them, and by overcoming our distraction, impatience, and growing detachment from the natural world.

Quit if you must. But hang in there if you can.

THE GOOD-ENGLISH DOG

PERSPECTIVE AND COMMON SENSE ARE ESSENTIAL TO LIVING WITH DOGS. For many busy and pressed people, there does come a point where training has resulted in a dog and a relationship that may not be the stuff of a segment on Animal Planet, but it's good enough. That's a personal choice that nobody else can make.

When is a dog good enough? That varies, of course, but for me, it's when the dog is safe and lives comfortably in the world. The dog comes when called, lies down when asked, sits when told. Chews its own stuff, not yours. Doesn't scare or jump on people, is reliable around kids, is unlikely to attack or maim another dog. Doesn't bite, bark continuously, or behave compulsively. You can walk it, rather than have it walk you. The relationship resembles a partnership, with mutual affection and respect.

I know many dog lovers who've taken in aggressive or troubled dogs. They take their responsibilities seriously, keep the dogs away from other people and animals, and have happy lives and relationships. For them, that's good enough.

A relationship with a dog is good enough when you can communicate with the dog without anger, when you've fulfilled your moral responsibility not just to house and feed a dog but to lead it into the community it has to negotiate. That state is defined not by fear or even obedience, but by affection and peace of mind. It's not an easy place to reach, but it's certainly reachable. Good enough is a big idea—the point where the owner and dog accept each other.

We are, most of us, harried and distracted, insecure about our jobs, worried about our health, separated from our original families and communities, struggling to balance a complex world against the needs of our dogs. As much as I believe in the power and long-term reward of training a dog well, perspective is essential. Sometimes good enough is good enough.

THE GOOD-ENOUGH OWNER

IF THERE'S SUCH A THING AS A GOOD-ENOUGH DOG, THERE IS ALSO A good-enough owner.

Often there's an enormous difference between what our dogs need and what we think they do. Our desire to provide everything they might possibly need sometimes becomes overpowering. This impulse can be great for dogs, but it can also lead us into excess.

One recent winter day in upstate New York—where I've suffered both frostbite and hypothermia on my farm—I got just such a reality check.

The temperature was below zero by evening, and my dogs and I had already been on three walks, one of them a forty-five-minute stroll into the deep, snowy woods, a hike I love. I'd also taken Rose out for our daily workout with sheep (another half hour) and worked with Orson, who doesn't really herd but circles the sheep pen with great gusto and enthusiasm. Clementine, as usual, had come along on each excursion to scarf up dead rodents and other gross Lab treats. So all the dogs had been walked, exercised, trained—yet here I was, suiting up in thermal outerwear again, until Paula brought me up short: "It's freezing out there, and you're tired," she admonished. "What are you doing?"

I knew the answer, though I didn't say it aloud: I was giving my dogs perfect lives, or trying to. It was I, not they, who needed the satisfaction of taking them for one more walk, giving the border collies yet another chance to run and play, tossing more balls and sticks for the energetic Clementine. The more I did for them, the better I felt. Sometimes I literally can't do enough for them. So I sometimes do too much.

Three long walks a day is more than enough, especially in sweltering heat or bitter cold. Yet I was actually feeling guilty because we hadn't walked still more. I'd like to get over that.

It was an important reminder that many of the things we're driven to do for and with our dogs are not necessary, at least not for them. Sometimes we try to fill the holes in our own lives by filling theirs—with treats, toys, too much food, too many activities. We can easily make them hyperactive and drive ourselves nuts in the process.

Good enough doesn't apply only to dogs, but to us. In fact, it's an elemental question for those of us who feel the full power of dog love.

"Your day has been good enough," I announced to my eager dogs, clustered at the door, taking off my coat. Separating human and canine needs, being aware that they frequently diverge, is one of the biggest challenges we face in our lives with dogs.

CASE STUDY: *Ernie*   Whenever we don't give much consideration to our needs and motives, our relationships with dogs can become miserable for both parties. If choosing a dog wisely and training him well has a payoff, failing to do either can have a poignant and painful downside.

Ernie, a fluffy golden retriever pup with heart-melting eyes, was originally a birthday present. The lucky recipient was Danielle, a pony-tailed eleven-year-old living in an affluent Westchester suburb.

Danielle's passions, for some time, had been soccer, Justin Timberlake, and instant messaging, but her parents wanted to give her a different kind of birthday gift, "something that you didn't plug in or watch, something that would give her a sense of responsibility." She'd often said she'd love a puppy, and vowed to take care of it.

Girl and dog, growing up together—what parent hasn't fantasized about that? Her folks envisioned long family walks around the neighborhood, followed by Ernie frolicking on the lawn while they gardened. They could see him riding along to soccer games.

Acquiring a dog completed the portrait that had been taking shape for several years, beginning with the family's move to the suburbs from Brooklyn. The package included a four-bedroom Colonial, a lawn edged with flowering shrubs, a busy sports schedule, a Volvo wagon and a Subaru Outback to ferry the kids around. A dog—a big, beautiful hunting breed—came with the rest of it, increasingly as much a part of the American dream as the picket fence or car with high safety ratings.

So Danielle's parents found a breeder online with lots of awards, cooed over the adorable pictures, and mailed off a deposit. They drove to Connecticut to pick up their purchased pup and returned to surprise Danielle on her birthday, just hours before her friends were due for a celebratory sleepover.

It was love at first sight. Danielle and her friends spent hours passing the adorable puppy from one lap to another. Ernie slept with her that night. Over the next two or three weeks, she spent hours cuddling with him, playing tug-of-war, and tossing balls while her parents took photos.

But the dog did not spark greater love of the outdoors or diminish her interest in the TV, iPod, computer, and cell phone. Nor did his arrival lighten Danielle's demanding athletic schedule; with practices, games, and victory celebrations, soccer season took up three or four afternoons a week. Anyway, she didn't find the shedding, slobbering, chewing, maturing Ernie quite as cute as the new-puppy version.

Both of Danielle's parents worked in New York City and rarely got home before seven on weekdays. The household relied on a nanny/housekeeper from Nicaragua who wasn't especially drawn to dogs and viewed Ernie as stupid, messy, and, as he grew larger and more restive, mildly frightening.

Because nobody was home during the day, he wasn't housebroken for nearly two months, and even then, not completely. No single person was responsible for him; nobody had the time, will, or skill to train him.

As Ernie went through the normal stages of retriever development— teething, mouthing, racing frantically around the house, peeing when excited, eating strange objects and then vomiting them up—the casualties mounted. Rugs got stained, mail devoured, table legs gnawed. The family rejected the use of a crate or kennel as cruel. Instead, they let the puppy get into all sorts of trouble, then scolded and resented him for it. He was "hyper," they complained, "wild," "rambunctious."

A practiced trainer would have seen a golden retriever that was confused, underexercised, and untrained—an ironic fate for a dog bred for centuries to be calm and responsive to humans.

Ernie did not attach to anybody in particular—an essential element in training a dog. Because he never quite understood the rules, he became increasingly anxious. He was reprimanded constantly for jumping on residents and visitors, for pulling and jerking on the leash when walked. He was big enough to drag Danielle into the street by now, so her parents and the housekeeper reluctantly took over. His walks grew brief: outside, down the block until he did his business, then home. He never got to run much.

Increasingly, he was isolated when company came or the family gathered. Complaining that he was out of control, the family tried fencing the backyard and putting Ernie outside during meals to keep him from bothering them. The nanny stuck him there most of the day as well, because he dirtied up the house. Allowed inside at night, he was largely confined to the kitchen, sealed off by a toddler gate.

Though abandonment and abuse of dogs is an enormous issue in the animal-rights movement, and quite properly, nobody is likely to talk much about Ernie. His abusers aren't lowlifes who mercilessly beat, starve, or tether animals. Quite the opposite: his owners—affluent, educated people—consider themselves humanistic and moral. But they've been cruel nonetheless, through their lack of responsibility, their neglect, their poor training, and their inattention. They never thought through why they wanted a dog, what they actually expected of one, how they would meet its needs. They presumed, instead, that Ernie would intuit and satisfy theirs.

I've seen Ernie several times over the past two years. I've watched him become more detached, neurotic, and unresponsive. I've seen the lively curiosity drain from the dog's eyes.

He's affectionate and unthreatening, but he doesn't really know how to behave—not around his family or other people, not around other animals. He lunges and barks almost continuously when anyone comes near. Increasingly, therefore, he gets confined to his backyard, out of sight and mind.

This family was shocked and outraged when I suggested that the dog was suffering from a kind of abuse and might be better off in a different home. "Nobody ever hits that dog," sputtered Danielle's father. "He gets the best dog food, he gets all his shots." All true.

But he lacks what is perhaps the most essential ingredient in a dog's life: a human who will take emotional responsibility for him.

I understand, but Ernie haunts me. He may be the most abused dog I know.

I FIRST WROTE ERNIE'S STORY—IN A DIFFERENT, ABBREVIATED FORM— for the online magazine *Slate*, and got thousands of e-mails after the column appeared in the fall of 2004. Many of the e-mailers offered to take the dog from his family. I forwarded some of the messages to Ernie's owners.

They were shocked, of course, and initially defensive. But, to their credit, they quickly came to understand the plight the dog was in.

Thanks to a rescue group in New Jersey, Ernie has been re-homed. His new family lives in a less developed area of northwestern New Jersey. He has a couple of fenced acres to run around in, but the bigger change is his striking connection to people, especially Kurt, the computer executive who took him in, and Kurt's wife and three kids.

Ernie is trained daily, exercised regularly, crated appropriately. He is being resocialized, taught to be calm and appropriate around people. He goes to the kids' sports practices and to obedience classes, for walks in the woods, and is deeply attached to his new owners. Because his contacts with other people and dogs are not so occasional, he is getting used to them, too.

I don't believe dogs have our kinds of emotions, yet when I drove out to visit the new, improved Ernie, it seemed to me that he was positively radiating calm and contentment, pleasure and gratitude. Ernie's second chance gives the lie to the notion that dogs like Labs or border collies are intrinsically and irrevocably "hyper" and "crazy."

I struggle against self-righteousness, a malady not unknown among dog lovers, yet I've come to believe Ernie's initial treatment is typical of a larger moral failure in our dealings with the species that's emotionally

and physically closest to us. Loving dogs is commonplace; taking responsibility for the care and training of dogs is still rare.

Ernie is by no means alone. Every American suburb is stuffed with
his like. I was shocked by the number of messages I got from people
across the country, reporting that they were living next door to that very
dog, or a reasonable facsimile.

The unconscious acquisition of dogs like Ernie, and the abrogation
of their training, is a growing catastrophe for dogs. The treatment Ernie
received in his first home is probably the most prevalent kind of abuse
dogs face in America. It's much more common for a dog to be abandoned at home than to be beaten or starved.

Unlike many, this story at least has a happy ending. Ernie has responded dramatically to being a wanted, trained, and loved dog in the
proper environment. It's a pleasure to see Ernie become the dog Labs
are bred to be, the dog he deserved to be. The dog we owe it to him to
let him be.

BLUE, HEATHER'S NORMALLY AFFECTIONATE AND OBEDIENT rottweiler (she had one brown and one bright-blue eye), began tearing up the house shortly after Heather went back to work as an accountant after several years at home. Her new office was just twenty minutes away, and her part-time schedule left plenty of time for dog walking. But after Heather's third or fourth day at work, she began arriving home to scenes of worsening carnage.

First, the contents of the trash cans were strewn all over the house. A favorite comforter was destroyed. Then Blue began peeing all over Heather's expensive new living room carpet, and systematically ripped through cables and electrical wires.

"I know exactly what's going on," Heather told her vet when she called, seeking help. "Blue is angry with me for leaving her alone, she's punishing me. She always looks guilty when I come home, so she knows she's been bad. She knows she shouldn't be doing those things."

Heather's assessment of her dog's destructive rampage is typical of many dog owners' diagnoses of behavioral problems. And her vet agreed, suggesting "separation anxiety" and prescribing antianxiety medication.

Heather, who adores her dog, also hired a trainer, who confirmed the diagnosis: Blue was resentful of her owner's absence and was misbehaving to regain the attention that she'd once monopolized. After all, Blue hadn't transgressed like this when Heather had gone out shopping or taken in a movie with friends. Blue might rummage through a trash basket or gnaw a stray slipper, but this level of destructiveness was new. It must be punitive. Heather's mother even recalled Heather, as a child, throwing tantrums when *she* went off to work. Heather and Blue had become so close, she joked, that they were acting alike.

So Heather shut Blue in the kitchen with a toddler gate, removing countertop food and garbage. Things calmed down. Heather began to relax, and gave Blue the run of the house again.

Heather—she's a friend of a friend of mine—had called me for counsel as well. But since she, her vet, her trainer, and her mother had all reached the same conclusion, and since the rampaging had stopped, I frankly didn't give the situation much thought. Besides, to be candid, I knew how fervently dog owners cling to their theories about their dogs' emotions.

A month later, though, Heather was back on the phone: Blue had relapsed, causing hundreds of dollars' worth of damage. She yowled piteously when confined to the kitchen or basement. Worse, she was showing signs of aggression with people and other dogs, and refusing to obey even simple commands that were once routine. On one late-night walk, Blue attacked a terrier walking nearby, opening wounds that needed stitches and cost Heather hundreds more in vet bills.

Blue's problems had grown so serious that kennels wouldn't board the dog and the vet wouldn't examine her without a muzzle. Heather was thinking of finding her another home, turning her over to a rescue group, possibly even euthanizing her. She was horrified at the idea, yet running out of options.

"She's out of control," Heather complained, exhausted, angry, and frightened. She sounded betrayed—a dog she'd loved and cared for was turning on her because she went to work. "I caused this by leaving her," Heather confessed, guiltily. But was she supposed to quit her job and stay home with her dog?

This time, Heather got my full attention. I took notes, asked questions, then called a canine behaviorist at Cornell and explained the problem in as much detail as I could.

"Everybody says the dog was reacting to her going back to work," I suggested.

"Everybody is probably wrong," was his blunt comeback. "It's theory of mind." Perhaps a dog's greatest enemy, he told me.

His analysis: "Being angry at the human and behaving punitively— that's not a thought sequence even remotely possible, given a dog's brain. The likely scenario is that the dog is simply frightened."

When Heather was home, she was there to explain and enforce the rules. With her gone, the dog literally didn't know how to behave. The dog should have been acclimated to a crate or room and confined more, not less, until she got used to her new independence.

Lots of dogs get nervous when they don't know what's expected of them, and when they get anxious, they can also grow restless. Blue hadn't had to occupy time alone before. Dogs can get unnerved by this. They bark, chew, scratch, destroy. Getting yelled at and punished later doesn't help: the dog probably knows it's doing *something* wrong, but it has no idea what. Since there's nobody around to correct behaviors when the dog is alone, how could the dog know which behavior is the problem? Which action was wrong? "This is what often happens when humans assume that dogs think the way we do," the behaviorist concluded.

He made sense. Dogs are not aware of time, even as a concept, so Blue couldn't know whether she was being left for five minutes or five hours, or how that compared to being left for a movie two weeks earlier.

Since she had no conscious notion that Heather's work life had changed, how could she get angry, let alone plot revenge? The dog was alone more, and had more time to fill. The damage was increasing, most likely, because Blue had more time to get into mischief, more opportunities to react to stimulus without correction, not because she was responding to different emotions.

I was familiar with the "theory of mind" notion the behaviorist was referring to. Psychologist David Premack of the University of Pennsylvania talks about it; it's also discussed in Stanley Coren's exploratory book *How Dogs Think*.

The phrase refers to a belief each of us has about the way others think. Simply, it says that since we are aware and self-conscious, we think others—both human and animal—are, too. There is, of course, enormous difference of opinion about whether this is true.

A theory of mind includes all the elements of consciousness, Coren says: active perception of a situation, a mental representation of the world, and self-awareness. "Self-awareness," adds Coren, "puts you in the position of using your own experience with your own mental processes to predict the mental processes and behaviors of others."

On some level, dogs do seem to have an awareness of others' thought processes. When I have finished my barn chores, I go to my study to work; there's a bowl of biscuits next to my computer. Rose is always sitting expectantly next to the desk before I get there. When I go out to the sheep pasture, I pull on a pair of rubber barn boots. Any other shoe: no Rose. Barn boots: she's waiting by the back door.

Has she connected the dots, read my mind, grasped my intent? Or simply been reinforced—taught to associate a treat with going to my desk, a certain shoe with going outside? Rose is the brightest dog I've ever had and I sometimes credit her with reasoning: a part of me needs to see her as intelligent. Still, when I stop and think about it, I decide that she's acting out of association, not higher mental processes or ESP.

When I used to leave him alone in the house, uncrated, Orson learned to open the refrigerator with his nose, remove certain food items, open the plastic container and consume its contents. Then he'd squirrel away the empty packages. Everyone I told this story to made the same assumptions: Orson was a wily devil taunting me for leaving him alone. We actually installed a child lock on the refrigerator door. But what changed his behavior was that I began to crate him when I went out. He has not raided the fridge since. Yet he could easily sneak in and do that while he's uncrated and I'm occupied outdoors or elsewhere in the house. Is he no longer wily? Or is he simply less anxious?

There's no convincing evidence I'm aware of, from any reputable behaviorist or psychologist, that suggests dogs can replicate human thought processes—use language, think in narrative and sequential terms, understand human minds, or share humans' range of emotions.

Yet that remains a powerful, pervasive view of dogs, the reason Heather's vet, trainer, and mother all agreed on Blue's motivations. It's almost impossible not to lapse into theory-of-mind reasoning when it comes to our dogs. After all, most of us have no other way in which to grasp another creature's behavior. How can one even begin to imagine what's going on inside a dog's head?

Most of the time, I don't know why my dogs do what they do. They seem aware that I have a way of doing things. They've learned that we don't walk in the street, that I don't distribute food from my plate, that there will be a bone or treat after dinner. But they are creatures of habit and instinct, especially when it comes to food, work, and attention. I often think of them as stuffpots wedded to ritual, resistant and nervous about change.

I don't believe that dogs act out of spite or that they can plot retribution, though countless dog owners swear otherwise. To punish or deceive requires the perpetrator to understand that his victim or object has a particular point of view and consciously work to manipulate or thwart it. That requires a level of mental process dogs don't have.

My dogs are keenly aware of where their food is stored, yet I doubt they have any consciousness, when I return to the house, of whether I've been gone for one hour or ten. Nor could Blue marshal the narrative reasoning to grasp that Heather was now going away to work, or for how long.

Our own favorite stories about how smart, wicked, or caring our dogs can be are rarely detached or unbiased. We see what we want and need to see.

The problem with this is that dogs often fare poorly at the hands of theory-of-mind adherents. If you think a dog is spiting or defying you, aren't you likely to get angry? To strike back somehow? Yet anger is almost always a poor training tool, and often leads to suffering, abuse, and abandonment.

Humans may not be as unique as we think; perhaps other animals also have a well-developed sense of self-consciousness. But probably not the animals that share our homes and menace our bedroom slippers. The more I've moved away from interpreting my dogs' behavior as nearly human, the easier it is to train them, and the less guilt and anxiety I feel.

To attribute complex thoughts and plots to their actions unravels the training process. Training and living with a dog requires a different theory: that these are primal, predatory animals driven by instinct. Rather than seeking animal clues to her dog's behavior, Heather had reasoned that if she, Heather, were suddenly left alone for long periods, abandoned by someone she loved and used to spend a lot of time with, she would feel angry and hurt and might try to get even, not only to punish her companion but to try to persuade him or her to return.

That's a lot of intellectual steps for an animal that can recognize a few dozen words but has none of its own, that reads human emotions but doesn't experience the same ones. Since the Cornell behavorist made sense to me, I conveyed his analysis and persuaded Heather—by now distraught—to buy a large crate. For weeks, she fed the dog in the crate, leaving the door open. Between meals, she left treats and bones inside.

The first time Heather closed the crate door, Blue threw herself against the metal, whining and howling. The same thing happened the second, third, fifth, and dozenth times. But Heather, cautioned that training and retraining often takes weeks and months, persisted. Sometimes she left the treat-filled crate open; other times she closed it.

After several weeks, Blue began to go into the crate willingly and remained there quietly for short, then lengthening periods. Heather walked Blue two or three times daily; when she was gone for more than three or four hours, she hired a dog walker to take her out an additional time and throw a ball. But whenever Heather left the house, she put Blue in the crate and left a nearby radio tuned to a talk network.

This time, Heather got it right, treating Blue as a dog, not a rebellious teenager. Blue never completely regained her easygoing geniality—it simply isn't clear why—but she improved dramatically, and the improvement continues. Her aggression diminished, then seemed to vanish, although Heather no longer lets her near dogs or children unleashed. It seemed the dog had comprehensible rules to follow, and felt safer.

Freed of the confusion and anxiety of figuring out what to do with her sudden, unsupervised freedom, Blue was off the clock. Once again there was little tension between the two of them. Heather's house wasn't getting chewed up, and homecomings weren't tense and angry experiences. Yet here was a case, I thought, where our seeing canine behavior in human terms nearly cost an animal its life.

Sometimes it does. Harry, a social worker in Los Angeles, wrote me that he had a great rescue dog named Rocket, and was happy enough with the experience to adopt a second. Rocket first attacked the new dog while Harry was feeding them, then bit a neighborhood kid. "He never forgave me for getting the new dog," Harry explained. "He was so angry with me. I couldn't trust him not to take out his rage on others, so I had him put to sleep."

We will never know, of course, what Rocket could or could not "forgive." Only dogs sometimes have an easier time understanding their position in a family. When another dog challenges them, especially when there's no acclimation or other adjustment period, instincts that weren't significant before suddenly arise. Any dog can bite a person or another dog, given the right circumstances.

But Rocket probably didn't attack the new dog out of anger at Harry. More likely, he was simply protecting his food or pack position. The creature in the household with the most to lose from a new arrival, he probably fought for what he had. Then, once aroused, he was more dangerous. As trainers know, dogs under pressure have two options: fight or flight. Rocket decided to fight, and paid for it with his life. Had his owner known more about dogs' true nature, he might have introduced the new dog more gradually, or not at all. And there might be one less bitten child. But this is all a guess. We will never know.

Usually, the consequences are more mundane. Sam, a Dalmatian in a Cleveland suburb, regularly enrages his owner, Gary, with his selective obedience. Sometimes Sam comes, sometimes not. Sometimes he stops at the curb as instructed, sometimes he lunges across the street. Gary has rejected a trainer's observation that Sam responded to food better than to verbal commands. "Sam's just being a jerk," Gary declares. "He's letting me know that he isn't one of those circus dogs who always does what they're told."

If Gary could put aside his imaginary power struggle, he might choose a different training approach—food sounded promising—then take on one behavior at a time, working with Sam for as many weeks or months as it took to develop a reliable and consistent response. Believe it or not, we *are* smarter than they are. But we are often more distractable and inconsistent, and a dog can often outlast his attention-deficit owner or decide that commands are multiple-choice games, not rules to be followed. Gary wants his dog to obey him out of respect and affection, so he only occasionally uses food. Yet food almost always works.

When I face such training problems—and I do, we all do—I try to adopt a Sherlock Holmesian strategy, using logic and determination. We have all sorts of tools at our disposal that dogs don't have. We control every aspect of their lives, from food to shelter to play, so we ought to be able to figure out what's driving the dog and come up with an individually tailored approach that works. And if it doesn't, to come up with another one.

Why will Clementime come instantly if she's looking at me, but not if she's sniffing deer droppings? Is she simply being stubborn, or is it, as many people tell me, that she's "going through adolescence"? Or because, when following her keen predatory instincts, she simply doesn't hear me? Should my response be to tug at her leash and yell? Maybe I should be sure we've established eye contact before I give her a command, or, better yet, offer a liver treat as an alternative to whatever's distracting her. But how do I establish eye contact when her nose is buried? Can I cluck or bark? Use a whistle or hoot like an owl?

I've found that coughing, of all things, fascinates her, catches her attention, and makes her head swivel, after which she responds. If you walk with us, you will hear me clearing my throat repeatedly. What can I say? It works. She looks at me, comes to me, gets rewarded.

The reality is, we don't know that much about what dogs think, because they can't tell us. You can make up your own mind about what you think dogs think. Behaviorists tend to believe that dogs "think" in their own way—in sensory images involving their finely honed instincts. They're not capable of deviousness or spite. They love routine: nothing seems to make them more comfortable than doing the same thing at the same time in the familiar way, day after day—we snack here, we poop there, we play over here. I am astonished at how little it takes to please them, how simple their lives can be if we don't complicate them with an overlay of human motivation.

Seeing them more and more as simple creatures, I try to regulate our activities. When I come home from an errand or dinner out, I wait four or five minutes before letting the dogs out of their crates, so that my coming and going isn't such a big deal, and we can avoid the jumping and circling of a multiple-dog household.

I try to give them three or four hours in their crates each day so that they can be calm, chew rawhide, and meditate on whatever it is dogs meditate on. I leave them in a fenced yard for an equivalent period to hang around with one another, play if they want to, stare at nothing in particular. We all go for three walks together each day. Sometimes we go for more.

It's a lot, and it is enough.

CASE STUDY: *What Katie Wants* SOMETHING ABOUT US WANTS and needs to believe our dogs think like us, but their welfare depends in many ways on our understanding that they don't—one of the great conundrums in the human-dog relationship.

Sandy, a medical researcher from Sacramento and one of my training volunteers, contacted me because her two-year-old Irish setter was driving her and her entire family berserk.

"Katie brings me rubber balls day and night, 24/7. Brings them to my kids at the school bus, all during dinner, to guests visiting, on walks. She's so hyper, she is making us hyper," was Sandy's e-mailed plea. "Somebody is always yelling at her to get off. She never gets the message. And I feel so stupid. Why can't I get her to behave?"

Sandy had a long litany of complaints about her dog. She thought Katie was defying her. She'd half-decided the dog was too obstinate to train. And it was hard not to sympathize. In her zeal to chase balls, the dog was jumping up on Sandy and others, knocking kids over. Peaceful moments had become nearly impossible, indoors or outdoors, with an aroused, slobbering dog dropping a slimy ball on everybody all the time. The dog, constantly in motion, was a source of embarrassment and aggravation.

Consequently, somebody was always yelling at Katie to stop. But dogs often don't differentiate between good and bad attention; they like both. Yelling can reinforce unwanted behavior, just like treats. Besides, yelling and shouting, along with games like ball tossing, are arousing. They crank a dog up, keep her in a state where communication and training become difficult. Nobody does a dog any favor by keeping it in a cranked-up state, when it's much more likely to bite, chew, bark, or fight.

"What do you do," I asked, "when Katie brings you the ball?"

"We throw it."

"Why do you do that when it bothers you and annoys everybody else?" I persisted.

She seemed incredulous at the question. "Because that's what Katie wants."

SOME AMOUNT OF COMPULSIVE CHASING AND RETRIEVING ISN'T SO UN-usual with hunting breeds. Sandy, unlike some owners, wasn't willing to call this a good-enough situation; she hadn't yet reached her personal

Quitting Point. But she didn't know how to proceed, how to break a dog of a bad habit without breaking its lively spirit. I wasn't entirely sure myself, but we agreed to talk weekly, to see what might work.

My first goal was to try to get Sandy to relax and to build her own confidence. My second was to stop her pattern of attributing motives and excuses to the dog. The third was to find a rational, pragmatic approach to calming the dog that fit Sandy's mild personality and the dog's obvious anxiety and arousal. Sandy loved her dog, despite the obnoxious behavior. The last thing she needed was to be made to feel clueless or incompetent.

"It's important that you don't feel stupid," I told Sandy, who, after all, did highly intellectual work. "You're not. You're simply struggling to learn a new way of dealing with your dog while handling a lot of other pressure and responsibility. It will be easier if you don't blame the dog, and don't blame yourself. You'll both get there a lot quicker. Nobody's at fault."

Another psychological factor was Katie's history: Sandy and her family had adopted her from a local shelter at seven or eight months, and their notion of Katie as a mistreated creature probably contributed to the reluctance to train her properly. Sandy's voice rose in a distinctly, aw-poor-baby tone whenever she talked about Katie. She was so skittish and flighty from the time they'd brought her home. Surely, Sandy thought, she'd been neglected and abused. She wondered if establishing any sort of authority or training was cruel, given Katie's possibly tortured past. Her theory of the dog's mind had polluted their relationship.

The cultural predilection to seeing dogs as abused or victimized has a lot to do with people's own wounds, traumas, and personal histories. For purposes of training, however, I believe in clean slates. Unless the supposed abuse is obvious, severe, or disabling, labeling your dog this way is seldom helpful. Sometimes dogs have truly painful histories; sometimes we invent such histories for them. Most of the time, we don't really know, and it doesn't matter much.

Adaptability is a dog's most distinctive trait. Even mistreated dogs can be trained and retrained. I don't refer to my border collie Orson as an abused dog, first because I don't really know what happened to him, and second because it's beside the point. He needs to be trained anyway.

It's taken three years, but as I'm writing this section, this dog, who could barely remain still for thirty seconds when he first came to me, has been dozing on the floor beside me for hours. My many triumphs—and mistakes—as I learned how to train him have been among the most satisfying experiences of my adult life. And I'm forever indebted to the trainer who raised one skeptical eyebrow at me when I told her I was sure he'd been badly mistreated.

"I don't care," Carolyn Wilki said. "Ask him to lie down, then reward him for it."

She also pointed out, as many other trainers have, that symptoms of "abuse" are difficult to diagnose because they're also symptoms of many other things—problems in the litter, poor breeding, the trauma of re-homing.

It was quickly clear, then, that Sandy had no idea what Katie really wanted. But we don't need to understand motive, even if that were possible; we need to react to behavior. Most likely, the dog was simply acting instinctively, as dogs, especially working and hunting breeds, often do. Her innate drive to hold something in her mouth and chase and retrieve it was then exacerbated by her well-meaning but confused family.

By assuming her dog wanted something badly, it became difficult for Sandy to say no; she didn't want to deny Katie. That response was not limited to her beloved pet. "I am a very lenient parent," Sandy conceded. "I hate to say no to my kids." Bedtimes, computer use, and TV-watching all provoked daily battles. "I'm not a good limit setter," she confessed. But she was a good human and a loving mother, and she could still, I assured her, have a great dog. The trick was to understand that her limit-setting problems were hurting, not helping, Katie, turning an energetic, hardworking animal into an anxious nut whose hunting instincts were cranked up all the time, who had no rules or limits she could follow.

"I don't want to hurt this dog," Sandy said soberly. "I love Katie."

The first thing we agreed to do was to stop all ball throwing in the house, cold turkey. Collect all but one or two balls, put them in a box, and donate them to your local shelter, I counseled. In the morning, after her first walk, Katie would get to chase the ball in the yard for ten or fifteen minutes, as part of her daily aerobic workout. Then, she'd come inside and do something else.

Confused and agitated by this change, Katie initially raced from room to room, frantically searching for her tennis and rubber balls. The hunt went on for several days. But since there was no payoff, Katie gradually stopped looking for them inside. Ball throwing happened only in the yard.

Without balls to tote around (and without having her hunting instincts constantly aroused), Katie began calming down, taking more naps, sitting by the family as they watched TV or played board games.

For the next step, Sandy began using the crate she'd puppy-trained Katie in, then stashed in the basement. She brought it up, and put bones in the rear of it so that Katie would rush in. She fed her some meals in the crate and kept it generously stocked with treats.

After a week of this acclimatization, Sandy very reluctantly closed the door, so that Katie spent an hour or two a day in the crate, doing nothing but settling down and napping.

WATCH ME

Then we began some grounding and calming exercises: five minutes of lying down and staying, rewarded by treats. Two or three walks, with no balls. If Katie got obnoxious or excited, Sandy calmly tossed a bone in the crate, let her run in, and gave her a peaceful timeout. She let her out only when she was calm and at ease. Because her retrieval drive was not in constant use, Katie was able to pay more attention, thus grew more responsive to Sandy's commands.

"She was a different dog in a week," Sandy reported when we next spoke. "Nobody was yelling at her, and she seemed to enjoy her time in the crate. She wasn't being obnoxious, so we could enjoy her. It was as if she'd morphed somehow." But Katie was simply being allowed to be the dog she was. Sandy was the one who'd changed.

Over the next couple of weeks, Sandy intensified her one-on-one obedience training, working on eye contact, sprinkling treats as Katie trotted by her side so that their walks would be pleasurable.

The crate gave Sandy a calm and comforting place to park Katie when kids were over playing, when company came, or when Katie reverted to a "hyper" state. Instead of constantly reinforcing her excitement by throwing balls, then yelling, Sandy worked at reinforcing her calm, praising Katie when she was still and relaxed. Like other dogs, Katie was a creature of habit; we were creating new habits. Balls in the house and on walks weren't part of the routine anymore.

Having a dog gradually became a pleasure again. Sandy no longer saw her beautiful setter as a piteous creature whose wants trumped her own, who menaced her home and guests, but as a proud animal able to live up to her higher expectations.

But other versions of Katie continuously appear in my travels and work, and their stories don't always play out in the same way.

GLORIA WAS A NEIGHBOR IN NEW JERSEY WHO WALKED A SCOTTIE NAMED Finnegan past our house every day. When I let my dogs out into the backyard recently for some exercise and leg-stretching, it was only a few minutes before I heard Orson's frantic barking and the thud of his charging at the wooden gate.

A dog who has demonstrated his ability to take out a lead-glass window can wreak havoc on an old wooden gate. The din was deafening and the scene, when I went outside to investigate, was disturbing, especially given Orson's history.

Both Finnegan and Orson were flinging themselves at opposite sides of the gate, teeth bared, bodies and tails stiff, barking uncontrollably. It had taken a couple of minutes for me to recognize the problem and make my way outside, by which time Rose and Clementine were beginning to join in. But Gloria, surprisingly, was standing at the gate, beaming, as if she were watching dolphins at play.

I yelled to Orson to lie down, and he didn't even hear me. I tossed a treat; he barely noticed. When dogs won't take food or hear commands, it's often a sign that they've entered a red zone of high arousal. Any group of dogs can be potentially dangerous; they're all predatory creatures capable of biting or fighting under certain circumstances.

So I was alarmed, but Gloria merely chuckled, "Oh, calm down, Finnegan, it's just your friend Orson."

I took Orson by his collar, pulled him back, had him lie down and stay. He was panting, wide-eyed. Finnegan was also out of control, barking furiously, snapping and lunging, pulling at his leash.

I brought the dogs into the house, and Gloria waved and moved on. I assumed she'd happened to pass by and felt bad that my dog had made a ruckus, one of those dog things that sometimes happen. Inside, I crated Orson with some treats; he needed downtime. It took a while before he was calm and responsive, breathing normally.

But the same thing happened the next morning, and then again the next. Each time the dogs became so excited that, I saw, they'd actually chewed some paint and wood off the gate.

Finally one morning the din grew especially fierce. This was becoming dangerous. Orson could go through the gate or jump over it, nip Sheila or her dog, or dash into the street.

I lost my temper, as I sometimes do when my dogs are out of control. I came rushing out of the house, roaring at the dogs to "get back" and then "lie down." They did, startled and alarmed. Dogs may not think like us, but they can read our moods quite well, and when I'm really angry, my dogs know it.

Still, it took three efforts before the three of them were stabilized and in a reliable lie-down. This is a crucial command, because most dogs will not bark or fight from that position; it's perhaps the most reliable method of defusing tense situations. When I see trouble coming—kids on skateboards, fire trucks with sirens shrieking, growling dogs off-leash—I order my three to drop to the ground and stay.

All the while, Gloria was beaming and Finnegan roaring. It was almost disorienting to see my neighbor enjoying a situation that was anything but healthy. "Gloria," I said, my voice rising, "what are you doing? Why are you standing here allowing all of these dogs to go nuts?"

She seemed surprised, and blew off the question. "Oh, Finnegan likes to visit Orson. He wants to walk by your house every day."

I took a deep breath and tried to calm myself as well as the dogs. My work had been interrupted, my neighbors disturbed, passersby potentially endangered, and much painstaking training undermined—by a woman I knew to be intelligent, hardworking, and responsible. I'd been spending most of my time with the dogs upstate at Bedlam Farm, and at moments like this in New Jersey I sorely missed it.

The frenzied barking, Gloria assured me, was just the dogs' normal way of greeting one another. She thought it cute. And of course, she would walk wherever her Scottie "wanted."

I asked her to tie her dog to a utility pole a few feet away while we talked; reluctantly she did. My dogs were calm enough now for me to praise them and for them to accept some treats. Finnegan quieted down as well.

I tried to explain without being accusatory. "Gloria, I'm bothered by what you said and I'd like to talk to you about it. I'm working here, my wife is working upstairs, and it's disturbing to have four dogs yapping and barking outside. The neighbors are at home, kids are walking by. Your dog is out of control, lunging at my gate, my dog is doing the same, and they're cranking up the others. You or I could easily be bitten if we got in between. Why are you letting this go on day after day? I don't want to make a huge deal about this, but I honestly don't get it."

Gloria looked hurt and surprised and said that if I felt that way, she and Finnegan could walk somewhere else. "He just wanted to say hello," she said. "He always wants to come visit." But perhaps, I thought, his motives weren't all that sweet.

"It doesn't look like a friendly visit to me," I said.

Still, I felt bad and regretted my impatience. Gloria had gone through a nasty divorce a few years earlier and had quickly bought Finnegan, who'd helped her through the tough transition and had, to her mind, become a literal member of her family.

I'd seen her talking to the dog, lavishing every conceivable kind of attention on him; I'd never known her to try any kind of training. She exemplified theory-of-mind notions about her dog, quoting his thoughts and feelings. There was no question he'd helped her tremendously, so it was hard for her to deny him anything she thought he wanted.

That she was completely misreading him—he wasn't visiting with his "friend" Orson, he was primed for combat—was, in a way, irrelevant. Gloria wasn't interested in grasping the animal nature of her dog, or in distinguishing her own experiences of loss from his instincts. And lectures from me weren't going to be of any help.

People generally do the best they can. In Gloria's case, she wasn't about to see her Scottie in a different light and treat him accordingly. It was thoughtless, almost arrogant of me, to even ask that of her.

I hurried after her and apologized. The real issue was noise interrupting my work, I said, not that she or Finnegan were unwelcome. She relaxed visibly, sighed, and thanked me. The next morning I heard the din again, but I didn't come out, and it didn't last very long. Gloria moved along, but not before Finnegan got what he wanted.

I F TRAINING IS THE SINGLE MOST IMPORTANT ELEMENT IN LIVING with dogs, the dialogue that either condemns them to struggle along in our world or shows them how to share it with us, it's also the most confusing, difficult, and challenging. The process fails more often than it succeeds, frustrates more than it rewards, and seems to generate more despair than joy. People often are made to feel foolish or inept at it. Yet I've learned from personal experience that this doesn't have to be the case.

Information about dogs is cheaply, readily, and plentifully available. I've included a reading list at the back of this book, and you can also meet with vets, trainers, breeders, shelter and rescue workers, and fellow dog owners. So why is this process so often painful and ineffective?

For me, having dogs is one of the most joyous experiences of my adult life (though getting married and being a dad were good moves, too), the source of enormous fun, satisfaction, and intellectual stimulation. It's an extraordinary pleasure to learn how to communicate with another species, as opposed to simply occupying the same uneasy space. It's deeply satisfying to work closely with a creature that loves you and wants to work with and for you.

Despite the ongoing political discussion about animal rights, dogs are not our equals. The truth is ethically much more challenging: we are stronger than they. They need us for food, shelter, and medical care. They are voiceless and utterly dependent on us; they can't leave us. So we owe it to them to help them negotiate our often cruel and chaotic world. As a culture, we are very good at acquiring things and then disposing of them. That ethos often proves tragic for dogs. Training is the most powerful antidote to the fate of those millions of dogs abandoned and put to death each year.

When training fails or is abandoned, much of the pleasure that can characterize the human-canine bond is threatened or gone. Much of the point of having a dog is lost. You have only to look around to see what I mean.

TRAINING APPROACHES: WADING THROUGH

JUST HOW TO TRAIN IS ITSELF A SOURCE OF CONSIDERABLE DEBATE. As I've discovered, various schools of thought preach their own stern gospels. Positive trainers reject any kind of aversive criticism or corrections. Dominance trainers believe we should sit on rebellious dogs, even learn to bark and growl like dogs. Pack theorists insist we should establish ourselves as leader of a hierarchy; behaviorists suggest studying our dogs' head and tail positions; and almost everybody has homegrown tips and ideas about getting dogs to stay off the furniture. Clickers and whistles are becoming increasingly popular as ways to reinforce desired behaviors.

Though these theories are very different in their underlying philosophies and styles, I've seen them all work to varying degrees and fail to varying degrees. They often reflect not what dogs need but how humans are constructed, which isn't a bad idea. Universal, all-encompassing training methods are too rigid; they can't take people's—or dogs'—individual characteristics into account. There's no point in telling an impatient, distracted, and easily frustrated person to remain all-positive-all-the-time. They can't stay that perky. Some people simply can't muster the chirpy vocal enthusiasm that many trainers like to hear during obedience sessions. I know quiet, fearful people from raucous and quarrelsome families who have trouble with pack and dominance theories: they can't bear to raise their dogs the way they were raised, with shouting, domination, intimidation. They can't stand to feel like bullies.

Absolutist training theories, because they doom people to fail, are counterproductive. Yet each of these theories has something to offer. It always makes sense, for example, to positively reinforce natural behaviors—cooing "good sit" to a puppy whenever he sits down, for example. But I know very few people who don't lose their tempers under pressure. Trainers, after all, work in controlled environments much of the time; a dog is in their class, or in their training school, or in your yard. As our dogs move into the world, we deal with a daunting list of uncontrollable factors—traffic, other dogs, strollers, squirrels. With all this to attend to, we're simply destined to lose it from time to time. Dogs can handle our occasional meltdowns, as long as we don't lose it chronically or brutally.

Reading training manuals, even the most useful ones, I've often thought that the writer really understands dogs but hasn't given much thought to people. Humans are so diverse, so individually constituted, that no single training approach can suffice. So we read, ask, grow, and learn, and weave what we're seeing and hearing into our own lives with dogs in the way that makes the most sense for us and is, therefore, most likely to work. We need a patched-together training method that understands the dog's nature and our own, and accounts for our unique environments. We need an approach that makes both us and the dog feel successful and connected. If that isn't happening under your current regimen, abandon ship. You've picked the wrong method for you. But don't give up on training.

BEGINNING THOUGHTS

REMEMBER (AND IT CAN NEVER HURT TO SAY BEFORE EACH TRAINING SESsion): "This is an animal, not a child." Most dogs are quite willing to follow the rules; when they don't, most often it's because they don't understand the rules. Communication is the key to training. Don't blame the dog for being confused. Challenge yourself to be clearer, more patient and creative about letting the dog know what you want. Try. Try again. Understand that real training takes many months, even years.

Dan complained to me that his beagle, an obsessive barker, yelped for forty-five minutes each time Dan left him in a crate. At that point, unable to bear the racket, he let him out. "I just couldn't stand it," he said. But what he'd done was trained the dog to bark—a lot—and then rewarded him for it, rather than wait for the dog to be quiet and *then* let him out.

The point of the story is that forty-five minutes of barking is nothing to a beagle. He doesn't know how long he's been at it. An alternative is to put the dog in a still place and leave him there until he quiets, as he eventually will. When he settles and stops barking, reward him with praise and a treat, then release him. People often quit on training when the dog gets frantic or loud. Some dogs (a few) can't handle confinement. But more often than not, they've been trained that way.

You have to muster particular patience and will to train some dogs. But if you start it, finish it. Think of training as a chess match: move, countermove, one strategy responding to another. If you fail or feel you're harming the dog, get help. But in the scores of cases I've seen and been involved with, when encouraged and informed, the human wins.

Keep training simple, focused. One command at a time; just a few minutes in each session. Training should be quick, clear, and fun. First, teach "come," then "sit," followed by "lie down" and "stay." When the dog understands one, move on to the next, then start mixing them up. Use the fewest possible words: "Come," "Sit," not "Petey, hey, come here now!" or "Sit down, goddamnit, how many times do I have to tell you?" If it doesn't work, forget about it. Try again five minutes later.

Since people are not dogs, dogs often have trouble understanding what behaviors humans are seeking and the ways humans communicate those desires.

When we tell a dog "Be quiet!" the dog has no clue what we want. If he were encountering another dog, he could learn a great deal by looking at the other dog's eyes, body position, tail. But when he encounters a person demanding, "Quit chewing the rug!" or "Bad dog, go outside," that's different. He hears a loud and angry tone and understands the human is not pleased, but often has no idea what this person wants him to do.

After intensive training, dogs can grasp somewhere between fifty and ninety words or commands, depending on the breed, genetics, the person, and the environment. Even the smartest dog has a lower IQ than a three-year-old child.

Another major school of thought, though, broadly sees dogs as instinctive machines that don't act with self-awareness or self-consciousness. Their thinking involves sensory images and ancient, self-serving, powerfully ingrained biological impulses.

Stanley Coren, one of my favorite (and one of the most valuable) writers about dogs, reports in *How Dogs Think* that biologists and psychologists are beginning to consider more seriously the possibility that dogs may have a conscious representation of their world. But there's nothing approaching a consensus on that idea. Nonetheless, Coren concludes, there are certain things almost all scientists agree on when it comes to dogs. Dogs sense the world and receive information from it; they learn to adapt their behavior to fit changing circumstances. They have memories, and the ability to solve certain problems. Their early puppy experiences shape their adult behavior. Individual dogs do seem to have distinct personalities, and different breeds have different temperaments. Social interactions, including play, are important to them. And, finally, dogs do communicate with one another and with human beings—if we can find ways to understand and to make ourselves understood.

That description does sound a little like us. I do believe dogs have some consciousness of themselves and of us and can exhibit signs of pleasure, fear, frustration, enthusiasm, and anger. But these traits don't obscure the elemental truth that dogs are predatory animals, driven primarily and overwhelmingly by food, attention, and attachment. That puppy we're oohing and aahing over is, on some level, really a killing and hunting machine. Our job is to suppress and redirect many, if not most, of its natural instincts.

To me, training a dog properly is impossible without understanding what instinctive animals they are. If you firmly believe that your dog thinks in human terms, or understands the deepest corners of your psyche, I'll try to help. But this may not be the best book for you.

NAMES

MAKE SURE YOUR DOG KNOWS HIS NAME; A SURPRISING NUMBER DON'T. When he first arrives, toss treats to him while saying his name. Repeat his name often while he is eating (usually his tail will wag). Say his name on walks and toss a treat when he turns to you. Name recognition is critical.

So is eye contact. The first step in teaching a dog anything is to be sure he's paying attention. That means knowing his name and looking at you. So hold food up to your face and call the dog's name. When he looks into your eyes, give him the treat. When he looks you in the eye at any time, praise him. Whistle and bark once in a while to get him to look at you, then praise him. Name recognition and eye contact are vital elements to training. Make sure you have both down before you begin the other stuff.

PAY ATTENTION

PAY ATTENTION TO YOUR DOG. DOGS BEHAVE DIFFERENTLY IN DIFFERENT environments at different times of the day. My dogs, for example, are extremely businesslike on their first walk of the day. They sniff fresh animal tracks, study the dew, eliminate and mark territory, orient themselves to the many things I can't see or smell that have happened throughout the night.

It's fascinating to me to watch my dogs methodically check out their environments first thing every morning, sniffing and circling. But that's not a good time for training. Late morning is better. By then they've sniffed every inch of ground, eaten, and eliminated, gotten their exercise, and are ready to do some work. Though, of course, your dog might have a different schedule.

FOUNDATIONS

BEFORE YOU CAN EXPECT A DOG TO COME OR LIE DOWN, YOU FIRST OUGHT to establish your relationship with the dog, a process I call "grounding."

Why should any animal do your bidding without first knowing and trusting you, and getting something in return? I love Coren's great training maxim: Never give a dog anything for free. We sit before we take a walk, we lie down before we eat, we stay before we go swimming. On the flip side to that, the dog ought to get something in exchange, too. It might be a walk, a scratch, a biscuit, work like herding or chasing a ball, or maybe just the company of other dogs.

The conventional wisdom holds that a dog will love you, no matter what. I sincerely doubt it. Behaviorists know that dogs are highly adaptable creatures who do what they need to do for food and shelter. But it's almost impossible to build a strong training relationship with a dog who's afraid of you or finds you remote, confusing, or inconsistent. It would be too much to say that a dog is capable of dislike—that's clearly a human emotion. But it's also a human conceit to assume that a dog will adore you regardless of how you treat him. Before I ask a new dog to obey me, I want him or her to know, trust, and like me. That means weeks of asking little, offering much. Hand-feeding is one of my favorite techniques for encouraging bonding with a puppy or new dog. Simply, I feed the dog his or her food from my hand, a half-cup at a time, sometimes one individual bit of kibble after another. Usually I sit on the floor, holding food out. When the dog comes running, I hold the food up by my eyes, so the dog gets used to making eye contact. Then, while the dog is eating, I repeat her name. If you hand-feed a dog for a few months while saying her name (half the time, I put food in the dog's crate to make her appreciate that, too), I can almost guarantee that the dog will know its name, pay attention to you, and be more receptive to what you ask.

Between feedings, I supply lots of treats, praise, play, and walks. Whether I'm trying to win over a new puppy like Clementine or an older dog like Orson, I want the dog to see me as a friendly, reliable, and consistent source of food, affection, toys, and exploration. A lot of training approaches quickly draw owners into making demands on their new dogs. Though training should start early, I prefer a first-things-first strategy.

THE CASE FOR CONFINEMENT

A DOG LEFT TO ROAM FREELY, INSIDE OR OUTSIDE A HOUSE, IS LIKELY, sooner or later, to get into trouble. The list of dangers is long: outdoor dogs can get hit by cars, fight with other dogs, menace passersby, eat rotten dead things or even poison, get skunked, squabble with rabid raccoons, even get lost or stolen. Indoors, dogs can chew your possessions and furnishings, including electrical cords, bark for hours and disturb your neighbors, steal your dinner, mess your carpets and floors. These aren't remote or paranoid possibilities.

If you're not equating humans and canines, the solution is clear: provide some sort of enclosure and put the dog inside it when you're not around.

For outdoor confinement, some owners like invisible electronic fences; some prefer physical ones. If you choose an invisible fence—the kind that delivers a mild shock to the dog—be sure your dog isn't so powerful or instinctive that she'll shoot right through it. Also, realize that while the fence usually keeps the dog in, it doesn't keep kids, dogs, or other animals out. But above all, don't refuse to give your dog a secure environment because you think *you* wouldn't like to be fenced in.

A woman called my radio talk show once to complain that her shepherd was rampaging through the woods, chasing deer, startling skunks, getting quilled by porcupines, fighting with other dogs, scaring neighbors.

What about a fence? I asked.

"Our yard is too big," she said.

What about fencing a *part* of the yard?

"Oh, she'd just get out of it."

Maybe a kennel and run, attached to the house or garage for shelter?

"My family is too disorganized. Somebody would always be leaving it open." Besides, the woman finally added, it would be "cruel to coop her up. She just loves to run."

I began wondering if this person should have a dog. Owning a dog is about understanding their animal nature and, just as important, about someone taking emotional responsibility for the dog's safety, training, and well-being. A dog like this one needed to be contained or it would get hurt or hurt someone else. Period.

CRATES

INDOORS, WHAT WORKS BEST IS A CRATE—A PLASTIC OR METAL ENCLO-sure, available in several sizes at any pet store. The metal kinds are collapsible, so you can move them from one part of your home to another, or stick them in the car when you travel. If you drape a sheet or blanket over the crate, it approximates the dim, cozy den that a dog would inhabit in the wild and screens out unwanted sources of stimulation. A pad or blanket on the bottom makes a crate comfier.

It's common, however, for dog owners and lovers to tell me they wouldn't dream of confining their dogs in crates or kennels, that it seems inhumane. They say their dogs "go crazy" in crates, barking and chewing to get out.

Those who've rescued troubled or abused dogs seem even more reluctant to subject their dogs to what they see as mistreatment in the form of further confinement, perhaps with unpleasant associations, even though they often have the very dogs who would benefit most from a calming confined environment. They can't stand it, people say, so they either abandon the process or never try it, nor do they learn how to correctly acclimate a dog to confinement.

This is too bad. Used properly, the crate or kennel is one of the best tools when it comes to training and living with a dog, particularly for housebreaking (more about that later), but also throughout the dog's life.

I've had Labs and border collies for years, and I've learned to never—ever—leave them loose in the house when I go out. My dogs get tons of exercise and work, frequent excursions, ample bones and toys, and plenty of companionship. They don't need to roam the kitchen or living room when I'm out shopping or doing farm chores. Unlike chickens, dogs don't need to be free-range; they benefit from quiet times in limited spaces where the rules are clear and they feel no pressure. Left out in the wild, almost every dog would seek out a space very much like a crate and voluntarily make it his headquarters.

Dogs are den animals, not restless kids. Crates are highly natural to them, especially when dogs are properly introduced to them. Confinement doesn't mean the same thing to dogs as it does to us. For appropriate periods, and as part of a balanced life with exercise, play, and companionship, it can often make the difference between a loving, easy, trained dog or years of barking, chewing, and anxiety.

An elemental law of dog training is to create environments where the dog can't help but succeed, to give a dog as little opportunity as possible to misbehave.

My friend Dave complained angrily when his chow, Gertrude, started pilfering food from kitchen counters—first the occasional loaf of bread, then veal defrosting for dinner, then a whole blueberry pie, which did not agree with her. But he objected to my suggestion of a crate. "I want her to be a member of the family, not a caged animal," he insisted. When his after-the-fact scolding had no effect, Dave tried a technique he found in a training manual: an array of mousetraps set atop the counter, whose snapping would startle Gertrude and deter her foraging.

If my friend is foolish enough to leave food lying around his kitchen, however, and leave a wandering chow alone with it, the dog deserves what it can get. To grab food is what dogs instinctively do; to ask a chow to do otherwise is to ask her to counter her powerful nature, and that's asking too much. Food needs to be shut away; dogs need to be in controlled environments. Mousetraps are for mice.

The same ideas apply to my border collie Orson. A dog that can open a refrigerator door, heist a container of meatballs, enjoy the contents, and hide the telltale packaging under a sofa doesn't need the run of the house. He needs a crate with a chewbone.

COZYING UP TO THE CRATE

AS WITH MOST TRAINING GOALS, ACCLIMATING A DOG TO A CRATE CAN take some care. For puppies, it's fairly simple. Put the food inside, and when the pup charges in, close the door behind her, then briefly disappear. Then take her outside on a leash, and when she goes, praise her. Bingo. Housebroken dog. And also one who sees the crate as a pleasant place, a source of food.

I often toss food into my dogs' empty, open crates so they will go in, eat, and either curl up and nap (which they often do voluntarily) or come back out. I position the crates in a quiet corner of the house, cover them with quilts or blankets, and sometimes leave a radio or TV on softly. I never scream at my dogs and force them into a crate; the crate is always a happy place.

When we've been herding, or after a vigorous walk, or when I'm busy or have company, I often toss bones into the crates and leave the dogs in their dens. They're happy to go; I'm happy not to be worrying what they're up to. Because of crates, all my dogs know how to be still, all were housebroken within a week or two, and my furniture and clothing are rarely disturbed or damaged. There's no better way to help a dog learn how to be calm and centered.

With older dogs, crate training can take a bit longer. Orson, my eldest dog, was one of those who freak out in a crate, pacing, barking, throwing himself at the latch. I talked to some trainers and read books, but then stepped back and decided to try my own method, based on what I'd learned, but more important on what I sensed about this particular dog and his response to stimulus and to me. None of the books I read described a dog quite like him, and of course none of the authors knew me.

I began by feeding Orson in the crate. The first day or two, he circled, but wouldn't go in. After five minutes, I took the food out and threw it away. On the third day, he rushed into the crate and devoured his food. I left the door open behind him. I broke up his feeding into four small meals and fed him this way—always leaving the door open—for two weeks. Then I bought a bag of beef jerky (one of my favorite training tools) and whenever I passed his crate, tossed a piece or two inside. When the dogs got bones or pigs' ears, several times a week, I put them in the crates and closed the other doors, leaving Orson's door open.

After a few days, I cooked a few marrow bones and placed them inside; when Orson charged in to chew them, I closed the door. He hardly seemed to notice. After half an hour I came and checked on him; he was asleep in the crate.

From that day on, I often found him napping in his crate, which was supplied with bones, beef liver treats, and jerky. He came to see the crate as a reliable cornucopia of goodies.

I rely on food, both meals and snacks, in training and acclimating a dog. People may choose to use praise instead, which is fine, but my dogs have always paid more attention to food than to anything else (except for Rose and her fixation on sheep).

Whatever works, works.

Given access to so much food over time, few dogs can resist seeing the crate as a friendly haven, especially since such spaces are natural environments for den animals. It may take weeks, even months, to bring about this association, but it can be done. For those very few dogs that simply can't handle crates, kennels or closed-off rooms might be an option, but controlled environments in some form are essential.

In his crate, and before my eyes, Orson has learned to chill. Whenever we've had too much company or play, he rushes into his crate (which is his alone, not interchangeable with Rose's or Clem's), curls into a ball, and sacks out. He used to sleep at the foot of my bed, but now most nights he stays in his crate until daylight, when he comes over for a snuggle. He seems to need his private space, and it's been good for him. I've watched him settle down, week by week. Not only is he calmer, but his calm has made the rest of his training regimen much easier. He focuses more on me; he listens more readily.

If I go out to dinner or the movies, Orson will be right where I left him. During busy times (workers in the house, dinner under way, kids ringing the doorbell on Halloween) I have a secure place that offers him privacy and protects mine as well. Orson feels safer as well as calmer, and the right of humans to spend time away from their dogs—a right I cherish—has been protected.

One caution: think of the crate as the dog's retreat, his sacrosanct getaway. It's not a place for punishment, a space to be dragged into while people are yelling. Crates won't work—as a calming tool, a place to park your dog when you're busy or away, or a learning device—if dogs associate them with punishment.

INSTINCTS

TRUST YOUR INSTINCTS AND PICK YOUR FIGHTS. YOU KNOW YOUR DOG better than anybody—a trainer, me, your vet. You know what makes him tick. If whooping and hollering (not in anger, just excitement) gets your dog to pay attention to you, carry on. If meatballs are more compelling, use them.

Many trainers tell you that if you give a dog a command, you must see that it is obeyed, no matter what; that's how you establish dominance. I don't agree. When my dogs blow me off, or flat-out fail to respond, I wait two or three minutes, and then try again. If I still can't connect, I leash the dog, then put my foot on the leash, maybe a foot from his neck. The dog isn't going anywhere until he does what I say. But I also assess his response: if my dog seems too stressed or nervous, I regroup and ask myself if this request is really worth it. I can usually come up with a different approach, or come back to the command when he's more receptive and at ease.

HOUSEBREAKING

HOUSEBREAKING'S IMPORTANT FOR MORE THAN THE OBVIOUS REASONS; IT'S usually our first significant training encounter with our dogs. So it's sad to hear people tell me, proudly, that they tie bags of dog feces around a puppy's neck. "They get so disgusted with the smell they want to go outside," one person explained. Maybe—but what an introduction.

People routinely yell, scold, thump their puppies when they eliminate—the most natural and uncontrollable of puppy behaviors. Others whack them with rolled-up papers, rub their noses in urine and fecal matter, and drag them outside by the neck, screaming meaningless (to the dog) epithets.

People who get non-housebroken puppies should understand they're likely to have occasional accidents. Puppies are messy and excitable; they have small bladders and undeveloped digestive systems. They can't control themselves for long and they go when they have to go. Holding it is something humans want from them, but not something they are naturally programmed to do.

Since this is among the first tasks you and your dog will work on together, it ought not to be a brutal, confusing, or hysterical undertaking.

Housebreaking is yet another argument for crates. When a new puppy arrives, I often feed the dog inside his crate, putting the bowl in the rear so the puppy rushes in, then closing the gate while he eats. The dog is automatically reinforced for going inside, and comes to see the crate as a good place. After the puppy eats, I wait fifteen minutes or so—the younger the puppy, the shorter the time—and then open the crate, slip a leash on the dog, and either carry him outside or walk him quickly to the nearest door. (It helps to set up the crate near the door.) Very few puppies will not eliminate soon after eating. I take the dog to the same spot every time, choosing places where we don't walk or play, so he'll associate the location with elimination.

When the dog pees or poops, I toss him a treat and praise him. For the first week or two, I keep the puppy inside the crate much of the day; when he comes out to play or join the family, he's on a leash. But whenever he comes out of the crate, I say, "Let's go outside," and we walk out the door.

Sometimes dogs won't make it to the door in time. Sometimes they will take a dump right in front of you. Ignore it; it won't be the last time, alas, that your dog does something gross. Clean it up and repeat the crate process. Usually the puppy can't help it, but even if he can, yelling and screaming just makes him more tense, more likely to have an accident.

The crate gives the dog owner an environment he or she can control, one in which the dog can make few mistakes. Dogs don't like to mess their sleeping quarters, so the puppy's crate should be small, big enough to turn around and stretch out, but not so spacious that he can eliminate far from where he sleeps.

As the dog grows older, his bladder and bowel control improve. If you stick with the crate method, you can have the dog mostly housebroken in a couple of days, though the process takes two or three weeks to complete. Even then, expect the occasional accident; don't panic or lose it. My dogs don't get to sleep outside the crate until they're six to eight months old, and they're rarely uncrated when I'm away from home.

Older dogs may have behavior problems from the past, and any dog can have physical or medical problems that cause frequent urination or diarrhea. These dogs obviously need to see a vet. But most dogs will be happy to go outside—that's their nature—if you simply take them there frequently enough during the day.

If you can arrange to be home for a few days when your puppy arrives, so that you can keep an eye on things—when a pup starts circling and sniffing, head outside—you can housebreak them quickly. If you can't, it may take longer.

Because housebreaking is your dog's introduction to training, the process ought to be calm, clear, and positive. It's a building block, your dog's first exposure to you and your rules. If you confine the dog after he eats and then take him outside, you are greatly reducing his opportunities to fail. You can simply reward him for succeeding.

CHEWING

CHEWING IS ANOTHER NATURAL, EVEN NECESSARY, BEHAVIOR IN PUPPIES; and some breeds—Labs and rottweilers, for instance—need to chew more than others. However, if adult dogs chew compulsively, it could suggest anxiety or behavioral problems that might require advice from a trainer or a vet.

Generally, my chewing strategy is simple: saturation goodies. When I get a puppy, I flood the house with bones, rawhide, and squeaky toys. A puppy that's teething and needs to exercise its gums will find something to chew. I'd rather it not be something I value, so everywhere the puppy goes he will find something acceptable. The house is a littered mess for months, but our bedroom slippers get spared.

When a dog turns to one of my things, like shoes or furniture, I simply take it away, sometimes with a hiss or growled "Noooooo," and substitute one of his own chewies. Their stuff is better than mine, so they're usually happy with the deal.

They form a habit of chewing on bones and rawhide or the many disgusting animal parts for sale in pet supply stores. Habit is key, whether we're talking about chewing, barking, or defecating. You want your dog to form the right habits, to reinforce those habits with praise and tangible rewards like treats and affection. Make sure to interact with your dog when he's doing the right thing, not just when he isn't.

As always, I reinforce this strategy with crates. When a dog has worked or played for an hour or two and is wound up or cranked, I toss a knucklebone into her crate. She not only learns to chill, but she also enjoys the bone and learns that this is hers, something okay to gnaw on. In the crate, there is nothing else for her to do, no trouble for her to get into. Eventually, the chewing need diminishes and so does the welter of semi-gnawed stuff on the floor. But I admit, the place never looks like Martha Stewart has taken up residence. It always looks like I have three dogs.

SLEEPING

THE PUPPY SLEEPS IN THE CRATE, PERIOD. NO CUDDLING IN BED, NO WANdering the house at night when I can't pay attention. They sleep in their crates for roughly eight months, through periods of housebreaking, chewing, and manic puppy play.

Only when they are housebroken, past their teething, and able to sleep calmly for substantial periods do they get to choose between the crate and other spots in the house—including my bed.

The more free time and room to roam a puppy has, the more trouble he or she will get into, especially when its humans are sleeping. It may learn to raid garbage cans, eat wires and DVDs, form the wrong housebreaking habits. So freedom to range around my house is closely connected to training progress; it's a reward, recognition for good behavior. The better training goes, the more choices I give the dog.

The best place for the dogs you live with to sleep is in their crates, leaving plenty of room in your bed, no fur on the quilts, no vomiting or worse in your bedroom in the wee hours. But that doesn't mean that dog owners—myself included—follow this impeccable logic.

My own dogs sleep all around the house—on the floor, in crates, in dog beds—but somehow by six A.M. all three wind up tucked in corners of my bed, especially in the cold of a rural winter. It's actually one of my favorite moments of the day, a time for cuddling and huddling together before life intrudes.

SOCIALIZATION

THE SOCIALIZATION PERIOD IN A PUPPY'S LIFE (ROUGHLY FROM FOUR TO twelve weeks) is "the most influential time in a puppy's life," Stanley Coren says. So those weeks are the period during which I take training the most seriously and work the hardest.

It's during this critical time frame that much of your dog's future behavior will be shaped. "Undoing any negative behavioral effects that result from experiences during this period of life may be extremely difficult and perhaps impossible," Coren cautions.

If you have a grounded, well-bred dog and you socialize the dog properly, you can avoid many of the most distressing problems that adversely affect our lives with dogs—especially aggression and confusion about how to live in our complicated world.

Just as training is about more than obedience, socialization is about more than manners. It's the process by which any individual—human or animal—comes to understand his environment, his social world. He learns—or doesn't—the rules and behaviors that will allow him to share our world. Wild animals only have to learn wild animals' rules. But because dogs are so enmeshed with people, they have to learn our rules as well. That makes their lives complex and stressful.

It's a gift to acquire a dog early in its socialization period. After that, socialization can be more challenging. With an older dog, however desirable for other reasons, we may never know what happened in the litter or during his socialization period. Sometimes that doesn't matter, sometimes it does.

Sociability also varies by breed and genetics. Breed differences are complex, write John Paul Scott and John L. Fuller in *Genetics and the Social Behavior of the Dog*. The hunting breeds they studied were strongly motivated by food but differed greatly in aggressiveness; beagles and cocker spaniels were much more "peaceful"; shelties "appear to have a rather high degree of aggressiveness but are relatively little motivated by food."

But environment also makes a strong contribution. Under normal methods of rearing, many puppies become fearful of humans at about five weeks. Yet this fear, note Scott and Fuller, almost completely disappears in response to daily handling by humans. (Good breeders are careful to handle puppies continuously.) In puppies with few human contacts, "the fear responses became progressively more extreme."

So during the socialization period, puppies urgently need contact with other puppies and with a wide range of humans. They needn't be overwhelmed, but they benefit from social experience and exposure.

One measure of successful early socialization is how easily a dog walks on a leash, a significant indicator of a dog's comfort level with humans. Well-socialized dogs feel safe around humans and like to be close to them, so they exhibit less pulling and straining. A study conducted in Maine found that puppies that spent time with humans between five and nine weeks had the fewest problems on the leash, following happily, with minimal coaxing.

Hand-feeding is an easy way to socialize your dog, not only within the family but also around strangers. The more people who approach your puppy with kibble in hand, the better. The idea is to expose the dog to a variety of noises and sights, people and animals, without overwhelming her. Obviously, if the dog is terrified by traffic, you need a longer, more careful sensitization process. But puppies are naturally curious, and you want them to learn early in life that other people are okay, that children are not small dogs, and that they have to coexist with airplanes, other dogs, and leaf blowers. Socializing is a passport to the world we and our dogs have to live in.

WHO'S WALKING WHOM?

NANCY CALLED ME FROM CAPE COD TO ASK FOR HELP IN A PROBLEM SHE was having with Lil, a boisterous boxer who for some reason had developed an insistence on eliminating in a thicket of rosebushes.

"It's killing me," Nancy complained. "I get cut by thorns and scratched by brambles. It's dark and messy and scary back there."

I laughed at the mental picture. "Who's walking whom?" I asked, knowing the answer.

"But I'm afraid she won't go if I don't take her where she wants to go. She pulls and tugs me until we get there."

It sounds silly to talk about a philosophy of walking, but good walking and elimination habits are essential to living well with dogs.

My philosophy: I walk the dog, the dog doesn't walk me. We go where I want to go. There are two things a dog will always eventually do, I told Nancy: eat and eliminate. There was no chance the boxer wouldn't eliminate anywhere but in the rosebushes. It might take a few days, but trust me, I said, this dog will eventually go where you take it to go.

Dogs should never set the agenda. I train my dogs to walk alongside me by dropping bits of kibble on the ground as we walk. Sometimes I use a choke collar; sometimes a gentle halter is all you need. But training methods aside (plenty of manuals offer instruction on walking properly), it's a matter of philosophy, as are so many things involving you and your dog.

This, to me, is a dignity question. I'm literally offended when my dogs try to pull and drag me. It's undignified and obnoxious, spoiling what ought to be a lovely, calm, and mutually pleasing experience. I don't permit it, and I make my disapproval clear through my voice and body language.

Nobody rushes out the door ahead of me, nobody pulls me along a path or lunges off in a direction I don't want to go in. I walk the dog; the dog doesn't walk me.

It's not only when walking that the human has to assert control. I don't want my dogs, puppy or adult, charging the door, rushing the food bowl, banging into my legs on the way outside, grabbing treats out of my hand. It's not just a matter of etiquette, but a question of setting a dignified tone for the relationship.

I believe I treat my dogs as well as my pocketbook and wife will tolerate. But when we go out in the morning, they lie down and wait until I've put my coat on. When I say, "Let's go out," if they rush toward the door, I stop, have them back up and lie down again; I wait until they are calm before we proceed. When I put their food bowls down, I first make them sit and wait. Maybe I make the coffee. Then I release them to eat.

I'm not trying to be prissy or ironfisted, only to keep things orderly—especially since I've chosen to live with three dogs. When your dog is pushing, you have a training problem. Push back, clearly and consistently.

CASE STUDY: *Training Clem*   I WANTED CLEMENTINE ALMOST from the moment her calm and sweet nature began to emerge. But I knew she wouldn't magically turn into a calm, sweet companion without a major commitment from me. Training Clementine was an opportunity I didn't want to blow, a chance to put my money where my mouth was. This beautiful creature came with all the advantages and blessings any dog lover could want or need. My mission was to do right by her.

I'd never chosen a dog so carefully or, to be frank, so thoughtfully. Few dog owners get to be in on every part of the process the way I'd been. Everyone had done her job well. The breeder was experienced and skilled, the breedlines stellar; the dog had been well cared for by her mother, socialized by Pam and Heather and me. She had every quality you'd seek in a new pup: she was bright, alert, approachable, with loads of personality. She loved treats and attention. She naturally made eye contact with humans. She was intensely curious and explorative, but she also, from the first, had the ability to pause and pay attention.

All the elements for good training were in place, at least on the canine side. On my end, I had all the proper physical equipment—crates upstairs and downstairs, rawhide chews in every room, training treats and puppy food in the pantry.

More fundamentally, I believed I knew why I was getting this dog: I wanted a calmer, more easygoing counterpoint to balance my two excitable working dogs. I wanted another outlet for affection—I was prepared to love this dog to death. And I also wanted to try out my hard-learned ideas about training and living with dogs.

On the surface, Clem would have it made: acres to run on and explore, other dogs for company, a human working at home every day, a stream below the meadow (to satisfy the Lab lust for water), donkeys and sheep to get to know, woods filled with raccoons, squirrels, and deer, and a cornucopia of smelly farmyard stuff to smell, eat, and roll in.

But there were potential pitfalls, too. Three dogs is a huge departure from one, or even two. Three dogs become a pack, and the other members of this gang were powerful, dominant, and complicated dogs.

The mere process of feeding them all would prove a challenge. Rose would much rather work than eat, so she picked and pecked at her food while keeping one eye on the back door, which led to sheep. She worked so intently and cared so little about food that I sometimes worried she would keel over. She needed her calories. Yet she was a tough creature who, hungry or not, wouldn't graciously yield the food in her bowl to a cheeky puppy. Orson, keenly interested in food and always eager to raid others' bowls when I wasn't looking, wouldn't take kindly to a puppy nosing around his bowl, either.

This wasn't a minor matter; feeding multiple dogs can be a struggle.

One gets too fat from grabbing all the food, another grows too thin. Nasty squabbles can break out. I know people who wind up serving three or four different kinds of dog food, because each dog likes a different brand. If you don't manage feeding well from the beginning, you can have headaches for years.

Clem had never really experienced a territorial, growling, protective dog. She wouldn't necessarily know what Orson meant when he warned her away from his food. Yet being a Lab—there is no greater chowhound in the animal kingdom—just the smell of food drove her nuts. Accustomed to competing for her share of a collective pan of puppy mush, how would she come to understand the new etiquette?

My farm presented safety concerns as well. A ticked-off donkey, protective of the sheep and mistrustful of intruders, could maim or even kill a small puppy if she wasn't introduced properly. Bedlam Farm was in a quiet hamlet but the old farmhouse, like so many of its generation, was built almost right on top of a road. Cars and trucks, snowmobiles and four-wheelers and SUVs often came flying down the hill. The border collies were street-trained, but I knew from personal experience

WATCH ME

how long that had taken. I couldn't consider trusting Clem near a road for at least months, and quite possibly years.

We also faced all the standard training issues: housebreaking, chewing, elemental obedience. But I laid the groundwork before I began more complex training; grounding was perhaps the simplest and most pleasurable part of the effort.

In Clementine's case, I not only hand-fed her but carried bags of treats around. I repeatedly called her name, tossed balls and toys, and took her on walks, alone and with the other dogs. She quickly came to see me as good news. I made sure to spend time alone with her each day, working on name recognition.

Only when it was clear she liked and trusted me—she often checked on my whereabouts, for instance—did I slowly, gently link her behaviors to training commands, praising her for coming when she came to me, saying "good sit" when she sat down, then tossing a treat. Slowly, without formality, yelling, or pressure, we began to work together.

For me, this is the beginning of a miraculous process that ought to be joyous and satisfying, a partnership. I lose my temper too often, but I want that to be the exception, not the rule. It seems to me inconceivable that trust and affection can really flow from bullying, scolding, yelling, shock, or intimidation. That tactic has never made sense to me, and in my experience, it is rarely necessary—which, of course, is not to say never. About all those treats: a major training decision is whether to use food or praise as a reinforcement. Many trainers and dog owners say they want their dogs to obey "for me," not for food. Some don't want the bother and expense of carrying smelly treats around with them.

I understand their position, but I'm more flexible. I don't really care why my dogs sit when they come to a busy street, or come when I call; I just want them to do it. If their motives are crass and self-centered, who cares? My ego doesn't need their approval. So I always carry a plastic bag filled with tasty thank-yous. Initially, the treats are pungent and expensive—I want the dogs to get used to paying attention. As training evolves, I usually end up using cheap puppy biscuits, small, dry, breakable, easy to carry and throw. Toting treats not only reinforces training, which takes years to really solidify, but is useful in case we run into other dogs. Nothing defuses canine tension better, in most cases, than sprinkling the ground with biscuits. Though some dogs will fight over food, most find it pleasantly distracting.

I haven't seen any scientific data on food versus praise. But while the dogs in my house like praise, they truly love liver treats.

ONCE OUR EARLY WEEKS OF HAND-FEEDING PAID OFF, I HAD TO CONSIDER how to feed my three dogs simultaneously. I hear more complaints and concerns from dog owners about eating than just about anything else. In multiple-dog households, near-riots can break out at dinnertime. And dogs slobbering at the humans' dinner table, begging and whining for food, isn't something I find cute.

The Rational Theory of Food Management posits that well-cared-for dogs in America do not starve themselves. They will consume what they need if their humans provide it without introducing competition, angst, or stress. Yet feeding these three would be dicey.

What worked: I put each dog's bowl on the floor for three to five minutes each morning, initially standing guard. When everyone has had a fair chance to eat, I pick the bowls up and throw the uneaten food away. I do the same thing for the second feeding at night. In a week or two, the dogs fall into line. The finicky Rose eats 80 percent of her morning chow and all of the evening meal, which is a bit heftier. Clementine will scarf up all of her food immediately, but I make her sit and stay for a full minute before she gets to move to the bowl. This teaches her to stay and to eat calmly, and it gives the other two dogs a chance to finish their food without being pestered, which minimizes squabbling and establishes separate eating spaces.

After a few minutes, the bowls go into the sink and we head out for a walk. If dogs are hungry, they will eat; but brief, focused eating with time limits helps the process along.

I never offer snacks from the dinner table, from a plate, or from any food prep area. The dogs don't get human food unless I put it into their bowls, either with their regular food or separately. Since they have no history or experience of eating our food, they don't bother to beg, and I don't feel even a bit guilty for not feeding them from my plate. They do fine.

I feed my dogs a mix of dry and wet food—to encourage quick eating, mostly. Busy and active working dogs all, they get one and a half to two cups of food a day, plus the biscuits and treats from my pockets.

And that's plenty. Too many U.S. dogs are chronically overweight because their owners—thinking of them as childlike—can't bear to "starve" them. But canine obesity is one of the most serious health threats American dogs face. Clem would eat as much as she could persuade me to give her. Her welfare requires that I—not she—know when to stop. For this reason, though I'm generous with treats, I use small dry biscuits without lots of calories.

Clem's housebreaking began as soon as I brought her home, and was made immeasurably easier by her affection for her crate.

This was no coincidence, of course. I'd been giving her a meal a day in her crate from day one, sometimes feeding by hand, sometimes not. Dogs associate food with good things, always; the more kibble, bones, treats, and nice smells that appear in the crate, the more the dog will associate it with sustenance, safety, and happiness. Perhaps it looked a bit strange when I plopped a bowl with a small piece of cooked hamburger in the crate, yelled "Let's go to the crate! Let's go to the crate!" and rushed into the room with Clementine charging after me. But so what? Her nose did the rest, and she would dash into the crate. I closed the door behind her and praised her. I made sure there was water inside as well as food. During her time in the crate, as long as she was quiet, I tossed in additional treats and chew toys. But she never—ever—got out of the crate if she was whining or barking (unless I thought it was a matter of needing to go eliminate, or of digestive urgency).

Roughly fifteen minutes after she ate, I let her out on a leash, walked her the three or four feet out the door, and made a considerable fuss when she urinated and defecated, praising her and giving her small bits of biscuits.

After a few days, whenever Clem needed to eliminate, I added another phrase—"Get busy"—along with the treats and praise. In a cou-

MY POCKET

ple of weeks, she would tend to her business, then come running over for her reward. Thus, she was learning to go to the bathroom on command—a valuable trait on cold or rainy nights, if you're in a rush to go out, or when you're staying at a motel or at a strange house.

She was fully housebroken in less than a week, and thereafter, aside from a bout with roundworm that caused diarrhea, she never had an accident inside. Of course, she was predisposed to eliminating outdoors because of her kennel-rearing. Pam Leslie had kept the puppy area so clean that the animals naturally wanted to go through the door to the outside to eliminate.

I made sure Clementine had no opportunity to learn otherwise. By not giving her many chances to screw up, I was not giving myself many chances to yell and scream. Knowing that I'm impatient, easily frustrated, easily distracted, I don't want the dog and her training to suffer for that, so I've constructed a training approach that allows her to succeed and prevents me from being an impatient jerk.

Along with Coren's "Don't give a dog anything for free," another of my favorite maxims is: Don't give a dog a chance to mess up. For the first month she was with me, Clem was usually either on a leash or in her crate. When she began circling or sniffing, a signal that she needed to go, we walked quickly outside, where I had the chance to praise her. If she dribbled or didn't quite make it, I ignored it, knowing she would get the idea quickly. There was some confusion: a straw mat at the door is stubbly, almost like grass, and Clem sometimes peed on it, waiting to go outside. I removed it.

THIS WAS A DOG THAT WAS DESTINED TO MEET THE PUBLIC. SHE'D ACcompany me to bookstore signings, encounter photographers and the occasional reporter, greet farmers and neighbors and workers and UPS deliverymen at Bedlam Farm. Her socialization skills would need attention.

So when she was nine weeks old, I brought tiny Clementine to Gardenworks, a local gardening center/gift emporium and high-level farmstand that also served as a community crossroads. She immediately bonded with Arlene, a member of the sales staff, who loved having a canine companion. And Clem loved hanging around with her (besides, there were lots of treats at Gardenworks), so I started taking her there two or three mornings a week for brief visits. Sometimes Arlene kept Clem next to the cash register with her; sometimes she positioned her by the front door, tied on a long lead.

A continuous stream of people—adults and kids, locals and tourists, gardeners and berry-pickers—poured past her, almost all of them delighted to see a puppy. They patted her, talked to her, gave her biscuits and ear scratches, all under Arlene's supervision.

Clem loved Gardenworks, so much that by the second week, she barely seemed to notice when I left. When I came to pick her up she was usually sprawled asleep on a blanket, exhausted from the attentions of scores of people. I rarely passed up a chance to take Clementine somewhere during those key socialization weeks. She came to dinner in strange houses, sat next to me during a noisy Fourth of July parade, even spent a morning at the friendly local pharmacy. She went for walks with friends and neighbors and met dozens of puppies and older dogs. I asked a friend to bring Arthur, an older black Lab, to the farm some mornings, and Arthur, Clem, and my other dogs played so ceaselessly and enthusiastically I often had to break it up and send everyone to their crates for rest periods.

I have never socialized a dog so determinedly, and I've never had a friendlier dog, one more at ease with others. Later that year, she came along on a book tour and, after greeting visitors, rolled over and went to sleep, snoring quietly while I talked and signed books.

Whenever a child approached us, I would stop, hand the child a biscuit from my pocket stash, and encourage him to give it to Clem. As a result, she loves kids, and has gotten used to their head-on approaches and herky-jerky movements (something my older border collie, Orson, has never quite become comfortable with). This is not only a good deal for her, but helps create fans who will be less fearful of dogs. Like my earlier Labs, Clem is something of an ambassador from Dogland, and she's very good at it.

THE OTHER BIG PUPPYHOOD BUGABOO IS CHEWING. I FLOODED THE house with puppy goodies. (Another of my training maxims: If they have lots of their own stuff, they won't bother yours.)

Chewing is good for puppies on several levels: it provides amusement and stimulation, helps with gums and teething, acclimates them to the places you want them to be—for me that's by my feet, in the crate, or on the porch. If I sat down to read or watch TV, I tossed a chewbone at my feet. Clem, still on her leash, would plop down and start gnawing away. Before long, the rug by my feet was her favorite spot. She was happy and busy, calm and settled, and there was no trouble she could get into. And I was making headway on one of my goals, having a settled dog content to hang around with me.

Because she had treats and bones littering the floor, she always had something satisfying to chew, and no inclination to switch to garbage bags, my shoes, or sofa legs. As of this writing, she is five months old, and she has yet to damage or destroy anything that was not meant for her.

· · ·

IN THESE FIRST MONTHS OF CLEM'S LIFE, I SEE ALMOST EVERYTHING AS a training opportunity. Whenever we come to a road, I ask Clem to sit. Then I walk ahead of her and tell her to stay. When I get to the other side of the road (you can do this while another person holds the dog on a leash if you're in a busier location), I say, "Heel to me," and tap my knee. Clem comes bounding over and gets her treat.

I make all this a game and she loves it (my family members, trying to enjoy a quiet walk, are less enthusiastic), but I'm laying the foundation for an even more important command: "No street." In a few more weeks, I'll hold my hand out, step off the curb, and if Clem stays, toss her treats. Each day, I'll lengthen the distance I walk into the road, saying, "No street."

The point of the exercise isn't to train her to walk off-leash, not even on country roads; that simply isn't safe in much of contemporary America. The idea is to get Clem to respect the street, to see it as different from sidewalks, yards, and lawns. After a few months, she'll automati-

GOOD GIRL—HEEL!

cally stop at anything that looks like a street. This may save her life one day. It also reinforces the notion that I am in charge of walks, and keeps them calm, pleasant, and controlled. A dog that will sit or lie down, at a corner or anywhere else, is a dog that can be brought quickly under control. A dog that won't, isn't.

BEHAVIORISTS SAY IT CAN TAKE UP TO *TWO THOUSAND* REPETITIONS BEfore a dog really understands a behavior. Very few people hang in there that long, underestimating the extended, consistent nature of good training. Americans are impatient, geared toward quick fixes and instant rewards.

Clementine now comes, sits, and stays (within the limits of her puppy attention span), but I expect to be training her most of her life. At the very least, the work we're doing will take years.

She has already rewarded me with calm, quick housebreaking, extraordinary sociability, and much affection. She knows her name, chews

SIT

NO STREET

her own stuff, comes when called, never runs off, and leaves the other dogs' food alone. Not bad, but we aren't nearly finished, either. We're not even close to the Quitting Point. I understand now what I didn't a few years ago: our training has just begun. At each stage of her life, and each stage of mine, we will be communicating our needs and responses. Environments change. People grow older, and so do dogs. I live on a farm now, but in a decade, I might well be in a different place.

My obligation is to prepare her to live with me—with us—no matter where. In return, she will adapt, weaving herself into my life and my family. That's the Rational Plan, anyway.

But there's a big "but" to this theory. I understand my own limitations too well to think I won't screw up. I will miscommunicate, make unreasonable demands, misunderstand and misinterpret her behavior. I will lose my temper, hiss, and yell. I will never be a perfect dog owner, and I'll never have perfect dogs. Total obedience is a robotic concept that doesn't seem especially relevant to my life with these animals. When I screw up, or they do, I want to be able to shrug, consider the vagaries of life, and move on. If my mistakes are not chronic or violent,

Clem will instantly forgive and forget, as Orson and Rose already have. I give them the same break. One of the nicer qualities of dogs is that they have memories but they don't hold grudges.

Training is an erratic and sometimes unpredictable path. The point is to keep making the journey, even if you never quite reach the end of the road.

CASE STUDY: *Colleen and "Shameless"* IT WAS ONLY TWO MONTHS before Thanksgiving, Colleen reminded me. Her whole family was due to gather from all over the eastern United States for the first time in years, and she would be hosting this important event. She did not want Seamus to spoil it.

We'd met a few weeks earlier at a book signing near my upstate farm; I was struck by her warmth, friendliness, and easy humor as we chatted about dogs. When I talked about my training volunteers scattered around the country, though, I saw her eyes widen. I wasn't surprised when, once everyone had left, she asked if I could spare a few minutes.

She approached apologetically, sensitive about my time; she seemed a person who didn't like to ask for things. I settled in to hear about a dog in trouble, and an owner's resultant confusion and anxiety. It was a refrain I'd heard many times.

Colleen was a municipal parks supervisor in a Boston suburb; her husband was also a town employee. They had two kids, one nine, the other entering college, and a twenty-two-month-old black Lab named Seamus.

Two weeks earlier, the dog—a powerful eighty-five-pound monster—had trashed the house, pulling down curtains, shredding the sofa, knocking utensils off kitchen shelves. More worrisome, he'd nipped their daughter Geraldine's hand when she tried to put a leash on him to take him out for a walk.

But the list of complaints went way back. The dog had single-handedly ruined a dinner party—the guests included her boss—by jumping up on arrivals and muddying their clothing, grabbing food from the table, barking and whining incessantly when he wasn't getting attention.

Seamus, in short, was wreaking havoc. Colleen's possessions were routinely damaged, her meals interrupted, her nerves frayed. Several sessions with a local trainer and a stack of manuals hadn't made a noticeable difference. Colleen was running out of things to try.

Her vet, who's been listening to Colleen's laments for months, was alarmed. Snapping and nipping at a child was a new problem. The vet didn't believe in putting kids in harm's way. Seamus, she suggested, should be euthanized before he could seriously hurt anyone.

So the stakes were clear. Colleen loved her dog but couldn't live with him. She'd decided that either the dog would be under control by Thanksgiving, or he'd be gone, taken by a rescue group or put down.

I don't know of any statistics on how many dogs live more or less out of control yet in close proximity to humans. But I hear about them daily.

These dogs and their owners dwell in a twilight zone of the dog world. Dogs that bite get publicity; for the opposite reason, so do dogs that rescue earthquake victims. Dogs that are much loved by their owners but also drive them crazy don't get discussed much—yet that may be the biggest subculture in the dog universe. So many people get dogs foolishly, attach to them, then grow bewildered, even desperate, over how to respond to their "misbehavior."

Many of these dogs live sad lives, constantly yelled at and scolded, locked away in basements and bathrooms to keep them out of trouble. But Seamus had a shot at something better; Colleen was ready to fight for her dog.

Though this drama seemed to be about a difficult pet, like so many dog-related problems it was really about something human: leadership.

Seamus's problems had been caused almost entirely by people: first the unscrupulous puppy-mill breeder and pet-store owners who'd helped damage a once-proud breed, then a person (Colleen) who'd further failed the dog in the most fundamental way. "This isn't about obedience," I told her at the bookstore. "This is about leadership. If you want to save this dog, you'll have to become a leader. You'll have to take responsibility for him, show him what to do, how to live. It's a long haul. A lot of people can't do it, or won't."

She was taken aback. Often people hear this challenge, mumble politely, then vanish or get off the phone. Colleen was surprised but wanted to hear more. She cared about her dog, despite his problems, had a profound sense of responsibility, and—often the case—did sense that the conflict was as much about her as the dog.

"I have a hard time being assertive," she acknowledged in a later phone conversation. "It's even a bit of a problem with my husband and my kids and my job, I know. I just dread fighting and confrontation, so sometimes I get pushed around."

I had no wish to function as her therapist, but I pointed out that without understanding something about herself, training Seamus might prove impossible. The problem, as trainers like to say, is rarely with the dog, almost always with us.

The double payoff in working with Seamus was that while helping the dog, perhaps Colleen could help herself as well.

"I get it," she said. "I want to try. I owe it to him."

I HAVE A SOFT SPOT FOR LABRADORS. I'D ARGUE THAT THERE'S NO BETTER family pet than a Lab, a distinction that has been the breed's blessing and curse. Because of their beauty, sociability, and loving natures, Labs are popular family and suburban dogs. Because they're popular, they're often mass-marketed by incompetent backyard breeders and puppy mills. As with other popular breeds, Labs have suffered genetically as a result; many now develop health problems, from allergies to bad hips to neurotic or aggressive personalities.

Yet like other working breeds, Labradors (actually first bred in Newfoundland) have a glorious history. They helped fishermen retrieve nets and fish in brutal weather. Then, exported to England, they became a favored hunting and sporting dog. The breed is marked by geniality, physical prowess, rapacious appetites and scavenging, and loyalty and sociability; and their work with humans continues and grows, from retrieving hunters' birds to guiding the blind to sniffing for bombs and rescuing lost hikers. They are among the most trainable of breeds.

So although their behavioral problems have worsened as their popularity has grown, the breed actually evolved in order to be responsive to people. Seamus may or may not have been damaged by poor breeding, but he'd returned enough affection and intelligence for Colleen to love him and, as she put it, "see the inner dog." That might be enough.

LABRADOR OWNERS OFTEN DON'T RECOGNIZE, OR LOSE SIGHT OF, THE fact that these are working and hunting dogs—strong, energetic, with a need for purpose, activity, and exercise, and therefore in need of lots of attentive, conscientious training. Poorly trained Labs are big, obnoxious, smelly garbage hounds with the ability to destroy, menace, and injure.

Though you often hear their humans describe them as "hyper," Labs don't come that way; they're *driven* nuts. Fortunately for this malleable breed, the damage, with patience and persistence, can often be largely undone.

Colleen understood that she'd gotten Seamus in exactly the wrong way, from a mall pet shop whose mass-produced animals—cranked out by puppy mills like CDs—were likely to have health and behavioral problems.

She'd gotten Seamus, in part, to fill the void caused by her elder daughter's leaving for college, in part because she'd always wanted a dog, and after years of nagging, her husband had finally agreed. Colleen envisioned companionship. She and her dog would take long walks in the country. When she retired, in five or six years, the dog could accompany her on volunteer activities. Yet her real-life dog was poorly equipped to do any of those things.

The process began chaotically. Her husband assured her that crates were cruel, so Seamus wasn't fully housebroken for nearly a month. At various times, he had his nose rubbed in fecal matter (another of her husband's contributions), got whacked with a rolled-up newspaper when he had accidents (this from a neighbor), got dragged around by a choke chain when he barked or pulled.

Already probably suffering from his origins and puppyhood, Seamus was then subjected to months of punishment, recriminations, and confusing signals. Colleen had no confidence in her own judgment, so she found herself deferring to others—"a bunch of people who had very strong opinions but, I see now, didn't know a whole lot more than I did." In fact, I told her, she probably knew much more. She saw the dog every day.

Still, as he grew older, Seamus seemed increasingly destructive and untrainable. He barked obsessively, grabbed food, refused to come, sit, lie down, or stay. When he could slip through the door, he ran off. Aggressive at times to other dogs, he drew blood fighting with a neighbor's golden retriever. "He just got worse by the day," Colleen reported, "and bigger and more powerful." The family began calling him Shameless.

After his run-in with the retriever, he bit a German shepherd, the resulting vet bills costing Colleen several hundred dollars.

Colleen read a training book on dominance that suggested she lie atop Seamus until he stopped moving. It was supposed to make him submissive. It didn't. A local trainer persuaded her to try a shock collar, and she jolted the dog for weeks until she saw that he was just becoming more anxious and out of control. (Who wouldn't?)

Another book urged her to show she was the alpha in the pack by barking and growling at the dog. "He looked at me like I was crazy. I felt the same way."

A positive-reinforcement trainer criticized her for reprimanding the dog and for being too negative. "She told me to wait until Seamus did the right thing and then to praise him. But this didn't really help when he was knocking my kid down or grabbing food off the dinner table. I would like to stay positive, but Seamus didn't seem to know about the program."

Several important psychological things were happening. Colleen was yelling at the dog so often it had become their primary means of communication, with the result that neither of them was cherishing that human-animal bond we hear so much about. "Fight or flight" is the term trainers use to describe the options facing confused or frightened dogs under pressure. Seamus was trying both, and Colleen was losing faith in him, in her ability to handle him, in the entire notion that dogs can be trained.

WHAT WAS CALLED FOR HERE, I THOUGHT, WERE SMALL STEPS. WE HAD to go back to the beginning, build the relationship between Colleen and Seamus, convince them both that they could work together and succeed.

Complicating this approach was her family. Colleen's husband proved a walking encyclopedia of animal ignorance, spouting dumb dog axioms from his family past. He decreed that crates were inhumane, that operant conditioning methods like positive reinforcement were "for wusses."

"I am getting no support for training this dog from my family," Colleen lamented. They'd undermined many of her training efforts, goading Seamus into barking, laughing when he jumped up on furniture, giving him treats and toys at the wrong times. They, too, loved Seamus, but they thought Colleen's efforts to rein him in were mean. Yet none of them showed any interest in training him themselves.

MY ADMIRATION FOR COLLEEN GREW, THOUGH, AS WE TALKED EVERY week or so. It's always seemed to me that dog training requires a certain inner strength on the human's part. Perpetually seeking answers from outsiders—as Colleen had been doing for months—reinforced the idea that some guru out there could tell her what to do. I was the latest candidate. But I'd come to believe that Colleen would have to be the guru. She knew herself and her dog better than any instructor.

We set to work. Colleen drew up a list of very attainable goals: first, create a quiet environment for the dog. She set up crates, one in the kitchen, one in the living room, one in the upstairs bedroom, three sites of frequent "Shameless" behavior. Colleen was surprised, as many dog owners are, at how quickly, with food and treats, Seamus adapted to the crate. By the second week, he was trotting eagerly inside to await a meatball or a rawhide chip.

For the first time Colleen felt she had some control. She confined Seamus when she was preparing meals in the kitchen, during dinner, when company was coming. The idea was to decrease his arousal and begin settling him down.

Next, we launched grounding and calming exercises. Colleen reinforced the dog's name recognition with handfuls of good treats, praising him for eye contact and for coming when she called his name. For almost the first time, he was enjoying interactions with her and doing something he could hardly fail at—coming to his owner for food. She began praising him and giving him attention when he was behaving, not rampaging. She also began hand-feeding him to strengthen their bond, offering handfuls of kibble, saying his name. Soon, a dog distracted by everything would turn on a dime when she called his name.

"The first victory was having him in the crate. My shouting decreased by half. The second was the ease with which he started coming to me. We both loved it. Whenever I said, 'Seamus, let's go to work,' he came flying. Suddenly it was fun." By succeeding at this simple command, Seamus was able to please his owner and give her reason to praise him. Soon he gave her more reason to be pleased.

I suggested that she attach a leash and then step on it, perhaps a foot from his collar, while saying, "Lie down," and then, "Stay."

Seamus struggled for a bit at first, but couldn't get up, so he had no choice but to lie down and stay. When he did, he was given rewards that escalated. First, he lay down for ten seconds, then fifteen. Before long he would lie down on command (with no leash necessary any longer) and stay for more than a minute, then two minutes while Colleen backed away.

Once or twice, Colleen called me in tears, frustrated and discouraged when Seamus wouldn't listen or reverted to his old craziness, which tended to happen when the whole family was gathered. Her husband and daughters thought she was being cruel, or just doubted this would work. They offered no help, just jokes and jeering, and predictions that she would soon give up. I didn't think so. The determination was evident in her voice. What was originally about the dog was now about something bigger. It's striking how often that happens when one is training a dog.

"This is a big undertaking," I reminded her when she flagged. "It's going to take a while. You have to have some faith. When Seamus doesn't obey, just don't reward him. Then go back and try again in a couple of minutes."

The fact was, the household dynamic was already changing. Because Seamus was out of sight during the most raucous times—dinner, visitors' arrivals, workmen coming and going—he settled in his crate, as dogs do, and finally seemed to learn how to do nothing.

"It was as if he was off duty," Colleen observed. "I felt like the crate gave him diplomatic immunity." The humans were behaving differently, too. Colleen wasn't yelling at Seamus all day, so their time together was more affectionate. And as he responded to her efforts, her family had less opportunity to undermine what she was trying to accomplish. In fact, she began to sense they were surprised and impressed.

Colleen began coming up with her own training ideas and games. She taught Seamus to not jump on people by tossing a ball over his shoulder when people approached. In a few weeks, if someone came to the house, Seamus turned to look over his shoulder instead of leaping at the newcomer. Colleen played hide-and-seek with him, subtly encouraging name recognition and eye contact. These weren't tactics I could have offered but things she herself was beginning to understand about her dog and capitalize on.

Next, having reserved playing and romping for fixed ten-to-fifteen-minute periods in the morning and at night, Colleen began finding work for Seamus to do. She taught him to retrieve the newspaper in the morning, for instance, and to bring back water toys she threw in a nearby lake. This brought dramatic change; Seamus was busy and successful and getting praise for his efforts. He was working with her.

And there was a spillover effect. "I really felt like I'd taken on some part of myself and conquered it," Colleen reported. "Every day, when I looked at this dog I was proud. It's a hard feeling to describe, but very satisfying, and it made me feel good about myself. I guess I needed that, though I was a little surprised to get it from a dog."

Through the fall, Colleen kept building on her successes. Instead of constant scolding, Seamus received praise and reward. She made sure he had quiet periods each day, moments when she would practice having him lie down while she massaged his back, brushed and petted him, praised him for being still, and rewarded him with a stream of his favorite snacks.

When she saw a dog coming, no matter how far off, she scattered the ground with food and noticed, over time, that Seamus looked to her for goodies rather than charging at the dog. They were having a good time; he was becoming the dog she'd long wanted. And, significantly, she was building on their work together. She began to develop strong instincts about timing and response: she knew what would work with her dog. So she became more precise and confident, something Seamus sensed and responded to.

"He is not perfect, and I understand he might never be. But he's pretty great. And you know what? We'll get there." Life calmed down. "Seamus is looking to me for direction, rather than my being his warden and cop all day. I got the leadership idea: you aren't always bellowing and yelling, just showing him the rules, insisting he respect them, and helping him get there."

Exactly.

He would regress and recover, she understood. Training wasn't a straight line; it was a general direction, a goal, her means of communicating with her dog. And you are never really done.

THE DAY OF JUDGMENT FINALLY CAME. THANKSGIVING BEGAN BADLY, with Seamus, perhaps sensing his owner's anxiety, making a lunge for the stuffing on the counter. Meanwhile, the kids demanded that he remain uncrated during dinner, since this was "a special day." Colleen noticed that her family seemed to side with Seamus when it came to training, as if training were too rough on him and they had to speak up for him.

But she held her ground. Training Seamus had become something of a family struggle, involving not only differing ideas on animal care but also the deeper perception that she was passive and somewhat weak. The dog had highlighted the fact that Colleen's opinions were not always taken into account, her ideas not always respected. "I didn't want to overanalyze it," she said, "but I almost got the feeling they were afraid of what would happen if this worked, of what it would mean for them. You know, if he had to change, then maybe they would have to as well.

"I never had much confidence in myself," she had to admit. But she was beginning to.

So, half an hour before the first guests arrived, despite familial grousing about how cruel she was being, how Seamus should be part of the festivities, she took some bones, called "Crate!" and, as Seamus darted in, closed the door.

Seamus sat quietly in his crate and napped for several hours. When he came out, he was "a bit excited," but happy to go for a peaceful walk. "It was a thoroughly enjoyable afternoon. I wasn't watching him, scolding him, worrying about him jumping on guests or on the table," Colleen told me afterward.

And what about her family and guests?

"They were all just shocked, even though my family had already seen some improvement. Last Thanksgiving was such a nightmare— this was a way to really measure our progress. Everyone said they'd never seen Seamus so calm and at ease. They all said they liked him more. His sweetness really seems to have come out in the last few months."

And her husband?

"Later that night, when we were cleaning up and getting ready to go to bed, he told me that I had done a great job with the dog and that I had been right. Hey, it wasn't the Nobel Prize, but from him that's a lot. There was respect in his tone."

Just before dinner, she confided, she'd felt so anxious about the dog, about everything, that she shed a few tears in the bathroom, feeling ridiculous. "I'm not a nut. I can handle situations," she said. "But not only was the dog's life at stake. I also felt there was something at stake for me. And I stood up to the dog, I stood up to my husband—it feels like something important has happened."

Something had. Seamus was on the road to learning how to live with his family. Colleen, having found her inner trainer, had gained confidence, not only in dealing with Seamus but in other contexts as well. Seamus was a living monument to her own growth and determination. She honestly hadn't believed, a couple of months earlier, that she could deal with this creature she loved. But she could.

In the following weeks, Seamus was by no means a model dog—as if such a thing existed. He raided the garbage, pulled on the leash, was still prone to jumping on people when excited.

But everyone who knew him was amazed at his growing calm, his attention to Colleen, the sharp decline in compulsive and neurotic behavior. The crate was now entirely his choice; he rarely needed to go in, but sometimes decided to.

The happy stereotype of dogs is that they are selfless, serving us for thousands of years out of noble motives. But those who know and understand dogs best recognize that they act mostly out of self-interest, not because they have absorbed Rin Tin Tin ideas about bonding.

To understand this isn't to diminish the human-canine bond but to cement it. Colleen had brought her troubled dog back by manipulating his yen for food, fun, and peace of mind.

As it happened, in her job as parks supervisor of her town, Colleen had been arguing for years that one or two of the town parks ought to set aside some time, early in the morning and again at dusk, when dogs could run off-leash. The parks commissioner finally agreed, but they told her she ought to set the example by being the first to bring her dog. It went without saying that they expected the dog to be well behaved.

On the appointed day, the local weekly paper, even a TV crew, showed up. Colleen was so nervous, "I almost couldn't go. I almost called in sick."

But she went, and Seamus put on quite a show. He hopped out of the car, greeted dogs and people calmly and warmly, chased and retrieved balls, sat and stayed on request. His picture appeared on the newspaper's front page, a testament to the opportunity for happy dogs to run free, as long as they and their humans both keep their parts of the bargain.

SEVERAL MONTHS LATER, COLLEEN CALLED ME. WE HADN'T TALKED IN A while and she wanted to share the news: she was planning to get another dog, maybe a golden retriever, possibly a border collie. The dog would have ample parks nearby with annoying geese to chase, and Colleen was planning to take it—and Seamus—to agility classes.

Seamus was doing beautifully. "Every day somebody tells me they can't believe his progress and asks for my help with their own dogs," she reported. They were about to take the AKC Good Citizen Test—sponsored all over the country by the American Kennel Club to test dog obedience and disposition. The Good Citizen certificates are often the first step toward dogs doing therapy and other advanced work requiring special training and reliability.

Colleen was increasingly coming to feel that the dog, a puppy-mill purchase of dubious background, had come about as far as she could bring him. She wasn't giving up, just trying to recognize the reality of her dog, much as I am coming to understand Orson's limits. Sometimes when we get dogs whose backgrounds we'll never know, we have to accept that they may have suffered breeding, behavioral, or other experiences that stay with them despite our efforts and commitment.

This was a different Colleen, as she agreed, and a different Seamus, and it was the work with the dog that seemed to have allowed a part of her to emerge. "I wouldn't have believed the two of us could do it," she said. "In fact, I was convinced we couldn't." Now that she'd seen that she could, she was ready for another challenge.

"Last year at this time, I was yelling at Seamus day and night and thinking of putting him down. With my new dog, I think I can go in a different direction. I'm very excited!"

I LIVE ON A FARM IN UPSTATE NEW YORK FOR MANY REASONS. I LOVE looking out at the mountains and meadows; I love caring for my donkeys; I love being outdoors, walking through the woods.

But one reason I live in the country—I might not have admitted this so freely a few years ago—is so that my border collies can embrace their destinies, or at least their ancestry, by loping through fields and herding sheep; so that my Lab can run and swim and eat gross stuff.

I may be edging toward the extreme in this, but the impulse is hardly unusual. I first learned to herd with my dogs at Raspberry Ridge, a Pennsylvania sheep farm and training center that offered a free monthly instinct test. The trainer put a few sheep in a fenced area and allowed people's dogs to circle the pen, while she evaluated the dogs' sustained interest in herding. I often helped out, and was perpetually amazed at

COEXISTENCE

the number of people who showed up, not only with border collies and other herding dogs, but with poodles, pugs, Newfoundlands, mutts of all stripes. Their owners were eager to expose their dogs to the ancient art of flock-tending, they often told me, so that the dogs could be "fulfilled."

People want much for their dogs, it seems, more all the time. The aspiring shepherds usually were fresh from other activities—obedience classes, agility training, tracking competitions, play groups. The owners often took their dogs on vacations and attended special programs and camps with them.

"I do agility and therapy-dog training," said the owner of a not particularly energetic sheltie (who looked at the sheep, lay down, and yawned). "I'd love to add herding. We have Thursdays and Fridays open." I wondered if the sheltie wouldn't be just as happy to spend those afternoons napping.

Middle-class America has relentlessly enriched its children with soccer and ballet, computer camp and Chinese lessons. If your dog isn't similarly fulfilled yet, it may be soon. "Fulfillment" has become a buzzword among trendy California dog lovers, the *Los Angeles Times* reported a while back, and I can testify that the phenomenon isn't limited to the West Coast. The idea is to figure out what a dog was born to do—herd, point, retrieve, loll decoratively on laps—and find ways to let him do it.

Dog fulfillment seems to me an inevitable development in our ever-deepening involvement with dogs. One of the Baby Boomers' more dubious ideas was the "gifted and talented child." In the seventies and eighties, schools across the country created programs to cater to this notion. As with our dogs, we had to figure out what our kids excelled at, then encourage them to do it. An unprogrammed child hanging around almost constituted neglect.

Nervous principals and anxious parents made sure that every child was defined as gifted and talented at *something*. This has evolved to the point where, in many families, too much is never enough. Every waking hour must be spent at a seminar or rehearsal; every drive, meal, and movie provides an opportunity to advance understanding of the world and our children's ability to compete and thrive in it.

As Americans who love their dogs become increasingly enmeshed with them emotionally, they grow more anxious about them, too. They feel pressure to do more, guilt about never doing enough. It's tough to watch other people shower their dogs with special diets, innovative health care, and stimulating activities and not feel crummy if you're not. "Is it okay to have a dog and still go to work?" one woman e-mailed me last year.

There is absolutely nothing wrong with doing things with your dog, from agility to obedience to therapy work or trialing. It's great fun and can be rewarding, if you have the time and the money. It spurs training and often strengthens the human-animal bond. There is, however, a difference between doing something you want to do with your dog and something you feel you *need* to do to qualify as a good dog owner.

People ask me all the time if a dog can be left alone long enough to go to a movie *and* dinner. "I have trouble enjoying my food, knowing the poor guy is sitting home, lonely and bored, waiting for me," goes the refrain.

A friend of mine has driven her beagle all over the Northeast in search of trials, hikes, camps, and classes that will provide further insight into the dog's potential and desires. "I just feel this drive to give her everything she possibly could need." A woman in Vermont e-mails me for advice about indoor games for an Australian shepherd. "On rainy days, I worry he doesn't get enough stimulation."

Dog owners vigorously search online and off for activities that will amuse and reward their pets. Dogs belong to recreational and sporting associations, sometimes organized by activity (tracking, herding, search-and-rescue), sometimes by breed or circumstance. Dogs have play groups and walking dates, annual conferences, regional get-togethers. They're acquiring service and therapy certificates by the thousands (along with the requisite accessories—collars, scarves, jackets, and vests).

Dog day-care centers have sprouted everywhere so angst-ridden owners can go to work feeling good that Max or Maggie (our dogs often have human names now, too) has sufficient exercise and companionship. The toy department at the local pet store now resembles a Zany Brainy store: not just balls, but balls that promote exercise and *learning*.

The conventional wisdom used to be that having a dog is a great way to meet people. The people who study companion animals call this the use of dogs as "social lubricants." It still can be a fine way to meet people, certainly, but I see more and more people for whom owning a dog is an end unto itself, offering a social life and structure in which people sometimes become beside the point. There's less impetus to link up with humans, more to share activities with the dog. A lonely single friend in the Midwest who for years had sought a companion through blind dates and dating services in the meantime adopted a rescue dog for company. When he eventually met a woman he liked, he was a bit stunned to find he enjoyed solitary walks with his dog as much as or more than their dates. "I don't know how Socks would take to another person in the apartment," he mused. "We would have less time together if we had a family."

Well . . . yeah.

A generation or two ago—in fact, for most of the species' history—the idea that a dog needed to be fulfilled would have shocked even the most attentive owner. As recently as the sixties and seventies, dogs were rarely even leashed or confined; they generally were content just to hang around, occasionally tiffing with other dogs, knocking over trash cans, or pursuing a mailman. No one I've met over the age of fifty remembers dog play groups—or any other sort of recreational activity with dogs outside of shooting the occasional duck.

Today's owners might pause to consider that their dogs may actually need less from them than they feel they need to give. And they may need to put less pressure on themselves. Most dogs require between forty-five minutes and an hour of exercise a day, depending on breed and size, not endless fetching or romps with packs of excited peers. A dog that chases balls, sticks, and Frisbees all day is often a codependent creature—obnoxious, aroused, or hyper, but not necessarily fulfilled.

Our dogs certainly need love and attention, but not always as much as we think. They need food and things to chew and play with, but not as much as we usually provide. It was my trainer and friend Carolyn Wilki who warned that I wasn't helping anxious Orson by rushing him around to sheepherding and other activities all day. "He needs to be socialized with dogs and people, but he also needs to learn how to be calm just as much," she cautioned. "I see people smiling all the time when they see their dogs racing around in packs like maniacs, but they aren't always doing their dogs a favor." Fortunately for Orson, and for our future together, I listened to her. In fact, I have come to believe that calming training may be the most important training many dogs ever get.

Dogs don't have "fun" the same way humans, or human kids, do, and people often confuse their excitement and arousal for yuks.

In natural environments, which almost no dog or owner can replicate today, dogs act like lions. They lie around much of the day, rousing themselves now and then for food or sex or to chase something appealing. They need activity, but don't get bored in the human sense. They may get anxious when left alone—being pack animals, they usually prefer company—but loneliness is a human, not a canine, emotion. Dogs can grow restless with too much inactivity, but they are not self-aware; they don't know they are bored.

With proper training and acclimatization, almost any dog can spend time alone happily, vegging out, smelling the smells and listening to the sounds of the world, chewing on rawhide, doing nothing in particular with great enthusiasm. One European study suggests that dogs left alone are smarter than dogs smothered by attention: they get the opportunity to solve problems by themselves.

The lesson, I think, is that once we've ascertained how much exercise and activity a dog needs, we need to examine our self-generated pressure to give our dogs perfect lives. We so often feel helpless to affect much of what happens in the world, in the workplace, in our own communities. *Here,* we think, is something we actually can achieve: we can give our loyal companions everything.

I preach common sense and simplicity, however. If tracking, agility trials, or play groups are fun for you and your dog and fit into your life, have a blast. But at times they may do more for you than for him. Moreover, dogs rarely need vacations. Almost any dog can happily survive in a kennel for a few weeks while you take yours.

I've spent some of the loveliest hours of my life out in pastures with my vigilant dogs, listening to the sound of sheep crunching away on grass on warm, breezy nights. But it's sometimes okay to relax and let our dogs just be dogs and spare them the fate of today's harried kids, stressed out about college before they're ten.

I've learned (almost) to stop obsessing over their psychological development. We've spent some of our happiest times together doing nothing.

AMERICANS NOW SPEND TENS OF BILLIONS OF DOLLARS EACH year on stuff for their dogs—health care, food and treats, toys and beds, clothes and collars and leashes, dog walkers, kennels, plus weirder and even more expensive things: pet cemeteries and spas, retreats and camps, designer booties and sweaters, cologne, oil portraits, psychics and channelers.

Our attachment potential is bottomless, and the great capitalist machine has geared up to take advantage of it. Meanwhile, the Internet has spawned a new generation of "experts" offering diets, studies, ideas; some of that material is useful, and some spirals into conspiracy theories and suspicions swirling around vets, dog-food companies, and training approaches.

Pet marts—multiplying in numbers and size—offer rows of bones, pig and cattle parts, balls that squeak and light up, and nearly as many stuffed animals as Toys R Us. We find learning and puzzle toys that spur development, animal toys that growl, audio- and videotapes to leave on when we go out to provide our dogs with companionship and amusement.

Consider the ante upped. "I feel like I'm abusing my dog because I feed him canned dog food from the supermarket," laments one New Yorker who takes her dog to a Greenwich Village dog run every morning. "People there make their dogs vegan diets and buy gourmet organic food that costs a fortune. Some of them feed their dogs only turkey necks. Everybody tells me I'm poisoning my dogs with ordinary dog food."

Almost everything about dog care is confusing and controversial. Do dogs need vegan diets? Expensive feeds imported from California or Europe? Do they actually benefit from annual shots and vaccinations?

Nobody—surely not I—is an expert on all those things. It's healthy to read books, talk to several vets, speak to nutritionists and behaviorists, and to other dog owners. All I can offer is my own experience and conclusions after a number of years of talking to literally thousands of owners, trainers, nutritionists, behaviorists, breeders, vets, and shelter and rescue workers.

There is nothing many of us wouldn't do for our dogs, and since they can't tell us what they need and like, we often project psychological issues and traumas from our own pasts onto our lives with dogs. The intensity of our relationships, then, pits boundless love against boundless stuff. I struggle often to find the balance between rationality—plain common sense—and my dogs' welfare.

I also consider my own time and emotional energy an important factor in the equation. I don't want to spend most or all of my waking hours worrying about my dogs, much as I love them. I can't provide them an environment entirely free of nutritional, environmental, or other dangers. I have to pick and choose.

So I work to find the balance that seems healthy for them and for me, and to maintain some perspective in an environment that offers unbounded goodies. I don't, for example, buy canine cookies from the gourmet bakery section of a pet store. My dogs' biscuits aren't shaped like pretzels or pastries—perfect examples of our being lured into thinking something is neat for our dogs because it resembles something *we* like. Such treats cost four or five times the price of perfectly fine biscuits available in any supermarket. Yet a number of friends refuse to buy commercially produced dog biscuits, citing chemicals and other undesirable ingredients. Some make their own, or order only organic cookies. I actually horrified one of my volunteers by suggesting she use sliced-up hot dogs for training. "My God!" she gasped. "Don't you know what's in those things?" We compromised on soy dogs.

Compromises are the stuff of life, but all dangers are proportional. I worry about the risk to my dogs from street traffic and from attack by one of the untrained dogs we often encounter, but I don't sweat their eating store-bought biscuits or franks.

In fact, I buy training treats in bulk from a farm supply store. My dogs have learned to love these simple treats, which are dry, comparatively odorless, easy to carry around, and last for months.

One challenge for dog owners is to figure out whom to listen to, what websites to frequent, which advice and warnings to heed. If life with a dog is going to be manageable and rational, for both human and animal, you have to put up your own boundaries. There is simply no end to people's concerns.

Though some dog stuff is frivolous—the decision to do your dog's astrological chart or not is of little practical consequence—diet is more serious. People do battle over their different approaches. Full disclosure: I give my dogs Eukanuba dry food, but half a dozen other upper-end dog foods are available through pet stores, vets' offices, and many supermarkets that would probably serve as well; and countless more exotic premium foods are available online and through specialty catalogs. Many dog owners have expressed surprise or dismay that I don't use them.

Conventional dog foods contain unwholesome by-products and chemicals, I've often been told. I've also heard warnings that the vets that recommend them are compromised, bribed, or influenced in some way by pet-food companies who lobby veterinarians and otherwise influence their recommendations. Dog-food companies, the conspiratorial whispers continue, help pay off vets' college tuition, maintain their offices, give them equipment and vacations. So I'm chided for not giving my dogs vegan or raw-meat diets, which, I'm told, reduce the risk of disease and allergies, and increase longevity.

Numerous vets, nutritionists, and breeders assure me, however, that the food I use and similar brands provide everything my dogs need. They are high in protein and low in fat, which is one of the primary nutritional goals for dog food. Beyond that, there is little agreement among vets about nutrition.

"Your dog food has everything your dog needs," a vet told me. That's an important phrase, a seminal idea in my life with dogs: I want to give them what they need, not what I think they need, not what I need to give them.

I'm not convinced that vegan or raw-meat or organic diets are necessary for my dogs, or that they merit the time and money required to obtain or prepare them. There's nothing wrong with using a different approach, as long as a dog is healthy and thriving on a diet, but for me, the question is how much time and engagement I want to put into every aspect of my dogs' lives. "These high-end diets are just not necessary for most dogs," a nutritionist at the University of Pennsylvania veterinary school told me (virtually pleading that I withhold her name). "It's just an example of people going to the max, believing they are doing right by their dogs. They are wasting money, and, in some cases, giving their dogs diets that are just too rich." As for standard supermarket dog-food brands, although I'm in no position to judge, I know many dogs that are living happy and healthy lives on them, and many vets who are quite comfortable recommending them. Seeking a medium between extremes, I go with slightly more expensive and nutritious pet-store brands.

If I thought my dogs were anything but vigorous and healthy, I'd switch foods. But they're flourishing. As they grow older, beyond puppyhood, I switch to a mix of regular and low-fat food, even for a working dog as busy as Rose. I want my dogs lean—you should be able to feel a dog's ribs—so they get one cup of food twice a day, morning and evening. Obesity claims far more dogs annually than abuse, mostly, I believe, because people can't say no to their dogs and don't give them enough exercise.

Because Rose is so finicky, and I want to encourage her to eat, I usually mix in some canned food or microwave a handful of hamburger and add it to the kibble. It encourages focus and quick eating, of importance in a multi-dog household. The dogs go right to their bowls, eat their own food, and don't get into the habit of moving in on anyone else's. To go farther is a personal choice, one I don't choose to make.

Living with a dog in contemporary America means having commercial companies bombard us with products from one side and an increasingly polarized, politicized dog culture bombard us with arguments and alternatives from the other. It requires some thinking about how far each of us wants to go down the caring-for-your-dog road. I do lots of things for my dogs, expend a lot of emotional energy on their welfare. I try to maintain some limits on how much.

TOYS AND BEDS

It's easy to see, when you enter my old farmhouse, that dogs live here, and fairly pampered dogs at that. I've put those pillowy cedar-filled beds from L. L. Bean and fleece-lined foam beds from pet chains in three or four rooms. The dogs could easily sleep on the floor, much of it carpeted, or in their wool-lined crates, but they seem more comfortable on softer surfaces. This isn't something they need—beds don't confine dogs or help train them—but an amenity they seem drawn to. And it helps keep them off the human furniture.

When they're so moved, they also can come pile into my bed at night. It gets crowded in there sometimes, but it's a loving gathering of the pack we all rather like.

I confess to spending a small fortune on toys: balls, chewbones and rawhide, tug toys and ropes and Frisbees. Whenever someone's up for hide-and-seek or a wrestling match with toys, indoors or out, there are plenty of playthings around. Debate gets heated about how much play or toys adult dogs need, but in my view toys are stimulating, promote exercise and socializing, help dogs figure out what to do with other dogs. Puppies provided with toys have outlets for their chewing, curiosity, and playful alertness.

I throw balls on walks; the dogs are happy to chase them to the point of exhaustion. Clem loves stuffed animals and waggles around the house with them day and night. The border collies prefer tug-of-war toys. They probably need about half of what they have (sticks in the woods serve some of the same purpose), but I'm a sucker for toys and can rarely leave a pet mart without picking up a few more.

Do dogs need grooming? Some do, to keep their coats clean and smooth. Do they need accessories, ribbons, painted toenails, and scents? Not mine. Those are human decorations.

Nor do my dogs need special video- or audiotapes for learning and soothing. That's my job as owner and trainer. I've heard of cases in which tapes that desensitize a dog to certain noises—gunshots or airplanes, for example—are valuable training tools. I haven't tried them myself. They will just have to deal with some anxiety. I do.

Sometimes I leave a radio or TV on when I go out, because I believe the low-level chat soothes the dogs. But I couldn't prove it. I remember asking a trainer I was visiting whether we should leave the lights on when we went out for dinner, putting our dogs in crates.

"What for?" she asked. "They don't read."

So I don't leave lights on when I go out.

As for dogs' psyches, I've learned a lot from behaviorists, but I'll pass, at least for now, on channelers and psychics. There is much about the world of dogs and people we don't understand, and I cannot say with certainty that those alternative practitioners aren't sometimes useful and valuable.

But it's enough that Rose herds sheep and runs the farm; I don't need to make her a therapist or high priestess, and she doesn't need to have her innermost herding thoughts interpreted for me. Our experiences together do sometimes feel spiritual to me, but that arises on its own from our shared lives and seems to require no professional intervention.

THE RATIONAL THEORY OF VETERINARY CARE

FOR THE PAST THREE YEARS, I'VE ATTENDED NATIONAL VETERINARY CONferences in Orlando and Las Vegas, where I've met and talked with hundreds of vets. I've kept up many of these relationships via e-mail and the phone. It's been enlightening.

One of their biggest challenges, they tell me, is dealing with dog owners who go online to find better! cheaper! miracle cures from other dog lovers.

"I love it when my clients are well-informed," one vet confided. "But so often they get information that doesn't work or hasn't been tested. And they believe it, and come storming into my office demanding to know why I'm not giving their dog herbs to cure their cancer, because somebody on a message board told them it works. Somebody online will tell you almost anything works. It's become a huge headache for us, and it isn't always great for their dogs and cats either."

Medical practitioners of all kinds face new and complex difficulties in our skeptical, yet demanding, age. Vets, like human doctors, are increasingly likely to face lawsuits, so their insurance rates constantly rise. As a result, they feel pressured to require tests and procedures that may not be necessary but might help them fend off charges of negligence or malpractice.

Meanwhile, the mass media in general, and the Internet in particular, have made instant medical authorities out of everybody. Consumers, better informed, no longer see doctors—of any sort—as omniscient or infallible. Good medical information is available online, of course, but so is plenty of junk. On the mailing lists and websites that have become an integral part of the dog world, all sorts of holistic remedies and other alternatives are constantly being discussed and recommended, but readers have little means of evaluating them. In this culture of suspicion and passion for alternatives, many have grown skeptical about traditional veterinary protocols. They believe that vets are too quick to vaccinate dogs, that they give unnecessary shots in order to make money, that they're under the sway of pet-food companies and pharmaceutical houses. Scores of heavily trafficked websites list the benefits of alternatives, from acupuncture and herbal treatments to stress reduction and massage. Many pet owners report good results.

Holistic veterinary care is a growing and respected branch of animal medicine, as interesting and worth investigating as human alternatives have proved to be. But this growing suspicion of conventions like ordinary dog food and mainstream veterinary care also reflects our intensifying emotionalization of dogs, their elevation to human status. How much time and care do we wish to lavish on our animals, no matter how wondrous they are or how much we love them? My own approach has evolved this way: though I'm interested in these alternatives and have heard friends cite success stories, I happen to like vets; I generally trust and respect them. It isn't easy to become a vet.

Most graduating vets today—nearly 90 percent—are young women who love animals, go to school for many years, pile up enormous loans and constantly enroll in recertification programs. Yet most don't make a lot of money, not from their clients, not from pet-food or drug companies. Their practices are labor-intensive. Unlike physicians who treat humans, they face a complex economic reality: medical care for their patients is optional, entirely the choice of their owners.

The clinic I use in upstate New York, the Borador Animal Hospital in Salem, is run by three women who are typical of the impressive vets I meet at national veterinary conventions. Mary Menard, Whitney Pressler, and Jen Steeves are all thoughtful diagnosticians and passionate animal lovers. They work hard to stay abreast of veterinary advances. They're good listeners who can also be blunt and candid if they feel I'm slacking at my dietary, health-care, or training obligations.

My dogs and I have been through innumerable procedures and crises with them, ranging from routine vaccinations and spaying to Orson's torn ligaments, Rose's shredded paw pads and Lyme disease, and attacks by feral cats. And then there was the time Rose got kicked squarely in the forehead by a donkey. I've called the clinic at all hours for help and advice and spent a small fortune on my dogs' health care. I don't regret or resent it.

The vets' compassion is striking; so is that of their staff. I trust them and generally do what they advise. But it is a partnership; we talk things over. They understand how well I know my dogs and so have altered treatment plans at my suggestion, just as I have acceded to some of their requests. I watch my dogs closely to see how they do on certain kinds of medications and report my observations to the vets. I trust them and listen to them, but I don't do everything they say. Good vets, in my view, are open-minded and flexible and want to have this kind of back-and-forth.

Their practice is also open to alternative and holistic approaches such as acupuncture and massage; some behavioral and medical problems are beyond the reach of conventional veterinary medicine, and a good vet will be the first one to suggest you might go elsewhere for more help.

But I'm not inclined to research dog health care on my own—I'm not competent to evaluate medical research. And I don't have time to become a real expert. Perhaps I'm giving my dogs short shrift, but I've rarely been disappointed by an experienced, professional vet. When Dr. Menard told me it was time for Clem to be spayed—the breeder thought we should wait—she explained that the procedure was easier on a dog when she was young, and that early neutering reduced the risk of cancer. We talked it over, and I agreed to go ahead.

When Orson seemed to have torn a ligament and was hobbling on three legs, friends bombarded me with alternative ideas and possibilities—this vet in Michigan, that holistic practioner in Vermont. Whitney Pressler said Orson might need surgery, and that the practice was comfortable performing the procedure.

I would gladly go anywhere for this dog, within reason, but I chose not to immerse myself in online discussion groups or drag him all over the Northeast for third and fourth opinions. I chose to have the procedure done quickly and locally, if that proved necessary. But we all agreed to wait a while and see what rest and time could do first, and his leg appears to have healed on its own.

NATURALLY, ANYONE WHO HAS DOUBTS ABOUT AN INVASIVE OR OTHER medical procedure for his dog has every right—and obligation—to satisfy himself that it's necessary and appropriate; second opinions are entirely logical.

But, personally, while I know that no practitioner is infallible, that mistakes can happen, I'll trust my dogs to vets. I'm happy to rely on their guidance in caring for my dogs' health. Maintaining a balance requires continuous tinkering, management, and reflection, especially given modern communications, the intensity of dog love, and a rising sense of empowerment these days in anyone who sees a professional about anything.

I elect to stay more or less within what I consider the mainstream dog community. If I run out of Eukanuba, I stop at the supermarket and happily fill in with Pedigree or Alpo, and my dogs have never skipped a beat.

Dogs tend to love what they know, accept what they are given. They respect their own traditions. If I adopted a raw-turkey-neck-only regimen, they would soon get finicky about dry kibble—so much easier to get, store, and feed, especially when traveling. I could spend hours researching and struggling to comprehend competing claims about inoculations, or consult my vets and respect their judgment. I don't think my vets have been corrupted by malign forces. There are lots of easier ways to make a buck, and most don't require nearly as much education.

WHY DO I WANT ANOTHER DOG?

The Multiple-Dog Household

ONE CHARACTERISTIC OF MANY OF US DOG LOVERS IS THAT WE are almost always thinking, secretly or otherwise, about another dog. Maybe there's a breed we've had an eye on, or we have trouble with those pleading-eyed pups the local rescue group totes to the mall on Saturdays. Maybe we've paid repeated visits to Petfinder.org.

A lot of those who love dogs will, at one point or another, consider two. Or three. The number of multiple-dog households in this country is increasing dramatically, says the American Veterinary Association.

Curiously, though, dog owners and lovers like me are often married to sane people who don't particularly want another dog and often point out the many sound reasons why another dog is unnecessary or even burdensome—including but not limited to increased costs, lack of time, lack of space, a dislike of chaos and dog hair, more vet bills, less freedom to travel, less room in bed. This discussion is eternal, in that it can't ever really be won or resolved. The dog lover never stops wanting more dogs; the sane person never stops resisting. In the best of circumstances, like mine, the discussion is (reasonably) affectionate and good-natured, though I've also seen it cause bad feeling and disappointment. Sometimes, after all, the sane person is right.

Individual circumstances vary so wildly that it's tough to generalize about caring for more than one dog. Nevertheless, having done so myself for many years, I can offer some general thoughts, a Rational Theory of the Multiple-Dog Household.

First, you need to spend some time considering your motives. A good friend upstate is always calling me up excitedly, telling me about a dog he's found and wants—immediately. Once it was a runt he saw in a pet store, more recently a collie tied up in front of a farmhouse with a FOR SALE sign.

Usually I get to Dan before he brings the dog home, and we talk about the situation. His impulses are familiar, not uncommon among animal lovers. Dan comes from a troubled, dysfunctional family whose members struggle with anxiety, depression, addictions. He loves taking care of creatures, both two- and four-legged. He dotes on his wife and daughters, and he's crazy about the two dogs he already has.

For Dan, acquiring dogs is a way of loving safely, of healing old wounds.

Lately, he's expressed some concern about his wife; she seems distracted, preoccupied with work and the kids, and it bothers him. It's a minor source of conflict in his marriage, he says. Still, it's very likely tied to the latest outbreak of desire for another dog. Perhaps, he concluded as we chewed it over, he ought to work out those problems.

In a marriage, minor conflicts can become major. Dogs, especially new dogs, can disrupt a home and its routines. It's risky to turn to dogs reflexively rather than grapple with people-related problems. If your kids think you're a jerk, or your husband doesn't understand you, getting a retriever to hike with you on weekends may not be the best solution.

In Dan's case, he was also starting a new job, and his younger daughter was still recovering from a broken ankle suffered in an auto accident. I thought the tumult and anxiety in his life was triggering a need for another creature to nurture and care for. I certainly understood the impulse, but it didn't seem a propitious moment. We both knew he would eventually get another dog, but we also agreed there would be better times for that.

Such self-awareness is not an argument against acquiring another dog, nor is this sort of exploration indulgent. As I've argued earlier, living well with dogs is easier when we understand ourselves. Had Dan gone ahead and grabbed the most recent dog he spotted, he would have had to put aside his marital concerns, or else tend to them to the exclusion of attending to the new dog. Yet new dogs often require lots of time and attention to adjust well.

People who have suffered, emotionally or otherwise, often make loving and sensitive pet owners. But there's a practical element to getting a dog that potential owners sometimes overlook—at the dog's peril.

It's important (maybe even more than when you first become a pet owner) that you find the *right* second or third dog. Dog lore—movies, books, myth—advances the idea of the impulse dog. He "finds you" on the street, or you stumble across him in a shelter and he's meant for you. These scenarios rarely bother to include the necessary months of training and acclimation. Myths don't always translate smoothly into real life. You need to know as much about a new dog as you can. Trainers, vets, breeders, and experienced rescue and shelter workers can all help you consider, choose, and analyze a second or third dog you're considering bringing into your home.

Be up-front with breeders or shelter and rescue workers about the dogs you already have—their number, kinds, and personalities. Let them help you find a compatible addition that's the right age, gender, size, and breed. This process might not be as resonant as the dog that finds you, but the odds are better it will work out.

Then do yourself and your existing pets a huge favor and take some time getting to know the new candidate before you bring him home. Take him for a walk, or to a dog run, or spend an afternoon with him. It's well worth a few hours, given that he'll be around for years. There's no reason to be surprised by a newcomer; usually you and a trainer (or shelter or rescue worker, vet or behaviorist) can make a decent guess about what he'll be like.

Think, too, about your other dogs. Untrained dogs, or dogs with behavioral problems, often suffer when additional dogs enter a household; it becomes even less likely that they'll get the attention and training they need. I once wound up relinquishing a dog I loved because I added an additional dog before I had worked through our lingering problems. It was a sad decision. In retrospect, I wish I'd squarely confronted some key questions. They're the ones I still ask myself when I think about getting another dog (which I do, on average, two or three times a day).

What's the point? Why now? Millions of dogs need homes, just as millions of humans need food and medicine; but that's a bottomless problem, not a coherent reason for acquiring an animal. Do I really have time for another dog? Time to get to know him, to bond, to train and exercise him?

Do I have serious, unresolved problems with any of my existing dogs? Are they well behaved and properly trained? If not, I wait. First things first: no more dogs for me until my house is in order. This is not only a sensible deterrent, but also a stimulus to continue the work I've started with my dogs, rather than simply moving on, leaving unfinished business. If one dog won't come, sit, or stop barking, adding another won't help.

What's the impact on my family? Is there serious resistance to the idea of another animal in the house? Can we afford another dog, when that can cost thousands of dollars a year? Is there space in the household? Places in the neighborhood or environs to walk and exercise several dogs?

Can I locate a dog that's safe, within reasonable expectations, and reliable? That won't endanger my family, friends, or neighbors—and their dogs?

I also talk to family, friends, and neighbors. Often they vote no, suggesting, as non–dog lovers will, that one or two dogs is plenty. But unless they raise an objection related to one of the real issues mentioned above, I make up my own mind and start thinking about the dog I want and how to find him.

Dog lovers who want another dog are likely to keep rationalizing until they get one. Often there's no stopping them. I'm just trying to slow the process down a bit.

HOW MANY?

I'VE LONG BELIEVED THAT TWO DOGS ARE EASIER THAN ONE, AND NOT just because I love having dogs around. Dogs are social animals; they seem calmer and more grounded in a pair, if it's the right pair.

They exercise each other, and the mentor teaches housebreaking and other dog skills to the newcomer. I even feel better about leaving dogs alone when there are two.

But there's a significant difference between two dogs and three. Two is a pair; three or more is a pack, with its attendant hierarchy and canine politics.

Though many dogs languish in the shelter system, and many good-hearted people want to save them, for most people, having three dogs or more is a journey to a whole other realm. If your work isn't centered on dogs, and you're not at home most of the day, it's nearly impossible to know, train, or control six, eight, a dozen dogs.

That's not the kind of life with dogs that would be meaningful to me. I want to know and train my dogs well enough to forge a particular kind of connection with them. It's tough enough with three. I can't imagine it with many more, and I don't recommend it for the average dog owner.

Everything about a dog's life changes when a new dog enters the picture. Three dogs are much more likely to quarrel over food and toys than two, and humans obviously have less time for individual attention and supervision. Three dogs charging a door that Grandma is about to come through can be obnoxious, possibly dangerous. Walking three dogs together or separately in most of urban or suburban America is a complex process. Even distributing treats inequitably can trigger a riot.

Add long work hours, small children, crowded city living, or other factors to the equation, and things can get chaotic.

True, there are various protocols and procedures people can follow to more smoothly manage multiple-dog households. But we already know that most people don't follow sensible training procedures for one dog, let alone two or three. Owners need to be realistic about what they will or won't, can or can't, do.

Harmonious coexistence with dogs requires self-awareness, perspective, and balance. If the humans are irritable, exhausted, semibankrupt, or overwhelmed, life with dogs will deteriorate. Yet it can be hard to return to equilibrium, because once people get a new dog, they find it hard to let go.

Everyone's threshold is different. I've seen some mothers shepherd four or five small kids with equanimity, grace, and unbounded patience; I couldn't do it without going mad. I have two insatiably busy, dominant border collies and a curious puppy constantly eating or chewing something, or trying to. Somebody always wants something. Rose wants to herd the sheep; Clem wants to play; Orson needs attention. The combination could drive lots of people nuts—and over much of my life, I would have been one of them. Yet at this point it works for me.

Still, it hasn't been easy, or cheap. When Clem arrived, everything about our daily routines changed: when and how the dogs ate, how often we went to the vet, how the crates were set up, how they played, where they slept. A multiple-dog household requires thought, research, and preparation.

PREPARING FOR THE NEWCOMER

TAKING SOME TIME UP FRONT CAN SAVE YOU AND YOUR BURGEONING canine population considerable grief.

Let's assume you've done your homework, learned as much about the dog—her breed, her history—as you can. You've ensured that the people giving or selling you the dog understand the animals you already have, your home and yard, your family dynamic, the time and energy commitment you're prepared to make. And you've been honest, because you and your pets will pay if you aren't.

Dogs are social, adaptable creatures, but first impressions matter. Don't just show up at the front door with another animal in your arms or on a leash and expect a warm welcome from your existing dogs. Walk the newcomer nearby or on the other side of a fence or across the street, or introduce him in a crate or kennel. Give everybody some distance and maneuvering room.

Most of the time, dogs work their differences out. Don't worry about squabbling, growling, pinning, or posturing. I do get concerned if a dog draws blood, or if fights and confrontations grow so fierce and prolonged, and the dogs so seriously aroused, that somebody (human or animal) could get hurt.

As always, crates or kennels, confined spaces, can help manage dogs' environments. Dogs in crates don't fight or lunge; they can get to know one another safely. Doors, gates, and entranceways can be flash points for dogs, transitional spaces where confrontations occur—places for caution when you're moving new dogs in and out.

Food management is critical. When a new dog arrives in my household, cooked hot dogs and hamburger go into the food to encourage avid and focused eating, thus avoiding the jockeying and foraging that can cause brawls.

Problems frequently occur around feeding. Dogs that didn't get enough to eat in their litters are possessive about food. (Likewise certain breeds—huskies and malamutes, for example—regardless of litter experience.) They get so little of it in their natural environments that when they see food, they grab it. Your kid or your other dogs shouldn't be too nearby when they do. They're not mean dogs, and few of them bite humans, but food means different things to different dogs. Dogs that are socialized properly—fed from human hands, handled while eating when puppies—rarely develop aggression around eating.

Other options: feeding dogs separately, in different rooms or crates. Or borrow my strategy: hamburger makes the food so appealing that everyone gets into the habit of scarfing it down quickly.

THE TWO-DOG RULE AND OTHER CAVEATS

THOUGH THREE DOGS SHARE MY HOUSEHOLD, I DON'T TAKE MORE THAN two at a time for a walk off my own property. I don't bring more than two into public spaces where there are kids, other people, other dogs. I can't control more than two reliably. Usually I bring one, leaving two behind. Many people are afraid of a single dog, let alone several. With so many people and dogs getting attacked and bitten and sued, I don't want to put people in the position of dealing with a pack. I can walk my three dogs on my own property, or in other secluded places. This protects them, too. I'm conscious of not placing them in circumstances that could get them in trouble. It's part of my job.

Living by the Two-Dog Rule, I crate one or another of my dogs at various points during the day. Two dogs are manageable, three on the outer edge. The dogs accept this and rotate willingly into their comfy and bone-stuffed crates while I answer the door, do chores, take the others to a book reading. I crate my dogs when school gets out, for example, because I don't like them rushing at the fence outside my New Jersey house, as border collies are wont to do, when kids come flying by on skateboards or bikes.

When people are coming to my house, unless they are certified, true-blue dog lovers, I crate one or more of my dogs. Sure, I could employ various "lie down" and "stay" commands to train dogs into calmness around visitors. But it's not a simple proposition. Doors, entrances, and gates have a way of triggering a dog's territorial nature.

One reason so many dogs make a ruckus when delivery people arrive or doorbells ring is that they think they've been successful, repeatedly: when the person leaves, the dog figures his barking has run off the intruder. This is a self-reinforcing behavior. The more the dog does it, the more enthusiastically he will do it again. Shouting at the dog to stop just cranks him up further.

Most people don't appreciate three dogs—or one—lunging, barking, or jumping on them when they come to the door.

It's best to stay calm, quietly get the dog's attention, and have him lie down and stay; then reward him handsomely for his restraint. In my experience, though, you can't rely on this 100 percent of the time, especially with several dogs encouraging one another. Dogs love chasing people away from their residences and their humans.

One idea for people with packs of dogs is to have friends and family members—people the dogs know—come to the door, bringing treats. The dogs will learn that friends and rewards, not just intruders, come to the door.

But if you, like most Americans, are too busy for this level of painstaking training, spare strangers the fear and paws and chaos. Don't give your dogs the chance to go crazy over and over again; it's a tradition you don't have to permit or encourage. Put the dogs in crates, kennels, or other rooms. Introduce them to your company one by one, when things have quieted down. Or don't. They can probably use the downtime.

As I was writing this chapter, a friend showed up at the farm and opened the door without ringing the bell. My three dogs were barking and tearing for the door before I even knew she'd come. Barking at

STAY

strange people and animals and other intruders is one of the most in-grained and natural behaviors in a dog's repertoire, so if I were concerned about a dog's aggressiveness, I'd keep the door locked.

It's not always a bad thing, this ruckus. If somebody comes to the door while your kids are playing in the backyard or while you're asleep, you'd probably *want* your dog to bark. Yet it's confusing to dogs when people ask them to be quiet around certain visitors at certain times of the day but to protect the property otherwise.

A gate near the door to hold the dogs back, crates when there's company and at other busy times, or a backyard kennel—these are all helpful aids.

ALL THESE CAVEATS ASIDE, I'VE SEEN MULTIPLE-DOG HOUSEHOLDS WORK well in various situations, from farms to crowded urban apartments. How well they function depends on the person, the dogs, and the work they do together.

The Rational Theory holds that one dog is fine for people with limited time, energy, and resources; two is a great combination for most dogs and many dog lovers. Anything beyond that becomes a life in which dogs play a more central, not a peripheral, role.

I love each of my dogs, but a three-dog household means continuous effort, from training to grooming to feeding. It's a rare week that we're not at the vet because someone cut a paw pad or sprained a leg. Or that I don't clean up some wretched mess. Every few days brings some nerve-racking encounter with an animal, another dog, or a UPS driver.

I have no regrets, but I wouldn't do this casually.

Life with dogs becomes much more demanding with population increases.

We can't buy or adopt perfect lives with dogs; we have to build them. It's demanding work, more so as the numbers rise. The monks at New Skete are right about this: approached properly, living with dogs can be a profoundly meaningful experience. Approached impulsively, carelessly, or thoughtlessly, it's a mess.

GINA'S ELEVEN-YEAR-OLD DACHSHUND RAN OFF RECENTLY, AND in the aching days afterward, she was a wreck. I could hear her voice quavering on the phone.

"I do not have words to tell you how much I love that dog," she said. "There's a hole in my heart and my life too large to measure. It sounds strange, but I've never known such love. Does that make any sense to you?"

It did. I feel the same wash of emotion all the time. Sitting on a windswept hill when Rose briefly leaves her sheep to dart over and lick my hand. Working in my office as Orson wraps himself around my leg beneath the desk and sighs contentedly. Lying in bed on an inky night when Clem puts her head on my shoulder and we both drift off to sleep. I understand the elation Gina felt when her dachshund wandered home days later, bedraggled and exhausted but unharmed. The way we feel about our dogs can be the purest of loves, and sometimes the most powerful.

But it also gives me pause.

I encountered Joshua, a young investment banker, and his dog Namath, when Josh responded to a column I wrote. He told me he loves his dog so much that it sometimes unnerves him; he's even considering moving out of Philadelphia so that Namath, a German shepherd–huskie mix he adopted three years ago from a shelter, can have more space to run.

Josh and Namath are both athletes and love sports. They jog together, play Frisbee, take long hikes in the Poconos. Josh was planning a Caribbean vacation last year, but decided instead to rent a cabin in New Hampshire so that Namath could come along. "I have to say it was great, one of the best times I've ever had," he reported.

Human companionship? Sometimes Josh dates, but he's as inclined to stay home with Namath, who's more fun to be with than most women he's met. He's rarely more at peace, he says, than when he and Namath are relaxing on the sofa with a bowl of popcorn, watching ESPN. "There is nothing I wouldn't do for him, nothing he wouldn't do for me," Josh says. "We understand each other."

About the same time, I also heard from a California couple in their late twenties who doubt they'll have children "because we are so content"—content with each other and with their two rottweilers. "We could not love any children more than we love our dogs, to be honest," the husband explained. "We see the dogs as the glue that helps keep our relationship strong."

A woman I've known for years, a former computer programmer, just sold her home in a Boston suburb, bought a ranch house on five acres in upstate New York, and moved in with her seven rescue dogs in various stages of ill health and disability. She intends, she told me, "to spend the rest of my life with these dogs. I want to take care of them and make them happy. Often in my life I've felt let down by people, but never by my dogs."

Dog love is a powerful thing; it can consume you. It can be comic or disturbing, painful or uplifting, neurotic, joyful, all of the above. Since dogs can't speak or put any limits on it, dog love can also be boundless, sometimes growing beyond our intentions. They can't tell us when to stop.

Managing dog love, seeing it clearly, is sometimes difficult. But understanding it seems important, for us and for these animals we share our lives with.

Love for human beings can prove difficult, unpredictable, disappointing. Dog love, by comparison, is safer, more satisfying: dogs can't betray us, undermine us, tell us they're angry or bored. They can't leave. Our voiceless companions, dogs are a blank canvas on which we can paint anything we wish. When it comes to love, that's a powerful temptation.

Dog love is also private, strictly between us and them. Much of our human-canine interaction goes unobserved by others. Our friends aren't likely to intervene with a "He's no good for you," and we never have to take our dogs to the office holiday party for our coworkers to check out.

Behavioral research suggests that men and women love dogs equally, but often in different ways. Men often love dogs because they *don't* talk, which makes them the perfect pals. A guy can have a close relationship, like Joshua does with Namath, and never have to discuss it. What a great deal.

Women are more likely to see dogs as emotionally complex creatures; it's disturbingly common to hear them say their dogs understand their moods better than their boyfriends; that their dogs know when they're upset but their husbands don't.

Amanda, an artist in Vermont, e-mailed me to tell me that her rescued border collie, Pix, had transformed the very nature of winter for her. "It used to be a lonely, tough time. Now it is my favorite season, filled with love and companionship, and Pix is the reason," she wrote. "I can't describe the depth of my love for her." I hear these words often: a love that can't be described, can't be quantified, can't be explained, only felt.

I've observed various kinds of dog love, distinct but equally powerful. Working dogs—herders, hunters, bomb sniffers, search-and-rescue dogs, therapy dogs—have a particular kind of connection with their owners and handlers, forged by intense experiences and years of training and working together.

Dog rescuers, meanwhile, those tens of thousands of people (mostly women) who scour animal shelters for dogs in trouble, see a lot of ugly human behavior and its consequences. The bonds between rescued dogs and those who foster, transport, heal, and adopt them are probably among the strongest on the spectrum of human-animal attachments.

This intensity often leaves me a bit ambivalent. A recent Yankelovich study for *American Demographics* found that nearly a third of respondents—and half of all the single people in the study—said that of everyone in their lives, they relied most on their pets for companionship and affection. That's a lot of weight for a dog to carry. Distressingly often, owners confess that they could survive the loss of a companion or spouse but they're not sure how they could live without their dogs. Sadly, they are likely to find out: dogs don't live nearly as long as we do.

If you believe, as I do, that our treatment of, and relationships with, dogs reflect our society, you can't help wishing we humans did a better job of loving and protecting one another, so that we wouldn't be as reliant on our dogs. Nor can you help being grateful dogs are around. But you have to wonder if there isn't such a thing as loving them too much. I think there is.

Part of our responsibility as people who live with dogs is to try to keep this love in perspective. Dogs are animals. When we love them like people, we can misunderstand them, confuse them, complicate their training, damage our lives together.

Many say they do struggle to manage their dog relationships, to keep limits and live rationally, to go to work and take vacations without letting such experiences get distorted by their feelings for their pets. For with love comes worry and concern: Is Rusty okay at home in a crate by himself? Will Phoebe do well in a kennel? What about taking Jojo to the dog run?

This is why I've become a dog-love rationalist: love them all you want, but maintain some common sense and balance about what dogs are and where these feelings originate.

On a recent business trip, I left my dogs in a Vermont kennel. It wasn't, I admit, so easy. I called my friend Anthony from the road a day or two later, and wondered aloud what Clementine must be thinking—in a kennel with Rose and Orson, but without me for the first time.

Anthony, a dog lover himself but also a wise man who knows me well, replied quickly. "Clementine is thinking, 'Good rawhide, I'd like some more. And when is dinner?' " Knowing the dog, and knowing he was right, I laughed.

This doesn't detract from my great love for Clem, but I want that love to stay grounded in reality, not to reflect my own emotional needs. Clem's simplicity, her great affectionate nature, her relentless and utterly indiscriminate appetite, are among her most pronounced traits. To love her is to understand that, not to deny it or to picture her pining for me in my absence. Cindy, the kennel manager, assured me when I returned that Clementine had done just fine, played often, and eaten very well (her own food *and* Rose's).

A couple of years back, a University of Kentucky psychiatrist who studies human-animal bonds sent me a classic work, *Twins,* by the late British psychoanalyst and author Dorothy Burlingham.

Burlingham explored the power of fantasies in children, especially lonely or frightened ones. A certain kind of child, she wrote, "takes an imaginary animal as his intimate and beloved companion; subsequently he is never separated from his animal friend. . . . This animal offers the child what he is searching for: faithful love and unswerving devotion. . . . The two share everything, good and bad experiences, and complete understanding of each other; either speech is not necessary, or they have a secret language; the understanding between them goes beyond the realm of consciousness."

This yearning is what I hear of so often from dog lovers. It's part of many of our lives from our earliest years. What begins as a potent, comforting fantasy later ripens. Dogs now at our sides, we escape from loneliness and solitude, find "faithful love and unswerving devotion." We feel, rightly or not, as if we share complete understanding; certainly we have a secret language. Our love goes beyond words; we've finally found our beloved companions.

How best to manage what can be an emotional deluge?

Some dog owners *don't* feel it. Professional trainers and breeders, hunters, people who show dogs or do search-and-rescue with them, often love their animals dearly but have a more pragmatic approach. Their work with dogs would be impossible without a clear understanding of their elemental natures, and it's tougher to anthropomorphize a dog whose instincts you know so well.

Working with Rose has helped me grasp this. She's a working dog through and through, with little interest in people outside her farm. Sometimes I can't believe just how much of an animal she is. Unlike Clem or Orson, she doesn't have a great need to stick by my side while I'm not with sheep. At night, when the flock is tucked in and the workday is over, she slips off to remote corners of the house. Unlike my other dogs, she has no need to cuddle with me in the dark. If I put my barnyard mud boots on, she is instantly there. Otherwise, she comes and goes, checking on things, peering out the window at the pasture, in her own world.

We have something of a business relationship, Rose and I. She loves me in proportion to my taking her to herd sheep, and she tolerates me fondly in between. It shocks people when I tell them that if I were gone and Rose went to live on another farm with sheep, she would adapt quickly and happily. But I'm quite convinced of it.

Yet we've bonded as closely as members of two different species can. If my bad leg buckles and I fall, she is at my side. If the ram makes a move toward me, she stares him down. When the sheep come too close, she drives them off. In the middle of the night, in the pitch dark, I feel her featherweight body hop gently onto the bed. She picks her way around Clem and Paula, circles around to the top of my head, and licks my forehead two or three times, quickly and lightly. Then she's gone. She keeps an eye on her shepherd. I do, indeed, lack the words to describe how I feel when that happens.

For those of us who grapple with dog love, then, what's important is to retain a sense of our pets' animalness, their "dogness." It is the essence of their spirit. I love my dogs not because they're human but because they aren't. I try to remember that they're alien creatures, not capable of human-style emotions. They are not thinking in my language; in the sense in which most people use the term, they're not thinking at all.

As sentient beings, they need to be loved and understood for what they are. Let dogs be dogs. Dogs hunt things. They roll in things. They smell. They squabble. There is a profound difference between companion animals and animals viewed as social companions.

We have to set rules and demonstrate how to live by them, but I try to let my dogs retain as much of their dogness as they can. That means understanding the fever that grips Rose when she moves sheep and sometimes fails to hear me. Or Orson's crazed look when he sees a squirrel dart down a path. Or Clementine's passion for garbage and gourmet donkey droppings.

I correct my dogs, I guide them, I lead—but I want to learn to truly love them for what they are, and to value my own, different needs. It takes constant work. I fail nearly as often as I succeed. I am getting there.

JACK, WHO SELLS ANTIQUES IN UPSTATE NEW YORK, IS NORMALLY A pretty upbeat guy. But when a vet diagnosed his twelve-year-old black Lab, Schuyler, with cancer of the jaw and told Jack the prognosis was grim, he burst into tears, so upset he had to call his girlfriend to come drive him and the dog home.

He called me later that night. Punctuated by sobs and silences, our conversation lasted nearly an hour. "I really don't know what to do," Jack said. "My friends say I should take him to Penn or Cornell for chemo. My girlfriend says I should try alternative medicine, maybe something homeopathic. I can't bear to think of it. When do you put a dog down? How do you decide? I don't want him to suffer, but I can't bear to lose him."

His nightmare worsened over the next couple of weeks as he considered what to do and the advice poured in. Don't listen to the vets, one friend urged; try changing the dog's diet. Chemo, another dog owner advised. Online discussion groups offered others' experiences with canine cancer, complete with heroic and miraculous efforts by dog lovers who simply wouldn't stop fighting for their dogs' lives.

When our companions fall ill, and they will, how much do we want or need to know? Or spend, in terms of money and time? How much can we absorb? How much searching, seeking, thinking, is appropriate for any animal, no matter how wonderful, in a world with so many human problems? It's important to think about.

When I perused many of the same websites Jack was visiting—and it seems a healthy impulse for people in that situation to reach out to other owners for information—I was struck by the profusion of confusing, contradictory data. Conventional wisdom teaches us to be suspicious and vigilant, but it doesn't show us how to process all this unfiltered information, or how to weigh it against professionals' advice.

Jack felt guilty as he read about people who drove to Canada or Mexico for special medications, flew their dogs to Europe to see specialists, imported herbal treatments from China, and sought out masseuses, psychics, channelers.

"The ethic I keep hearing," he reported, "is 'Don't give up. Ever.' "

We spoke a few times, Jack agonizing over the many options he was hearing about. His vet had suggested that he euthanize Schuyler before the dog's condition worsened, but Jack had clearly decided against that. He would put the dog down "when he [Schuyler] was ready," he said. The vet respected that, but warned Jack that in his opinion, there wasn't much anybody could do for Schuyler.

JACK DROVE SCHUYLER TWO HUNDRED MILES TO A SPECIALIST WHO SEConded his vet's opinion. He consulted an alternative practitioner in Massachusetts who disagreed, suggesting acupuncture and a radical change to a raw-turkey diet.

Jack also talked to a friend who counseled that Schuyler would tell him when it was time to go, that Jack should watch and listen to the dog for cues. Did I think that was the right course?

To be honest, I didn't quite say what I was thinking. Jack was in enough pain; he didn't need a lecture. Each decision about the death of a dog is personal, dependent on context and circumstances.

But what I was thinking was this: Dogs are voiceless. Dogs can't speak. It is the most elemental difference between the two species. They can't tell us when it's time to die, even if they were capable of such abstract thought. That's something we have to decide for them, wielding our love, compassion, and common sense as best we can.

The best vets understand that we know our dogs better than anyone, including them. "When somebody who loves his dogs as much as you do tells me it's time, I usually accept that," my vet told me when I was about to put down one of my yellow Labs. "I can listen to his heartbeat, but I can't really say when he's not living a meaningful life."

I couldn't look to my wonderful Labs, one diagnosed with heart failure, the other with cancer, to tell me when it was time. The responsibility and decision, it seemed to me, were mine.

I put them down before they endured prolonged suffering—my choice, not necessarily a recommendation for others. But people who share their lives with dogs should know from the outset that they'll face this situation one day.

It's probably the most personal decision any dog owner ever makes. Jack kept Schuyler alive for two more months, as the dog's jaw swelled further. When he called again, he said it seemed time and he was going to ask the vet to put the dog to sleep. Later, he called this the most wrenching decision of his life, so painful he'd decided never to get another dog. I told him that would be a shame.

It's in the nature of dogs to live much shorter lives than ours—just eight years, on average. To own and love a dog is to understand, and accept, that along with loyalty, love, and devotion come the specters of grief and loss. This is as integral a part of the experience as going for walks.

There's no "idiot's guide" for this question, no handbook. The many points of view are all strongly held. One vet I know says a dog should be euthanized "when it can no longer live the life of a dog." Another vet believes dogs ought to be killed before they really suffer; others will not put a dog down at all. A breeder says she puts her dogs down when "their suffering exceeds their ability to take pleasure in life." A trainer I respect believes her dog should live as long as it can eat.

Another friend and dog lover says she always knows when it's time: "When the soul goes out of their eyes."

I'm not among those who believe dogs have souls, or that we will meet them in the afterlife, but I know what she means. Most of us know that visceral "dogness" in our pets, an interest in people, food, squirrels, swimming—whatever—that's part of their individual spirits. When that disappears, it does seem the "soul" of the dog is gone.

When Orson stops wanting to be near me, I will wonder if it's time—or when Rose stops following the movements of her sheep or Clem loses interest in splashing in mud puddles.

But I know other owners—a growing number, according to vet studies—who fight to keep their dogs alive as long as possible.

Researching a previous book on dogs, I visited an emergency-care clinic where six dogs lay in a rear room, attached to respirators. Their owners, the vet there said, simply could not bear to lose them. She was uncomfortable with the sight of the dogs' inert bodies. I was, too. Was this kindness?

Perhaps such attitudes should come as no surprise when we come to see our dogs as human members of our families, companions that provide us with more emotional support than friends or spouses, more satisfaction than work, more support than we can find elsewhere. People become devastated by the loss of their dogs, thus more uncertain about how and when to put them down, and more inclined to search desperately for remedies that might prolong their lives.

Decisions about putting a dog down touch the deepest parts of our attachment, stir all our complicated feelings and needs. As with much else about living with dogs, we need perspective, an internal check-and-balance system to keep our love in proportion, to honor our responsibilities to make good decisions for our dogs. Are we doing what's best for them? Or for us?

This is not easy stuff.

As the owner of three dogs, I spend more than I can truly afford to keep them healthy and vigorous. There's not much that I wouldn't do to keep them well and by my side. But as my conversations with Jack and many others have reminded me, they are not people. They do not live as long as we do. Their deaths, though terribly painful, ought not to be conflated or confused with human losses. One of the more striking differences is our role as decision makers.

To love dogs is to know death, and to accept that there's never a time we are more morally obliged to speak for them than when they face the end of their lives.

RE-HOMING

IT'S SOMETHING OF AN ARTICLE OF FAITH IN MUCH OF THE DOG WORLD that you never give a dog up, no matter what. The bond between the two of you is eternal, unbreakable. Part of the Disney dog myth is this notion of us and them, forever inseparable.

Since dogs can't contradict our accounts or offer their own, we often fashion stories for them, stories that make us feel good about ourselves, but which may not be helpful for them.

Part of the responsibility of living with a dog is ensuring that the dog is in the best possible environment—for him, not just for us.

We've seen how many people choose the wrong dogs for the wrong reasons at the wrong point in their lives; it's unfortunate, but commonplace. The dog pays, however. A dog living the wrong life with the wrong people can be a very unhappy animal, destructive and aggressive, compulsive or obsessive, frightened, scolded, shunted aside.

Yet choosing reality over myth has nearly become a taboo.

I'm lucky in dogs, and I don't think there could be a better home for any of my three. But I haven't always been so careful in my choices; and my dogs haven't always been so lucky.

SMART TRAINERS ALWAYS TELL YOU TO WATCH OUT FOR "THE GOOD DOG," because he's the one nobody is paying much attention to. Homer was my good dog, and everyone else's, too, one of those dogs who fit most people's image of what a great pet should be.

A fluffy little border collie with ears that stood at attention, he was beautiful and good-natured. He didn't chew things he wasn't supposed to chew or mount strange canine females. He wasn't overtly needy or intrusive, didn't jump or slobber. In fact, he did few of the things most dogs naturally love to do.

He was what behaviorists would call a submissive dog, a dog that reflexively and instinctively defers to other, more dominant, dogs, a dog that learns early on how to stay out of trouble.

He was also a wary creature. When he first arrived at the Albany Airport five years ago, twelve weeks old and fresh from the Southwest, I opened his airline crate to reach for him. He seemed startled by the sight of me, and backed up. When I finally got him out into the lot where my car was parked, Orson pounced on Homer, barking and snapping.

This was a foolish way to introduce a puppy to his new world—I know better now—and a harbinger of things to come. Orson, I would learn, didn't like puppies and cut them none of the slack most older dogs do for nonthreatening new dogs. Orson craved attention, especially mine, and seemed to be signaling clearly that he had no intention of yielding any of it to the newcomer.

Homer, a sweet pup, was sent to me in the first place because his breeder believed him one of the few dogs who could live peaceably with this tempestuous housemate. This turned out to be true, but the price— for Homer—was high.

Studies of submissive dogs show that they often adapt by becoming background pets, living on the periphery, staying out of the way, waiting to edge toward the food bowl, looking around before they dare to chew their biscuits. They do what they need to do to stay out of trouble. This is what Homer soon learned—or, more to the point, what I allowed to happen.

The irony of this behavior is that the dog seems unusually well behaved. Trainers and behaviorists know, of course, that the "good dog" (like the "bad dog") is a construct of well-meaning but sometimes self-serving humans. Dogs are neither good nor bad. They're shaped by all sorts of factors, and adapt to their environments depending on train-

ing and circumstances, and on varying degrees of luck, instinct, and skill on the part of human beings.

So this wasn't a case of Homer being good or bad but of how well I'd taught him to live in our world. And the truth is, I'd ducked dealing with the real struggles this dog faced. I already had a complicated dog with many difficulties we'd yet to work through; I brought a submissive, somewhat edgy puppy into this environment before it was appropriate.

Orson had been unstrung by his unfortunate early experiences as an obedience show dog. He was needy, highly aroused, dominant and ferociously territorial, especially around me. He sometimes acted like a deprived creature who, once he got what he wanted, would hang on to the death.

At first, he went after Homer whenever he came within three feet of me, blocked me whenever I reached for Homer, growled Homer off the couch or the bed. Homer would stare at Orson for permission before eating, would drop biscuits and toys at the sight of him, and quickly learned to avoid where I sat or slept.

Homer learned to avoid me, because the farther he stayed away, the less trouble he got into. Like the shy, awkward kid growing up with a more charismatic older sibling, Homer lived in Orson's shadow.

The striking thing was how little trouble he caused. While Orson jumped through windows, raided refrigerators, went after other dogs, and was a genius at getting me to react to him, a trap into which I repeatedly and continuously fell, Homer was affectionate with everybody.

You couldn't help loving Homer. A profoundly amiable creature, he would collapse with joy at the sight of the mailman, his favorite UPS driver, and every other kid getting off a school bus. Each morning, he braved Orson's possessive wrath to hop onto our bed and wrap himself around my wife's head for a snuggle. He and Paula were crazy about each other, seeing in one another the stability, predictability, and sanity so often missing around them. Unlike Orson, a pest in his affections who never knew when to quit, Homer was gentle and discreet, crawling up to offer a few licks, then skittering away.

While I loved Homer dearly—he was irresistible—I'd known for a

while that in some ways our relationship was incomplete, troubled. I'd spent time working alone with him, but not nearly enough. I spent so much time talking to, yelling at, and dealing with Orson, that Homer often assumed my commands and directions were not meant for him.

HAD I WAITED ANOTHER YEAR—ORSON HAS BECOME A DIFFERENT DOG after intensive calming and positive training—things might have been different. But it's often difficult for dog lovers to wait.

Although it's heresy to say so, we don't love all our dogs the same way, any more than we love all people equally. Nor do dogs love us in the uniform, unwavering way often depicted in dog lore.

So while some of my and Homer's problems resulted from incomplete training, some belonged to the peculiar realm of chemistry, as is often the case with love. At the core, I was no longer sure I was really the best owner for Homer; I also wondered if he was the right dog for me. My other dogs and I seemed almost eerily in tune. Homer and I never seemed as in sync.

As I moved deeper into the world of dogs—training, writing, sheepherding—I came to see other people clinging tenaciously to relationships like mine and Homer's. I remember a couple with a troubled, aggressive cattle dog who was being trained at the Pennsylvania sheep farm where Homer, Orson, and I practiced herding. I had the odd sense that Marge and Tim didn't really like Hammer, nor did the dog seem to relate to them in any way that I could see. They often rolled their eyes at his odd behavior; he was often as far from them as he could get.

Yet they repeatedly vowed to "keep working at this as long as it takes, because it's our responsibility." As one who preaches about taking responsibility for our dogs, I should have been impressed. But I always went away thinking all parties involved might be better off if the dog lived somewhere else. There seemed little pleasure in their relationship, little progress being made.

I wasn't making much with Homer, either. We had wonderful times sheepherding together. Otherwise, he seemed disconnected from me. He lagged behind on walks and showed poor name recognition and eye contact, despite hundreds of dollars' worth of liver treats.

He didn't seem—something that only someone who knows and loves a pet well can discern—a happy, attached dog.

And how ironic. Orson opened screen doors, escaped over and under fences, moved household objects around just because he could. I loved him beyond words. Homer would never dream of doing any of those annoying things, yet our relationship had become a struggle.

Could I have trained my way out of this? Maybe, especially knowing what I now know. A number of trainers have told me that any dog can be trained properly, no matter what his history.

But I realized that at some point I began to enter the murky area where the boundary blurs between a human's troubles and the dog's. I became increasingly annoyed with Homer, his avoidance, his lagging, his timidity, and, yes, his rejection of me. I found myself scolding him, urging him to hurry up on walks, to pay attention. "C'mon, c'mon," I'd hiss in a scolding voice I rarely used with my other dogs. "Let's go."

Friends, assuming I would hang in there with Homer to the end, advised me to stop worrying. "Look, he's just a dog, and he's living a better life than 99.9 percent of the dogs on the planet. Life doesn't necessarily have to be perfect, even for dogs. You do the best you can, and he's fine."

But does that philosophy really serve the dog, or it is designed merely to make the human feel better? My duty went deeper, I thought. The day I took on this dog, I accepted responsibility for his care. I hadn't done right by him.

Was he happy? I wasn't sure; how could we really know? Was he as happy as he deserved to be? I didn't think so. Was he getting the attention he craved? Did he feel calm and safe? No.

On some level, I'd reverted to my own complicated family history. I was scolding and chiding Homer in the same way my father jeered at me, and for some of the same reasons—timidity, lack of athletic ability, disobedience, rejection.

I'd concluded Homer wasn't good enough, not as adventurous or resilient as the other dogs. He didn't react as quickly, herd as competently, love me as much. He suffered in comparison to my ferociously instinctive new puppy, Rose, as agile, confident, and grounded as Homer was slow, submissive, and cautious. And I shouldn't, it's clear in retrospect, have tried to resolve matters by introducing a new dog to the mix. Poor Homer, I thought. No wonder he slept in another room.

Things began to change the day we started the school-bus ritual. I was looking for things Homer and I could enjoy together; it worked differently and better than I'd imagined.

Homer loved school buses, mostly because kids came pouring off them, and he loved kids. He was especially fond of one of our neighbors, Max, a sweet ten-year-old with a shy but affable nature. In a funny way, he was much like Homer, which is perhaps why the two connected. Homer adored Max from the first, and vice versa, so I thought it might be pleasant for him to greet Max at the bus stop.

By the third day, all I had to say was "Let's go see Max" and Homer would go nuts, wriggling as happily as if there were sheep outside. The other schoolkids also loved Homer, who was nearly drunk from all the sudden attention. And since I left Orson at home, Homer didn't have to fight for it or look over his shoulder.

He soon realized that greeting Max's bus was his daily task, his work, his moment, without competition from siblings or criticism from me. There was no part of this task that Homer could fail at, and it was delightful to see those two guys fall in love. It was also instructive. Homer's demeanor and behavior could change, I saw, under different circumstances. He could be more animated, more connected, less submissive. And, perhaps most important, he could succeed.

It occurred to me, after a few days, that this was the kind of relationship Homer could thrive on, and the kind I couldn't provide. In a few weeks, Homer was visiting Max's house, getting to know the rest of the family.

One afternoon, taking Homer to Max's house to play, I sat on the back porch with Max's father. Hank, perhaps sensing what I was thinking, told me how much they all loved Homer and what a great dog he was. In the yard in front of us, Max and Homer were lying face-to-face. Max was throwing a ball over Homer's shoulder; he'd rush to grab the ball, lope back to Max, and slurp his nose.

He was having a blast, running in circles, tearing around the yard, smooching Max in between. I'm sure Hank noticed that I was affected by the sight, although I didn't say why. The reason was that I'd rarely seen Homer so uncomplicatedly happy and at ease.

When I headed back to Bedlam Farm later that month, Orson and Rose came along. Homer stayed behind—a trial separation.

The next few days and weeks were rough for me, and, I'm sure, for Homer. I suffered guilt and sorrow. But I learned, over the coming months, how adaptable dogs really are.

Homer is a much-loved dog. He walks with Hank, runs with Hank's wife, Sharon, greets the kids Sharon tutors in their home. He is profoundly connected to Max, in a way he was not to me. He sleeps in a different bed in his new house every night. He thrives as an "only" dog, without the competition and intimidation of more dominant dogs. I can keep an eye on him, feel comfortable about his new family, visit and keep some connection.

But there are other ways to relocate dogs. Groups found on websites like Petfinder.org, breeders, vets, shelter staffs, trainers, and local rescue groups often know of people seeking dogs and are usually glad, even eager, to help with re-homing if things aren't working out.

Dog lovers are often right to struggle through difficulties rather than quit. It is a wonderful thing—as I've learned with Orson—to work with a dog through trouble and hard times.

But there are times when it just isn't going to work; to me, it seems responsible and compassionate to recognize that. Homer is a happier dog now. I am a happier dog owner. He has the home and family he deserves. It's not mine, but it's better for him.

WHEN TO GET ANOTHER DOG

PEOPLE WONDER, AFTER THEY'VE LOST OR RELINQUISHED A BELOVED PET, whether and when they should get another.

I remember being upset, during an appearance on a California talk show, to hear the host compare the death of her cat to the loss of a human being. "I will never get over it," she said. "I may never get another cat."

My unsought advice: Get over it. Millions of animals need homes.

We mourn our dogs when they leave us, but finding a new dog promotes healing, helps us recover. In the best tradition of dogs, having served us, they have moved on; let others take their places. It is the natural order: dog lovers should have dogs.

When the awful day comes—as it surely will—that I lose Orson, Rose, or Clementine, I'll be a mess. But soon, age and health permitting, I'll dry my tears. I'll remember my dog with sorrow and deep appreciation. And then I'll reach for the phone book.

CASE STUDY: *Candy*　THE CALL CAME ONE BITTER WINTER EVE-ning. Kirsten, a young woman from a nearby town, the friend of a friend, sounded angry and agitated.

Her brother, a town highway worker, had a young Irish setter, a rescue dog that had developed all sorts of behavioral problems in the few weeks since she'd arrived.

The dog was sweet and sociable, but had never been trained. She'd never really settled into her new home or developed an attachment to the family. Perhaps that wasn't surprising: it was a busy household, with two hardworking adults and two small children.

So Candy was barking compulsively, drooling with anxiety when left alone, and having accidents all over the house. She'd also developed a particularly miserable habit of appearing by the bedside in the wee hours and whining to go out. If the sleepers didn't respond instantly, Candy wet the floor.

After a few days of this, Kirsten's brother took to leaving the dog outside at night, in all kinds of weather, where she barked and whined to come in. That was equally disturbing, so the family tried shutting her in the basement, where nobody could see or hear her. Not surprisingly, this made things worse.

Many of these problems are commonplace—to varying degrees, and usually for short periods—with newly re-homed dogs. Sometimes the dogs have been ignored or mistreated; sometimes they're understandably frightened by their new environments. Candy showed all the symptoms of an anxious dog that didn't understand her new owners and their rules and hadn't yet adapted.

Experienced rescue groups evaluate their dogs, spot such problems, and prepare new owners to deal with them. And group members are also usually available to help out if trouble arises. These difficulties usually can be worked through with training, and there are few more meaningful or satisfying experiences with dogs than to see them settle down, attach, and become loving pets and companions.

But Kirsten's brother didn't have the time or patience to work with a dog with such problems. And the backyard rescue group that had passed Candy along—one person working valiantly, if not always competently, to save strays and abused dogs—hadn't noticed the dog's traits or the owner's shortcomings.

Clearly, this dog was a poor fit for such a man; he shouldn't have taken Candy, nor should a rescue group have given her to him. He knew little about dogs, was unwilling or unable to invest time in training. Now, furious at the dog for waking him up every night, he was tired, cranky, and disappointed.

"This isn't what I wanted when we decided to get another dog," he told Kirsten. "This isn't what I bargained for, and I don't have time to deal with it." He was, in fact, working two jobs to feed his family. His life was already difficult and distracting; he did need his rest.

His expectations had been off base, as is often the case. He thought he was getting a beautiful purebred dog, old enough to already be well behaved and housebroken. Instead, he was cleaning up messes and hadn't had a full night's sleep for two weeks.

So when Kirsten happened to call to say hello, he was heading out of the house with the setter on a leash and his deer rifle in the other hand. He was sick of disrupted nights, he said. He had no time for training. Nor did he want to call some other rescue group, either—probably, Kirsten thought, because he was too embarrassed to admit he couldn't control the dog. So he was going to shoot it.

"I screamed at him to stop," Kirsten told me. "I knew he was serious. His idea about dogs is, they work out or you get rid of them. I told him these are all problems you can fix with training. Isn't that right?"

Without seeing the dog or having her evaluated by trainers or vets, it was hard to say. It was possible, I pointed out, that Candy had a urinary-tract infection or kidney problems.

The term "separation anxiety" has become a handy rubric for dog owners, trainers, and vets. Technically, the term applies to the anxiety a small child feels when separated from a parent, especially a mother; there's no equivalent response in a dog.

Dogs often get anxious when left alone, but that can reflect multiple causes—past mistreatment, previous punishment for misbehavior (so the dog fears scolding or retribution when the people come back), confusion about what to do when left alone, or the general trauma of being moved from one home and owner to another. People are often drawn to the idea that their dogs love them so much they can't bear to see them leave, but often this amounts to our projection, not their problems.

Candy might have also become anxious if previous owners had subjected her to brutal or foolish housebreaking regimens. Many dogs find that traumatizing, including puppies who are screamed at or dragged around, or whose noses are rubbed in their waste. And a few dogs, I warned Kirsten, simply cannot be crated or confined, the usual housebreaking techniques.

But Kirsten couldn't bear to think of Candy, a graceful dog with a coppery coat and beautiful brown eyes, facing an angry, one-man firing squad. She pleaded with her brother to let her take the dog instead. She wanted to see if she could keep her; if not, she'd find a more experienced rescue group to re-home her.

So we set out on the by-now-familiar calming and training program, slowly introducing Candy to a crate in a quiet corner of the house. Kirsten faithfully undertook eye contact and grounding exercises. And she took Candy to a vet who did, in fact, find a severe urinary-tract infection and prescribed antibiotics.

The accidents stopped, but the barking continued. Left alone, the dog threw herself at doors and walls and tore up curtains and garbage. Her drooling left pools of spittle in different parts of the house. Occasionally, Candy quieted long enough to be praised and rewarded for being calm. Over several weeks, some things got better, some got worse. Kirsten was learning firsthand that training doesn't follow a straight line.

Candy turned out to be one of the most difficult training problems any of my volunteers encountered. She still barked compulsively when left alone, and developed sores in her throat and jaw. Her anxiety was such that Kirsten came home to find pools of spittle in Candy's crate and had to spend a half hour cleaning up. The stench became pronounced, and there were stains on the carpet and the walls. When Kirsten opened the crate, Candy barked and raced around the house frantically, sometimes peeing on the floor.

To her great credit, Kirsten always reacted calmly, waiting for Candy to quiet, then reinforcing her with praise and treats. She had a training plan, and stuck to it. But Kirsten was getting weary, and we both were growing pessimistic. Dogs with severe behavioral problems like Candy's can bounce from group to shelter and back to rescue group, and most end up being put down.

After more than a month, the vet and a trainer Kirsten consulted both suggested medicating the dog—a perfectly appropriate remedy under such conditions. But Kirsten's instincts said no, wait. It would take a lot of medication for a long time to help Candy, she reasoned. She also doubted she would have much motivation for training if Candy quieted down. Besides, Candy *was* calmer than when she'd first arrived, despite the barking, clawing, and drooling. She was clearly attached to Kirsten, and vice versa. In many ways, Candy was what Kirsten described as "the greatest dog. She loves to walk with me, and when I'm home, she curls up at my feet and goes to sleep. If I could leave her alone without all this trouble, we'd be fine."

For the first time in my experience, I suggested a citronella anti-bark collar. It sprays citronella, a scent dogs dislike but not one that harms them, into the dog's face if it barks.

Often, just one or two sprays can quiet the dog.

Like Kirsten, I generally prefer to train my way through problems; devices like collars don't address the causes of the behavior. But the clock was running down on this dog, as well as on Kirsten's patience and energy.

. . .

SO SHE BOUGHT AND ATTACHED THE COLLAR, CRATED CANDY, AND THEN promptly left the house, pausing to listen outside. Candy barked once, got sprayed, and never barked in her crate again.

The transformation was sudden and stunning. The collar kept Candy from cranking herself into a frenzy. It reduced the drooling and scratching in the crate, enabling her to calm down to the point that she could be praised and reinforced for quiet and calm. Because she wasn't panicking, she wasn't getting skin sores any longer. She drank less, slept more.

Kirsten—somebody with no previous training experience—had pulled off one of the toughest challenges I'd ever seen. Perhaps it had been more a matter of persistence than of following the wisdom of gurus or adopting some complex training theory. Kirsten, trusting her instincts and her developing knowledge of the dog, was willing to experiment with different solutions.

That this dog came so close to getting shot was a jolting reminder of the plight of dogs, of how much at our mercy they are. It's also a reminder that training can be, literally, a matter of life and death.

The example was extreme, but only because Candy was about to be shot. Vets and trainers will tell you that behavioral problems are now a leading cause of death for American dogs. According to veterinary statistics, more dogs are now euthanized for behavioral problems than for cancer.

But not this one.

Kirsten wasn't willing to keep Candy at all costs, however. We both knew there might come a point when time, money, and emotional energy were exhausted.

But Kirsten did commit to a serious training approach, had faith it would work, and was willing to try almost anything that seemed likely to get results.

The upshot was a beautiful dog, a contented owner, a peaceable life together. And something millions of dogs and their owners don't ever get to experience—a happy ending.

11

CONTINUING EDUCATION

Things My Dogs Won't Do

ALMOST EVERYTHING TO DO WITH DOGS THESE DAYS—HEALTH care, food, toys, training—has become a big, profitable business. Some elements of the training industry maximize those profits by advancing the dubious idea that success—working with dogs to train them well—can be achieved in short order, no muss, no fuss.

Books, videos, classes—many tout themselves as alluringly simple. It reminds me of the way diet plans are marketed to overweight humans.

This idea—that training your dog requires but a few hours or weeks of classes—plays perfectly into our distracted, quick-fix culture. You will rarely see ads touting a two- or three-year training program for dogs. Yet that would be much more realistic. Training a dog is not a quick and finite process.

"When we got our older dog," Georgia e-mailed me from Los Angeles, "we had the time and energy to train him consistently. At six months, we started with an excellent trainer, and we worked with him steadily for two years. Now with our newer dog, we're both too busy for regular training. So we taught her the basics—but, boy, the difference in behavior is noticeable. Training is an ongoing experience, not something you can perfect in six dog training classes. It's a shame people don't get that."

People don't. I didn't get it either, not for a long time.

My dogs are great. I take them all sorts of places, from assisted-living residences to the local library. They generally come when called, lie down when asked, stay when told. They are affectionate with people, do not damage things that are not theirs, never run off, allow vets to handle and treat them, and leave me alone when I work. Yet I am constantly regrouping, reconsidering, evaluating. Whenever I stop to think about what we've yet to accomplish, where I've gone wrong, what I want to correct and reinforce, how much remains, I realize just how continuous a process this is.

There are many things my dogs won't do, that I still can't induce them to do, despite my deep involvement with training, despite my access to experts, vets, and behaviorists, and despite being with them on a huge farm nearly all day, nearly every day.

These failures and abandoned efforts on my part are worth listing, not as a mea culpa, but to make two points.

One: that a perfectly trained dog is rare and, for most people, probably both impossible and unnecessary.

Two: that training a dog well is complex and demanding, even when you have all the time, resources, and goodwill in the world.

Personally, my biggest training problem is that I have three dogs and spend too little time training each one individually. My other big problem is me: as I've said, I am impatient, easily distracted, and viscerally disorganized.

Though I spend my workdays reading, learning, training, and writing about dogs, like most people I am busy with other matters, too.

I have the myriad responsibilities of running an active farm, from birthing lambs to trimming the donkeys' hooves to distributing water, hay, and medicine.

My aging farmhouse and four barns in various states of disrepair require constant attention. Farmhouses built before the Civil War are picturesque, filled with character, and also filled with peeling wallpaper, rotting window frames, mice and other pests, and numbing heating, drainage, and septic concerns.

Barns, even more atmospheric, present still more of a nightmare, with crumbling foundations, sagging floors, and large and diverse populations of pigeons, bats, squirrels, and hornets.

At various times, therefore, I'm involved with handymen, masons, shearers, farriers, vets for animals large and small.

I have a wife and a daughter and a slew of friends I want to communicate with regularly. I get lots of phone calls, receive and answer several hundred e-mails each week, stay in touch with the volunteers training their dogs and helping me with this book.

And did I mention I try to keep writing?

None of this is by way of complaint. I choose to do all this; I love doing most of it. I'm lucky to have this strange little empire. But it also explains why I—like many people—struggle to train my dogs as well as I would like and they deserve.

I have nothing but sympathy and admiration for anyone who seriously tries to train a dog. It always competes with other demands, and is often not especially appreciated. It does not, in my experience, proceed in a straight line.

My dogs, like most, would benefit from two or three ten-minute training sessions a day. But when I do the math, it's sobering. I don't have that spare sixty to ninety minutes on most days. So I mix and match, training in fits and starts.

I'm doing it myself, at this point. When I've taken my dogs to professional trainers for one reason or another, I've always bristled a bit at their implication—or their outright statement—that I, too, could do what these trainers do with their dogs, if only I would bear down and concentrate. Maybe—but dogs are all different, and so are their humans.

Orson is easily aroused and sometimes loses control. Clapping sends him into a frenzy. So do men in hats approaching the gate or doors. He is too overwrought to herd sheep, so I work with him alone, usually training him in the morning, when he is the most focused.

He will now, after four or five years of training, lie down—but almost never the first time he's asked and almost never around sheep. He will stay—but only after I repeat the command three or four times. He simply cannot yet control his excitement at working, especially at working with me. He barks and nips, spins and lunges.

A former obedience show dog who fell into the hands of an inexperienced trainer (me) who yelled at him repeatedly to stop herding buses and jumping through windows, it was his arousal that was reinforced. So he still pops up and down like a windup toy before (if I am sufficiently patient) he settles down.

LIE DOWN

STAY DOWN

Orson responds quickly to commands when I show food, less quickly when I don't. He can't herd sheep effectively, he is unreliable with other dogs (he may charge and nip at males), and his responsiveness is severely compromised if he's on the trail of a squirrel or some other critter. He has never bitten a child, but if he got excited enough, I fear he might nip one. As relentlessly as I work to calm him, I also make sure he never gets the chance to harm anyone. We work often with kids, but I may never fully trust him alone with them.

When I'm out of sight, Orson won't yet reliably stay. Either he simply can't, or I haven't done enough work to make him at ease away from me. People often remark on how much Orson loves me and adheres to my side, but I know the sadder truth: he feels safe nowhere but with me. It's not a matter of devotion, as many of us would like to believe, but of anxiety, a training failure on my part.

This dog and I have bonded in an almost primal way, but I'm never sure if this is as wonderful a thing as movies and TV shows—and many dog lovers—suggest. The happiest and healthiest dogs I see (Clementine comes to mind) like lots of people, not just one.

My major wish for Orson, our primary training goal, is to help him feel okay in the world apart from me.

So every morning, when I can, I do exercises aimed at calming. I brush him, lie on the floor with him, praise him for being calm. I give him two or three quiet hours a day in a crate with a blanket on top. I've even tried the spinal massage used by horse trainers. Two or three times a week, I take him out on a leash near the sheep, have him lie down, pat him and give him treats when he stays quiet.

I sometimes feel that Orson and I have hit the training wall, my own Quitting Point, that very personal juncture where human and dog have gone about as far as time, commitment, and individual circumstances permit. Is it better to keep working with this wonderful but damaged dog, who nevertheless lives quite happily under my roof? Or to invest that time in Rose, a supremely competent and rewarding working dog? Or Clem, a dog that can go anywhere and be with anybody?

I don't really know. My time and energy are limited. But it's a matter of faith to keep going. I see small signs—calmness around sheep, better eye contact, a growing sense of ease—that we are still making some progress.

I usually take Clem and Rose together for our daily sheepherding, and while this is enormous fun, it is also problematic in a training sense. Clem usually sits by my side, dozing or having her belly scratched or chewing sticks while the intensely focused Rose chases the sheep around (who says border collies are smarter than Labs?). Clem understands that "come bye," "away to me," and "bring the sheep" are not commands intended for her.

The good thing is that I can simultaneously give Rose commands and hang out with Clementine. We all enjoy this time, a lovely dog-human experience and a training triumph in itself. My only regret is that Orson can't come along; some day I hope he can.

The problem is that I have inadvertently taught Clem that she need not necessarily pay close attention to what I am saying, that many of my commands are optional. When she drifted too close to the road one day and I heard a truck rushing down the hill, I yelled "Clem, come!" and she completely ignored me. Rose and the sheep were nearby, so she assumed I wasn't talking to her.

I tossed a stick in her direction to startle her; as soon as she realized I was calling her name, she came to me quickly, moving away from the road. But it was too close a call.

When I'm alone with Clementine, this isn't a problem; her name recognition is excellent, the payoff from a big investment in pungent treats. So I'm trying a series of "signal" commands to alert her that I'm speaking specifically to her. When I hold a treat up, I say, "Watch me," or I whistle. Increasingly, when I do one of these things without a treat, her head swivels and she focuses on me.

As for Rose, we've worked together so much that our relationship is nearly wordless. She always knows when I'm talking to her, and when I'm not.

Yet as great a dog as Rose is, I've come to realize I've only done part of my work with her. She's queen of Bedlam Farm, supremely confident around sheep, rams, cows, and donkeys. Away from the farm, however, she's as ill at ease as she is poised around her flock.

Bringing her back to New Jersey, when I spend time with Paula or when I have business in New York, has become difficult. The noisy garbage trucks and school buses, the throngs of people and other dogs, all unhinge her. She cowers and pants. Utterly at home in her farm element, she's grown uncertain and uncomfortable almost everywhere else.

I didn't socialize her nearly well enough. She is in no way aggressive; she simply has little interest in things not related to me, my family, or sheep. This is somewhat a trait of the breed, but it's also true that I never worked as hard at socializing Rose as I later did Clementine. So I've begun bringing Rose more places, into different homes, on walks in congested suburban areas. We have more work to do, however. It's become a common refrain.

I am committed to doing right by these dogs. I hope one day Orson will be calmer and more responsive. I want Clementine to have a better recall and react more promptly to commands. I'd like Rose to learn to live more securely in the world beyond the farm.

My life is such that I'm not sure we will all get there, but I've come to understand that these goals are important. Dogs have to share our complex, distracting, and fast-paced world. Yet all I can do is the best I can, one dog at a time.

Training is continual. It matters less that we meet our goals completely than that we're conscious of the lives our dogs are leading and the lives we want them to lead, and that we work to bridge the gap.

This requires patience and commitment, a willingness to observe our dogs and how they are doing, plus some candor about our own limitations and shortcomings.

To me, training is as much a way of thinking as a matter of methods and procedures. There's no surefire training program, any more than there's a dog who never misbehaves or annoys or troubles us.

We think about the lives we want to lead with our dogs, the things that have worked in our training, the things that haven't. We draw from conventional methods, taking what makes us comfortable, leaving behind what doesn't. We do the best we can, and we don't quit because we think training should be over in a matter of weeks, or because we haven't gotten the results we want or were led to expect. We see the process as more than a route to simple obedience. We recognize that success in training is as much about us as it is about them, and we take responsibility—rather than blaming or punishing society, other people, or our dogs—when we fall short.

How far we go is an individual choice. A single working parent is less likely than I to have a dog capable of a spit-spot response to "lie down." But she can craft a training program that makes her dog comfortable around her children and reasonably well behaved in a busy household.

The important lesson is, training isn't finite. It won't be over in a few weeks. The rewards can be great, your life with dogs a joy. However you do it, whatever your objectives, however you choose to live with your dog, training continues on from the day the dog arrives to the day he leaves.

12

COEXISTENCE

Boundaries and Limits

T O ME, TRAINING IS ABOUT DOGS AND HUMANS LIVING IN PEACE with one another—a phrase with many definitions, varying from one person, dog, home, to another.

A significant element of peace, though, is the definition of limits. These two species need boundaries, just as in any healthy relationship, as between lovers or spouses, parents and kids, bosses and employees, teachers and students, coaches and players.

With dogs, it's especially critical because, as many of us forget from time to time, they *are* another species. They have innate limits, and also imposed ones, frequently a matter of health and safety. I respect my dogs as wonderful embodiments of this other species, and I want them to respect me, too, within their ability to grasp our differences.

How else can we live harmoniously, exist together in sometimes narrow spaces? When the boundaries between people and dogs get blurred or eradicated, life with dogs becomes troubled and problematic.

Warren and Donna live on a twenty-acre farm near Bennington, Vermont. Having learned early in their marriage that they couldn't have children, they decided against the long dramas of fertility treatment or adoption and threw themselves into their work. They had talked for years about getting a dog but put it off because both were so busy. But last spring, they finally found a good breeder and acquired a springer spaniel puppy—and found themselves instantly overwhelmed by the intensity of their love for this little creature. Samantha seemed to fill a major hole in their lives, and they both sensed their lives were about to change. The dog, from the first, became the recipient and focus of all of this intelligent, affectionate couple's nurturing and caretaking instincts.

Together, even before they brought her home, they pored over training books, consulted friends with dogs, bought crates, toys, and balls. They worried about everything—food, vets, training. Each took a week off from work to ease Samantha's transition to her new home.

A month or so later, they asked me to come visit their new arrival and offer some training help and suggestions.

I drove over with the amiable Clementine.

When we came into the playroom (now turned into a puppy suite), Samantha went charging at Clem, who, her tail wagging, gave a low warning growl to tell the boisterous puppy to back off. Samantha stopped gnawing on Clem, and the two were about to begin ritualistic sniffing and playing when Donna rushed across the room, yelping, "No! No!" She grabbed the startled Clementine by the collar and yanked her back. Clem was stunned; the puppy, also startled, retreated into a corner.

"What's the matter?" I asked.

"Clementine was about to attack her," Donna said worriedly. "I had to stop her."

I pointed out that Clem's behavior was not only appropriate, but useful. Samantha needed to learn how to behave appropriately with other dogs, for her own safety. Clem, who loved all living things, except squirrels, was the perfect dog to teach her, as she would correct her without hurting her.

"Let them work it out," I said, and repeated one of the common trainer mantras: If you don't see blood, stay out of it.

Donna was unconvinced. "I hear what you're saying," she said, "but I don't really agree. I have to protect Sam."

Already, here was a lack of boundaries. Donna saw her dog as a child being bullied and did what any responsible parent would do—step in. But Samantha wasn't a child. Dogs work out differences differently than we do; they growl, posture, pin, challenge, send signals we don't see or understand.

In this way, they establish dominance and resolve conflicts, and usually avoid harming one another. When humans rush to intervene in dog squabbles, yelling and pulling dogs apart, they risk injury to themselves and their dogs. They're joining in the fray, getting everybody—especially the animals—even more excited.

But I dropped the subject, not wanting to seem critical. People are often sensitive, even defensive, about the way they deal with their dogs. They seek help but often don't like what they hear. Good trainers know how to tread gingerly.

So we talked for a while, then let the two dogs out into the freshly fenced yard. As Clem and Samantha started chasing around, Donna tapped on the window to get Samantha's attention.

Warren soon joined her at the window and tapped even harder, until Samantha turned to look at him. Within five minutes, one or the other of them had tapped to draw her attention half a dozen times.

Another boundary undefined: they couldn't allow their dog to amuse herself. She wasn't alone; she had another dog to keep her company. How would she learn how to feel calm when they were gone? I could envision, months down the road, long discussions about "separation anxiety" (also known as "My dog hates it when I go out").

It may seem a bit lonely if a puppy is outside by herself, but the puppy will soon become a dog who will need to be okay when you are not there. This was the time for Samantha to begin learning that; as an only dog, she was going to be by herself at least some of the time.

Anxious dogs are often created, not born. When dogs are off playing by themselves, dozing in their crates, or chewing a bone in another room, this is a good thing: you have a secure dog.

If you can't leave a dog alone for five minutes without calling him, playing or cuddling with him, you are creating more than a loved dog—one possibly too uneasy to be by himself.

I later noticed another boundary lacking. Samantha was already being overfed. Every time she waddled into the kitchen and put on that pleading Lab face, Donna put down a bowl of food. Samantha always had water in her playroom, too, day and night. Because of all this food and water, the puppy was having accidents all over the house.

Though they had bought a crate, a valuable housebreaking tool, neither Warren nor Donna could bear to put Samantha inside it. If she did go in and they closed the door, they opened it again the second she began whining. On those rare occasions when they didn't let her out, they still tried to soothe her, clucking and calling to her reassuringly. The behavior being reinforced was whining, not quiet acceptance of a crate.

Crates, one of the bedrock training aids, serve to establish boundaries in themselves, giving the dogs their own separate spaces, establishing some limits. Too many free-range dogs have total run of the house at all times, including the bed. That's too much dog freedom, in my opinion, providing too many opportunities for a dog to be annoying and messy, develop bad habits, or get into other kinds of trouble.

Crates give me a safe place to put my dogs when I am otherwise engaged, overwhelmed, or just not in the mood. They have their inviolate territory; I have mine.

Donna and Warren, however, didn't seem to want inviolate space. In fact, after Samantha arrived, Donna, who worked as a sales executive at a regional retailer, told her boss that she didn't want to travel so much anymore; she wanted to work at home more. She wasn't comfortable leaving Samantha alone for more than a few hours. "Now I have something to stay home for," she told me happily.

It was wonderful that Samantha was so loved, and that these two people had something to love so devotedly. But for me, alarms sounded. This couple obviously saw Samantha as a child, not a dog. That meant more anxiety and tension for them, more training challenges for the dog, more trouble defining boundaries.

Crossing my fingers, I decided our friendship could withstand some candor, especially since they'd asked for my counsel. But I've learned that dog love is sometimes much more powerful than well-intended advice or even common sense.

"I have to say," Donna said, showing considerable self-awareness, "that I am afraid this puppy won't love me if I don't feed her what she wants, or if I force her into a crate. That's hard for me."

Me, too, I said. It's hard for many people who love dogs to say no, to deny them things they want, to train or coerce them into doing things they don't want. But people who know dogs well do it anyway.

Dogs are almost unique in the animal world in their skill at reading humans and eliciting attachment from them, I pointed out. Dogs are naturally affectionate to us, as well. They show all sorts of loving signals: wagging their tails, drawing their ears back alongside their heads, rubbing against us, licking our hands, bringing us gifts. The arrival of a favorite human is often cause for joyful, noisy celebration by a dog.

True, this attachment is likely to be sparked by the dog's association of the human with food, walks, toys, and play, but that hardly matters. People react very powerfully to this seemingly unconditional acceptance, which they get from few humans. Dogs are just as happy to see us if we blew a big project at work or gambled away the grocery money, and that affection is not contingent upon appearance, status, or personality. Such behavior not only makes us feel loved and appreciated, it causes us to attach even more to our dogs.

Warren and Donna melted whenever Samantha bounded over to them to lick a hand or crawl into a lap. The couple clearly loved each other, but this was the additional something they'd needed for years. And that made observing boundaries and setting rules very tricky.

So our conversation was cordial, but just as ineffective as I feared. A few months later, I paid another visit and encountered a bigger, manic, obnoxious dog—loving and much loved, but in many ways an intrusive mess. Samantha was a poorly trained dog, the kind I wouldn't want in my home; I wasn't even crazy about seeing her in hers.

She played appropriately with Clementine but was otherwise almost completely out of control, jumping on people, barking and whining, offering her paw for a handshake every few minutes, dropping slimy balls in everybody's lap. She wouldn't go out into the yard unless Donna or Warren came along. She wouldn't go into her crate. She was already overweight.

"We weren't really able to do all the things you suggested," Donna said, shrugging a bit ruefully. "But we love her to death. And she is happy."

And that was true. I don't take it personally when people don't follow my advice. They ought to train their dogs in their own ways, using the approaches that work for them. And certainly this household came closer to peaceful coexistence than those where dogs are malnourished, abused, constantly confined. But because the dog didn't get the leadership—or boundaries—she deserved, Donna and Warren weren't living in what *I* would call harmony. They seemed her servants.

Was this really so bad? Was my view self-righteous, judgmental? The couple loved this dog, and she was better cared for than the vast majority of animals on earth. The scene did bother me, though, maybe because I believe it is the fate of a growing number of good dogs.

There was nothing these two wouldn't do for their dog, but little they asked *her* to do. They structured their weekends around walks, hikes, and treks to the ponds that Samantha liked to swim in. She wouldn't tolerate the crate, so on those now rare occasions when she was left alone in the house, she was confined to the kitchen, where she had fun trying to claw her way into cabinets and the garbage.

Maybe what bothered me was that Warren and Donna had, with the best of intentions, relinquished much of their own dignity. They couldn't quite preserve their own sense of a life apart from the dog's, something I think essential to living well with one. They still needed an income, so they went to work. But they stopped doing as much of the other things they'd once enjoyed—travel, movies and theater, visits to friends—because Samantha couldn't come along.

This might make sense for those who believe that dogs are our equals; that we should call ourselves their "guardians," not their owners; that they should have a human notion of rights.

But I can't agree. To me, the relationship works best when dogs serve us, help us, support us, as they have for thousands of years.

The happiest, most grounded dogs I know are those who literally *know*—and are taught—their places. I lavish all sorts of attention and other goodies on my dogs, but in the final analysis, I put my interests, and my human family's, first. That this is itself something of a controversial idea now says much about how enmeshed dogs and humans have become in America.

Samantha had no clearly defined place. Or, rather, she did: her perceived needs—not her actual needs—controlled the household and its occupants. When we subordinate our lives to dogs, it seems to me, the natural balance has been upset.

I'm exempt from none of these impulses and struggles. My dogs also fill holes in my life, raise emotional specters from my past, challenge the lines that ought to exist between humans and dogs. But maintaining some separation is important, for their sakes as well as mine.

On howling winter nights, I get invitations that initially seem less appealing than sitting in front of a woodstove with Clementine's head in my lap and the border collies dozing by my feet. We are so comfortable together.

It's often difficult for me to leave my dogs—Orson especially—in a kennel when I travel. It's taken me quite a while to grasp the value of crates and to use them appropriately, to learn the importance of denying dogs too much food, constant play, too many treats.

But we have come a long way. I do manage to keep boundaries; in fact, I'm getting better at it all the time.

My dogs can stay behind, for instance. I rarely bring them to other people's homes, where there's often some tension between visiting and resident dogs. I want my time with humans to be pleasant and relaxed.

When I'm visiting friends, I don't want to be constantly monitoring dog behavior. Somebody who's invited me for dinner is entitled to my attention, and I'm entitled to human interaction that doesn't involve dogs. And dogs are often a lot less happy to have canine company in their homes and territories than people think.

There are exceptions, of course. Some of my friends have dogs that

WATCH ME

are happy to play; some love having my dogs visit. But Orson, Rose, and Clementine get plenty of exercise, stimulation, and play. They can accompany me lots of places, but they don't need to go everywhere. There should be some social space between us, time when I can concentrate on people.

When I'm working, I stop paying attention to my dogs. That is a major, inviolable boundary for me. While I clack away on the keyboard, they're usually slumbering nearby, sometimes an inspiration, but not a bother or intrusion. That's my time, and it's important. "This is how I pay for your sheep," I muttered to Rose one day when she showed up at my desk while I was working. "Beat it." (Aren't I tough? We will herd sheep two or three times in a given day.)

When I leave the house, I put the dogs in their crates, usually with bones or treats. It's a nice feeling to know they're holed up next to one another safely, munching and crunching. I don't want to come home and look tensely around to see what has been moved, chewed, or damaged. In crates, they stay safe, and I have peace of mind.

When I leave the farm and go to New Jersey, I generally leave my dogs in a kennel in Vermont. My New Jersey town has grown too congested for my dogs to run much, and we encounter too many aggressive, obnoxious, and untrained dogs there. I want to spend time with Paula and with friends uninterrupted, see movies, go out to eat, enjoy a more urban life than usual. Two border collies now accustomed to living as farm dogs and a new Lab puppy don't always fit into that routine, so they usually stay behind.

I've worked to acclimate them to the kennel, taking them first for short periods, then for lengthening visits. Now when we pull up, they race out of the car and into the office, then sprint down the walkway and into their kennel area. The staff report that they usually skip food the first day, then eat heartily; they occupy themselves trying to play with the other dogs in the kennel—or, in Rose's case, push them around.

Dogs are obsessive creatures of habit; they tend to be easy with things they do often. Staying in a kennel is something Rose and Clem, especially, first experienced when they were young, so it doesn't seem to unnerve them.

It's always hard for *me* to leave them, but once I do, I'm quite secure knowing that they will be precisely where I left them. I don't want a dog walker—no matter how conscientious—or a friend to bear the responsibility of caring for three curious, active creatures while I'm gone for days.

Though the departure is a bit of a wrench, I figure I've earned some time away. It's healthy for them, too, to learn to be apart from me, to trust the loving, experienced staff at the kennel, to see that when I leave, I will return. The less anxious I feel about it, the less troubled they seem, a not uncommon reality in dogs' lives.

DOGS ARE ADAPTABLE, RESILIENT, FORGIVING. A RESPECTED SHEPHERD and trainer I know has twelve working dogs, mostly border collies. They go out in the morning for fifteen to twenty minutes to exercise and eliminate. Breakfast is a cup of kibble waiting on the floor of their crates when they return. They spend much of their days in crates in various corners of her farmhouse and barn. Three or four times a week, each dog gets some herding work and training. They go out again briefly in the afternoon, then again at nine or ten at night.

Their lives might strike some as extremely circumscribed, even abusive: they are always either working, exercising, eating, eliminating, or resting in their crates, period. When the farm is busy—as during trials or training classes—their out-of-crate time is even briefer.

Such a life is startlingly, even embarrassingly, different from mine with my dogs, but I've learned over time that these are happy, well-behaved, extremely affectionate dogs. They've been socialized with dogs and people; they're fit and energetic; they have work and companionship and care. They don't seem to need much more.

Boundaries are personal things, and we have the right to define our own. Still, I find it healthy to remember that dogs thrive when they fit into our lives, not when we subordinate ours to theirs.

Such inversions are especially striking because people so often acquire dogs these days in order to satisfy their own emotional requirements. Studies show that dogs meet the needs of widowed, separated, and divorced people especially well. One survey conducted in New England found that households with children at home tended to have more pets than those of either widows or of families with "empty nests" or with infants. Yet the same studies indicate that levels of emotional attachment to the dogs were lowest in families where children were at home.

The reasons validate what common sense tells us: people who have kids to attend to, care for, feel responsible for, don't need to lavish as much love on their dogs. Also, they're just too busy to devote all their energies to their pets.

DOGS DO PLAY DIFFERENT ROLES AT DIFFERENT POINTS IN OUR LIVES. It's no surprise to me that my love for dogs intensified when my daughter went off to college. Nothing in life has given me more meaning and pleasure than caring for her, ferrying her to school and her lessons and movies, cheering her triumphs and consoling her when she stumbled. When she left home, as she should have, an enormous void opened. She can't be replaced, not even by border collies. But my dogs have helped me move beyond that sense of emptiness and loss of vital purpose.

That's part of the miracle of dog love, which can do us a lot of good. But such love also requires thoughtfulness. The more I love dogs, the more I write about them, the more my life revolves around them, the more I understand that I cannot be solely defined by them. Good fences, as Robert Frost wrote in a different context, make good neighbors.

CASE STUDY: *The Dog Run*

MY FRIEND HENRY FOUND SNOOP, a two-year-old basset hound, through a vet he knew. It had been a long search. Henry had been visiting websites and shelters for several years. Some rescue groups and breeders refused to give or sell him a dog because he was away from home so much: he left for work at 7:00 A.M. and often didn't get home until eleven or twelve hours later. Some didn't think Manhattan was the proper environment for a dog. Yet Henry's Chelsea co-op permitted dogs; in fact, a surprising number of dogs were in residence, not only the little Yorkies, Westies, and miniature poodles that people associate with urban life, but plenty of working breeds—mastiffs, rottweilers, Labs, retrievers.

The idea of a dog kept growing on him. Living alone in New York was rough for Henry, and he often felt lonely. He thought a dog would get him outside more, give him a companion as he walked his neighborhood. He wanted something to come home to.

Talking to vets and shelter workers, he'd come to see an older, housebroken dog as a good choice. His neighbors, he'd learned, all had elaborate support systems—dog walkers, dog-friendly doormen, dog-loving friends, dog runs—to help keep their dogs exercised and cared for. Their routine often sounded chaotic, but Henry thought he could make dog owning work.

His plan was to get up at 5:30 A.M., take his dog for a long walk, then crate him or confine him to the kitchen. He'd hire a dog walker—at a cool $15 to $20 an hour—to come at midday and walk the dog, then he'd take the dog out again when he got home for a final evening walk.

On evenings and weekends, he'd take advantage of the surprisingly extensive network New York City dog lovers have concocted—out-of-sight park corners, vacant lots, abandoned piers—in order to gather with their dogs.

Snoop would mark a significant step in Henry's life. He wanted—needed—to make a change.

Though few of his friends or coworkers at a midtown ad agency knew it, Henry had suffered sexual abuse as a young boy in Ohio. His family, a confrontational, unsupportive lot, was of little help, then or now. After years in therapy, he'd quelled some of his worst fears, gotten past his panic attacks, and achieved success in his career—but he struggled still with loneliness, anxiety, and a dread of intimacy.

This legacy had so far isolated him socially—kept him from making many friends, from dating or marrying, a painful state for someone who yearned for a family. But it remained a struggle for him to trust people, to form healthy relationships, to overcome anger and fear.

So when Henry called one day to say that a neighborhood vet had told him of a basset hound whose owners were divorcing and leaving the city, it was happy news. Snoop was living in a crate in the vet's office, and was, Henry said, affable, sedentary, and reasonably well trained.

Part of Henry's plan was to introduce the affable basset to a dog run downtown. What did I think of dog runs and dog parks? he wondered.

Well, in the first place, it doesn't make sense to me to have hounds, border collies, and other working breeds in the city, where they can hardly get the kind of space and work they need and love.

As for community dog runs, though puppies urgently need to be socialized and to mingle with other dogs, I'm never quite at ease with people bringing strange adult dogs together in confined environments.

When I went with Henry to see the dog run, I found it the very opposite of my own situation with dogs—it was small, crowded, and noisy. Busy New York dog lovers are nearly desperate for some room, somewhere, to let their dogs loose; their commitment to this smallish rectangle of fenced, packed earth was touching. The dogs within, all barky and aroused, were having a good time, it seemed, running, sniffing, circling. But it was chaos.

In many ways, urban dog runs are about as far from dogs' natural lives as one can get. There's potential for all kinds of difficulties, from transmitting parasites and fleas to rumbles that arise from lapses in knowledge about dogs and their histories.

I've seen people stroll into runs and parks with newly acquired but highly aggressive dogs, fresh from shelters, who melt down in the mayhem and immediately tear into other dogs—and sometimes people. I see dogs cranked up, made hyper, by people working overtime to amuse and entertain them. Other people, ignorant of dogs' real natures, are overprotective. At some runs, breed snobs bristle at sending their expensive and groomed dogs to run around with various unkempt mutts.

Then there's the larger and sadder reality: very few owners train their dogs, so most can't reliably call their dogs back from unpleasant or dangerous situations—a real problem at a dog run.

"I thought this would be a good place to socialize Buster," one such owner told me and some friends at a dog park in New Jersey. He was apologetic: Buster, an Akita mix he'd adopted the day before, had just mauled a Scottish terrier. No, we told him, the time to socialize a dog like Buster is *before* you let him off-leash at a dog park. Like many dog lovers, the guy had the best intentions but didn't understand how to train, socialize, and acclimate a dog like the one he'd just acquired, and hadn't sought the help that could've prevented the incident.

Yet nothing speaks to the remarkably adaptive nature of dogs more than their ability to adjust to these confined spaces and to actually enjoy them. Dogs, creatures of routine, love almost everything they do every day. Standing outside a city run like Henry's, you can see dogs straining to get there, eager to run around and greet their pals. It is touching to see their pleasure—and the pleasure their "fun" brings to their owners' faces. Dog runs and parks sometimes seem to benefit people as much as dogs—not an insignificant function.

Yet people bring their dogs into runs expecting everyone to behave as if they were at a Buckingham Palace tea party. They get outraged or horrified when dogs challenge each other, squabble over toys, nibble on others' feces, hump or gang up on one another. These are all things dogs do naturally when they assemble—they *are* the canine equivalent of tea-party etiquette, actually—but people aren't prepared for them. One woman at Henry's run seemed ready to call the police when a golden retriever mounted her cockapoo. "My God, don't you see what's happening?" she wailed.

Fights, confrontations, misunderstandings among canines and humans—dog runs are just too unpredictable and tumultuous for me. I find it more comfortable, for me and my dogs, to skip public facilities. The idea that anybody can control large groups of excited dogs milling around tiny spaces has never seemed persuasive. And, of course, I have the luxury of not needing them.

But Henry did need a place to exercise Snoop and to socialize him quickly. So from the day Snoop left the vet's office for his apartment, Henry took him to the run early in the morning, whatever the weather. Usually, they found the same group of dogs there, so they all got used to one another. Snoop seemed eager to go, got a good workout, and did, in fact, become more social.

Both Henry and Snoop had their run-ins. A pit bull stalked Snoop repeatedly while his owner "apologized" by saying his dog had been too abused to train. The owners of some other dogs thought Snoop was too aggressive; they wanted him to leave their dogs completely alone, with no sniffing or circling, an unrealistic expectation for a curious and social dog.

But Henry felt Snoop needed the exercise, so he put up with both ill-behaved dogs and difficult owners. It dawned on him, after a few months, that he was enjoying the run along with Snoop. He got to know the people he met each day; they shared newspapers and talked about the day's stories while their dogs chased around the run. He met some fellow movie buffs with whom to compare opinions on the weekend's new releases. The run even hosted a Christmas party (sans dogs) at a nearby pub. Henry realized he had some new friends, people who helped one another find kennels and vets and deal with dog problems.

In his own apartment building he'd rarely spoken to any of his neighbors. Now he knew a dozen—dog owners, mostly—and was being invited to dinner parties, Netflix screenings, and Sunday brunches. Even his non–dog owning neighbors greeted Snoop and knew who Henry was.

Serious about learning about dogs, Henry took to watching dog shows on cable, read shelves of books, grilled fellow owners, and observed their dogs. He worked through the squabbles at the dog run, mediated differences of opinion, shared his growing knowledge. "In a different context, I would have fled," he admitted. "But I couldn't do that to Snoop. I stayed for him, and then recognized that I was also staying for me."

Some of the consequences were unexpected. Henry hadn't dated much in years, too anxious to risk it, afraid of rejection, possibly afraid of acceptance, too. But he met a woman he liked at work, and she asked him out for a drink. After some torturous back-and-forth, he was startled to discover himself in a relationship.

"I owe the dog and the run for this," he told me. "I learned to talk to strangers there, to resolve disputes, to make friends. We share information, talk about our dogs, worry when they get sick, help with training tips. If I hadn't been going to the dog run, I'm not sure I would've had the confidence to talk to Arlene, or spend an evening with her. But because of Snoop, I'd had lots of practice talking to people. And a lot of those people liked *me*, not just my dog. That isn't something I could believe before Snoop came along."

Was this really true? Join a dog run and change your life? Maybe Henry was overstating the case. But perhaps by getting Snoop and taking him to the run, Henry *was* able to break through some painful and difficult issues.

"Going to the run made me happier," he said. "I think it benefited both of us."

Henry also avoided some of the emotional pitfalls he saw his fellow dog owners struggling with. While training Snoop, he had no problems leaving him in a crate, and felt little guilt about leaving him home alone so much.

"He gets plenty of exercise, is well cared for, and is much loved," Henry reasoned. "We are very happy together. I owe him, because he got me through a tough period. But he owes me, too! I gave him a home for life. It's a very mutual relationship."

Henry had made the important discovery, one that eludes many

Americans as their attachments to their dogs grow: dogs are simple, adaptable creatures. Snoop wasn't living a textbook life for a basset hound—they were bred for hunting, after all—but he had a good life nonetheless.

Henry's story illustrates the danger of absolute theories. I know lots of dogs in suburbs with big yards who aren't flourishing like Snoop, or bringing their humans as much satisfaction.

So I admit to having been too reflexively negative about Henry and his dog run. My notion of densely populated cities as poor environments for dogs needs adjustment, as well. As I should know, theories and conventional wisdoms are fluid. If you'd asked me, in theory, whether being crated in a Manhattan apartment much of the day, exercised mostly on crowded sidewalks and in a tiny dog run, was satisfactory for Snoop, I would have huffed and puffed in disapproval. That's no life for a hound dog. What could Henry have been thinking? But if you spend any time with the two of them, such preconceptions crumble quickly. They fit together beautifully; they enhance each other's lives.

Theories about dogs—choosing them, training them, living with them—are useful, but the effectiveness of the people involved matters more. It's an important lesson: do your homework; make choices thoughtfully and knowingly; bone up on theory, by all means; but, in the end, make your own decisions and take responsibility for them. Consider your life and your dog's and the things you want to do, separately and together. Then patch together your own approach. Chances are it will be as good as mine, or anyone's.

13

VIOLENT DOGS

S PICE, A THREE-YEAR-OLD PIT BULL—LAB MIX, WAS A GOOD BUDDY of my two border collies. At the single park in my New Jersey town where dogs can run off-leash, they shared toys and snacks, tore after Frisbees and balls, wrestled tirelessly, played tug-of-war.

Spice's owner, Jan, a member of several rescue groups, thought it immoral to buy a purebred dog (like my two) when so many dogs are in shelters, many more than there are people willing to give them homes.

Accordingly, she'd plucked Spice out of a Brooklyn animal shelter days before she was slated for euthanasia. "I definitely was drawn to Spice because she was a pit," she told me. "The other dogs there had a shot at being adopted, maybe, but I didn't think she would." Jan knew nothing about the dog, apart from the fact that she was a stray found half-starved on the street. But that's often the case with shelter dogs:

without knowing their environments or histories, you have to take a lot on faith.

That Jan had rescued the dog seemed to deepen their relationship. Jan had a difficult childhood: her brother was killed in a crash when she was ten, and her mother died of cancer a few years later. "I am one of those people who identify very powerfully with the plight of mistreated animals, and I understand it has a lot to do with my own life," she's acknowledged.

Though Jan grew very attached to Spice, she didn't use the dog's hard times or her own as an excuse. She trained the dog conscientiously and consistently.

And it paid off: Spice was a great pet, obedient, easygoing, affectionate, and playful. I never hesitated to let her romp with my dogs, nor did Spice give me any reason to.

Yet Jan complained constantly about what she called "breed prejudice"—that fear of pit bulls that caused people to grab their kids or dogs and dash across the street when they encountered one. Though Spice had committed no sins, petitions circulated around the neighborhood, Jan's landlord threatened to evict her from her apartment, and her liability insurance doubled. "If the dog even sticks her head outside," Jan moaned, "somebody calls the police." It seemed unfair.

Last fall, however, during one of Jan and Spice's daily walks, a Pekingese slipped its lead at a county park and ran toward Spice and Jan, growling and barking.

Spice, startled, almost reflexively grabbed the dog's head in her mouth, bit down, and hung on. Neither Jan nor a dog trainer passing by was able to get the dog to loosen its grip; they watched, horrified, as the smaller dog screamed, then was still.

Its owner, an older woman strolling with her little grandson, shrieked at the sight and rushed to intervene. Spice, always previously friendly and reliable around children, was aroused, almost frantic. Jan and the trainer were shouting; the grandmother and child were rushing at her, the child screaming in fear. Spice struck back.

She bit the woman's arm, which later required thirty stitches. And then she bit the child, who was lower to the ground, on the face and neck; after two surgeries, small but permanent physical scars remained, along with who knew what psychological scars.

The local animal-control authorities seized the dog and placed her in a kennel for observation. When a dog bites and causes serious injury, local ordinances usually lead to euthanasia; the fact that the dog was a pit bull didn't help.

Jan, distraught, hired a lawyer and went to court. She would fight for her pet's life. "It was terrible, but it wasn't the dog's fault," she said. "The Peke threatened her, the woman and child charged at her. I'm so terribly sorry it happened, but Spice is a wonderful dog. She doesn't deserve to die."

Jan believed the woman and her grandchild were at fault, since their dog was off-leash and came at her and Spice. Spice, Jan argued, "was walking calmly, on a leash and under control."

Her view is widely shared in the dog world. Many dog lovers—especially those whose breeds are feared—insist that it's generally the people who get bitten who are responsible, not the dogs.

With proper education and more understanding, they argue, fewer people would be bitten. Children should be taught to avoid strange dogs, to approach them only with care, to adopt certain postures if they are confronted. Anyone who learns a few simple rules about dog safety can avoid injury, in this view. So those who won't learn these simple rules are therefore to blame when dogs bite them.

The offending dogs' owners get angry at the victims: *their* dogs are aggressive; *their* kids are careless. "People should stay the hell away from my dog," the owner of one especially aggressive rottweiler told me, unrepentant, after the dog had bitten a deliveryman.

Jan spent several thousand dollars fighting for Spice, money she could ill afford. But she lost her case. A local judge, in consultation with two local vets who work with the town shelter, ruled that the dog was dangerous.

While Spice was being held, Jan e-mailed and phoned, asking me, "as a dog lover and dog writer," to help. She wanted me to testify at an appeal, to send letters to the judge, the vets, and the shelter, affirming that the dog was gentle and playful, urging another chance. She promised to muzzle Spice when they walked, to build a new fence around her backyard. Jan even offered to leave town and move in with her mother, who lived in rural Sussex County, if the court would spare Spice.

AS AMERICA'S LOVE AFFAIR WITH DOGS HAS DEEPENED, MORE PEOPLE acquire dogs for all sorts of reasons from all sorts of places: professional and backyard breeders, shelters and rescue groups, puppy mills and malls.

Some elements of the rescue and animal-rights movements have advanced the idea of "no-kill" shelter policies—keeping virtually all dogs alive, even for years, until they find homes or die naturally. Dogs bred for hunting, fighting, and security, and those with strong jaws and sometimes aggressive behavior—pit bulls, rottweilers, Akitas, chows—are the focal point of many of these efforts, precisely because they are most in need of rescue. Often—usually—they make wonderful and loving pets.

Meanwhile, even traditionally gentler breeds like retrievers have become less reliable as their popularity increases. So many are poorly bred that they're less genetically stable, and now more likely to bite humans than the traditionally "aggressive" breeds. Nevertheless, it's important to acknowledge that all dog bites are not equal. When the fighting and hunting breeds do attack, they often cause much greater injury than other dogs. While Labradors, poodles, and Pomeranians are more likely to bite, rottweilers and pit bull mixes are most likely to kill or maim. Violent dogs have quietly but steadily become a significant issue for the dog world, and a mushrooming public-health problem for Americans.

The U.S. Centers for Disease Control and Prevention report that in 1994, the most recent year for which published data are available, an estimated 4.7 million people suffered dog bites and approximately 800,000 of them required medical care as a result. The U.S. Humane Society reported that in 2003, more than 400,000 people were bitten seriously enough to go to the hospital for treatment.

The injury rates are highest by far among children. Bites are especially traumatic for them; adults tend to be bitten on the arms or legs, but 80 percent of injuries to children are facial, the CDC found.

And of course sometimes the worst happens. From 1979 through 1994, reports the CDC, attacks by dogs resulted in 279 human deaths. These fatal attacks, up dramatically in just a few years, were concentrated among small children and the elderly.

According to the Dog Bite Law Foundation (www.dogbite.law), perhaps the most comprehensive resource in the country for information on dog violence against humans, the median age of patients bitten was fifteen, with boys ages five to nine having the highest incidence. A five-year study showed that the following breeds had killed at least one person: pit bulls, rottweilers, German shepherds, huskies, Alaskan malamutes, Doberman pinschers, chows, Great Danes, Saint Bernards, and Akitas.

These dogs are not, for the most part, wandering marauders. Biting dogs, 77 percent of them, belong to the victim's family or to a friend. When a child under four years is the victim, the family dog is the attacker half the time, and the attack, 90 percent of the time, happens in the family home. The chances that the victim of a fatal dog attack will be a burglar or human attacker are 1 in 177. The odds that the victim will be a child are 7 out of 10.

Dog-attack victims in the United States suffer over $1 billion in monetary losses each year, says *The Journal of the American Medical Association.*

Yet the implications of these awful statistics don't seem to have seeped into many quarters of the dog culture. Dog lovers don't like to view dogs—their own or anybody else's—as dangerous. Though the news media report, often sensationally, on serious or fatal attacks, the image of dogs most Americans cherish is shaped by popular culture, where dogs are always beautiful, clean, friendly, nonmenacing.

A vet I know even objects to the very term "violent dog." "Dogs are never violent," she protested. "They just get into situations where they don't know what to do."

Within the rescue movement, I've encountered various schools of thought about aggressive dogs. Most rescue groups take the matter of aggression very seriously, either euthanizing violent dogs or placing them very carefully in homes and environments where they're unlikely to harm people or dogs. Yet others insist that dogs are inherently blameless, that publicity about dog-related injuries only decreases the odds that the millions of dogs in need of adoption will find homes.

Though it's impossible to generalize about a culture as vast and diverse as the dog world, my sense is that many dog lovers are in denial about the growing numbers of attacks and the damage that dogs are doing to humans. Significant numbers of people who love dogs blow this off, either blaming the victims or rationalizing the circumstances. So the problem is either sensationalized by the media or ignored by the individuals, institutions, and agencies that comprise Dog Lovers' Nation.

Our reaction to this subject reflects the growing intensity of the human-dog bond, the struggle to balance canine and human concerns, and the increasingly complex ethical dramas and contradictions involved in the care, rescue, and welfare of dogs in America.

Not only are violent dogs brought into the mainstream population by the thousands each year, but it has become something of a moral imperative in some quarters to adopt and save them. Among some dog advocates, it's considered immoral to euthanize violent dogs yet humane to either promote their adoption (thus bringing them into contact with children) or keep them confined in shelter crates for years until they die. It's a confusing idea of morality.

The non–dog owning population is increasingly confused, terrified, and enraged at the growing toll. All kinds of dogs, violent or not, are being banned from public parks and spaces, apartments and buildings, as a result. The quandary of the non–dog owning population is quite real: If these animals are attacking millions of Americans each year, how are nonowners expected to ascertain which of the dogs they encounter are safe for them or their kids?

Obviously, as many dog lovers advocate, it would be helpful to teach children how to approach strange dogs: to not look them in the eye, approach them straight on, or grab them suddenly; to stay away from their food. But this doesn't absolve dog owners of moral responsibility.

It's almost impossible to teach a three- or four-year-old to always behave appropriately when encountering a strange animal. Do we really want to tell kindergartners that it's their fault when their own dogs injure them? Does anyone with kids seriously expect children this age to remain calm and remember the rules of dog safety when a large, strange dog is rushing at them, or when their own dog suddenly turns on them?

The grandmother whom Spice bit was a recent immigrant to America, it emerged. She spoke little English and had no time or resources to take a dog-safety course or teach her grandson the supposedly preventive behavior. And would that have worked, anyway? Children are already bombarded with messages—meant to deter drug use, for instance—but often the results aren't encouraging. That doesn't mean education is a poor idea, or that we should stop spreading such messages. It does suggest that it's unrealistic to expect children to memorize and employ the rules of dog safety.

As adults and dog lovers, this is our responsibility, not theirs. I find it repugnant to slough off responsibility for my dog's behavior and blame children instead. When I live with a dog, it is my job to do everything possible to see that my dog never harms a human or another animal. Any dog can bite under certain circumstances—no one with a dog should kid himself about having a dog that will never, ever bite—but in choosing dogs and training them we can reduce the odds. The epidemic of dogs biting children suggests that something is seriously wrong with the way many people acquire, train, and understand their dogs.

Surely dogs with histories of aggression in their breed or their individual histories are in urgent need of rescue. But that ducks the real question: Is it appropriate to breed, sell, rescue, and re-home so many dogs capable of causing so much damage?

The animal-rights movement sees itself as deeply moral, a powerful advocate for animals. But who is fighting for all those kids with face and neck injuries? Or for the right of nonviolent dogs to move freely about society, to be integrated into our work lives and homes? Who speaks for those violent dogs doomed to spend years, perhaps all their lives, in noisy confinement, as far from a dog's natural state as it's possible to be?

The subject of morality and dogs is complex. It's true that there are no "good" or "bad" dogs; dogs are incapable of moral choices. Spice was by no means a bad dog; she reacted reflexively, instinctively, when another dog approached her owner and intruded on her space. Of course the incident wasn't her fault, nor was it the fault of Jan or the poor grandmother who led her grandchild into such a horrific scene.

Still, when people buy, rescue, or otherwise acquire a dog with a history of violence, or a particular capacity for violence, they are making a profound choice. They have a bedrock responsibility to gauge the dog's behavior, to train it thoroughly and rigorously, to protect other humans and dogs from harm—whether the potential victims are behaving responsibly or not.

I don't want to own a dog that inspires fear or concern, nor do I ever want to be responsible for maiming another dog or child. My dogs are chosen carefully, their temperaments tested and observed by trainers and vets, and they are rigorously socialized. But should they ever cause harm, I'd consider myself responsible, except in the rarest of circumstances (if someone actually attacked me or the dogs, for example).

We need to show our dogs how to live peaceably in the world and among its inhabitants. Most dogs of all breeds can be trained to do so, though few are. But some dogs simply can't, for reasons of genetics, abuse, litter experience, or human handling. Such dogs ought to be permanently removed from society, not recycled again and again into the mainstream of life.

We have lost our moral perspective when we don't recognize that the rights and welfare of children take precedence over even our most beloved pets. If any of my dogs ever bit a child and caused serious injury, I would put him or her down instantly, unwilling to take the chance that it might ever happen again. It wouldn't matter whose "fault" it was.

Violent dogs not only represent a crisis in public health, they threaten the welfare of all dogs and the people who love them. That is not, for me, a moral position.

We want to live harmoniously with our dogs, and we want them to live harmoniously in the world. As a goal, that will never be universally obtainable. And the statistics remind us that we are currently heading in the wrong direction.

I told Jan that, heartbreaking as the whole incident had been, I couldn't in good conscience join in the fight to save Spice. The dog was duly euthanized. Jan was willing to turn her life upside down to save her dog, but I worried about Spice's demonstrated ability to turn other people's lives upside down. The risk, I thought, was too great.

CONCLUSION

My Life with Dogs

THE END OF THIS BOOK SEEMS A GOOD POINT AT WHICH TO TURN from the utilitarian toward the spiritual, from the how to the why. There's a potentially rich payoff to living well with a dog, a reason for all the work involved.

I've never been a particularly religious person, but I'm very drawn to the spirituality possible in the long common journey of people and dogs. For almost as long as there have been humans, dogs (or their ancestors) have been with them.

Our current relationships would likely surprise or amuse our forebears. Dogs have become companions or guardians that keep us company, that offer tangible assistance most contemporary owners will never require or use. They should logically inhabit the peripheries of our lives. Yet the dialogue under way between human beings and dogs is an extraordinary exchange between two distinct species, thus much worth thinking about.

Dogs have transformed my life. I've always had dogs and loved them, but this deeper connection was first forged when Orson arrived at Newark Airport, terrified, destructive, and apparently beyond my ability to train. Once I decided that I would do anything to help and keep him, that decision changed my work, the place I live, the nature of my friendships and my relationship to much of the world. It took me years to realize who had rescued whom.

My relationship with Rose, the working girl, is different. She came as a puppy shortly before I bought and moved to Bedlam Farm. I'd never had a true working dog before, nor needed one so badly. In her own way, she was as difficult to train as Orson, her instincts so consuming and relentless that she sometimes seemed beyond my reach.

Clementine, as she evolves past puppyhood, reinforces for me the idea that dogs are worth thinking about, especially before you get one. It's no easy thing for a puppy to enter my domain, live with the ferociously focused Rose and the sometimes thoroughly whacked Orson. Yet almost everything about Clem has been a joy, possibly excepting her fondness for all things rotting or fecal, and the consequent, sometimes explosive intestinal responses.

These three very complex and distinct dogs have presented me with some of the most challenging experiences of my life, and the most rewarding. It demonstrates daily why understanding them, working with them, loving them, fitting their needs into my already busy existence, has felt worthwhile.

They have taught me faithfulness and responsibility. At fifty-seven, I am still plagued with foibles and shortcomings; an enduring intolerance and anger always smolder just below the surface, controlled after much hard work but never entirely obliterated. We can change and grow, but I don't think that, beyond a certain point, we can become different people.

Yet sticking with Orson has taught me patience beyond my imagination. Rose has given me faith and the satisfaction of working hard and persistently, of rising to challenges and mastering them. Clementine brings me a rare contentment. That's a lot of happiness, even when my leg aches and my back twinges, even on a lovely morning when I wish Paula were here to share the view.

Animal ethicist James Serpell writes about what he calls the psychospirituality that increasingly underlies humans' connection to dogs and other pets. He's not referring to something religious or supernatural but to the point where psychology and spirituality fuse and forge a new kind of bond between people and animals—especially dogs. That's the very point—the emotion, sometimes spiritual space—that fascinates and compels me.

I LEARNED, ONE DAY LAST DECEMBER, THAT A FRIEND HAD DIED SUDdenly. No friend's death is easy to bear, but this one seemed particularly cruel: a dog lover in a San Francisco apartment building that banned dogs, she turned to friends and neighbors, borrowing their dogs to care for and play with. She was walking one of those dogs on the morning a truck hit her and killed her instantly. I had talked to her a few days earlier. The news hit hard.

Reflexively, I called Paula, who said how sorry she was. Then I put on my parka and headed out the back door, all three dogs with me. We walked up the steep incline behind my farmhouse, over the crest of the hill.

I couldn't work, I wasn't in the mood to move sheep around, and it was much too cold to cry. So I sat on an ancient bale of hay at the top of the world and stared out at the clouds rushing over the valley.

I don't believe the dogs understood that someone I cared about had died. I do think they read my moods well. Clem swore off donkey droppings for a few minutes to sit by me; Rose ceased her eternal vigilance over sheep and settled on the grass; Orson, as always, stayed Velcroed to my side.

The four of us sat together as the wind whirled, picking up a thin veneer of snow from the dried-out grass, dusting us all in a light blanket. It was almost painfully beautiful to see the winter farms, squared off like patchwork quilts, below us.

When my fingers and toes began to scream in protest, we trooped back down the icy hill and into the house. I fed the woodstove with logs, made some hot chocolate, passed out three marrow bones. We huddled together in front of the fire, sipping and chewing, mostly enjoying our togetherness.

My dogs were learning when to work, when to play, and when to do neither. It was always gratifying to see, but now, opened up by the death of my friend, it moved me even more.

I thought of Beverly, of her warmth and many kindnesses to me, of her unflagging generosity and spirit, even in the face of disappointment.

Then it was time for another of those transitions that are the stuff of life, with dogs and otherwise. I got up, let the dogs out into the yard, watched them turn to the pleasures of rope toys as naturally as they'd consoled me moments before.

I walked into my office and back to work.

A FEW WEEKS LATER, ON A SUNNY FEBRUARY AFTERNOON, A FRIEND pulled into the driveway at the side of my farmhouse. Orson, asleep at the other end of the house, heard the truck, came charging across the living room to see who'd arrived, skidded on the hearth rug, and plowed right into a floor-to-ceiling window, shattering a couple of panes of antique glass.

It was a dramatic but increasingly rare glimpse of the old Orson, who routinely crashed through windows, opened cabinets, and leaped fences. Years of calming and grounding training had ensued. I can't begin to count how many times we practiced our calming rituals: make eye contact, lie down, and get treats; sit quietly by the sofa or stay calm around sheep and get rewarded for it. He's seen trainers and behaviorists; I've even begun taking him to a holistic vet in Vermont.

Yet there is that part of him that I've never reached, perhaps can't ever reach, a broken part, a part that cranks him up beyond training, reason, and experience and sends him crashing into a window. I know that now, I accept it, and I love him just as much as if he were whole. Perhaps more.

That's Orson. That's who he is.

. . .

THE NEXT MORNING, A NEARBY FARMER CAME TO COLLECT THREE OF MY sheep. I was reducing the flock before lambing season. The farmer pulled her truck up to my pasture, and I sent Rose roaring up the hill to round up the sheep.

Rose dashed to the corner of the fence where they'd bunched up and cannily moved behind them, pausing to back up the stomping ram. She pushed them down the snowy hill, through drifts, over slippery rocks, around trees, rounding up stragglers, keeping the group moving, while I waited silently at the foot of the hill.

She escorted the sheep to the truck so those who were leaving could walk up a plank and into the pickup. Anyone who dawdled or tried to bolt got promptly disciplined. Once the sheep were aboard, enclosed in a plywood container in the truck bed, Rose and I followed behind in our own truck, as the farmer drove home.

At her place, we opened the box and guided the sheep out. When they took off, confused and frightened, Rose headed them off. The farmer opened the pasture gate; the new arrivals rushed in—but about a dozen other sheep dashed out. Meanwhile, a ram in a nearby pen circled and huffed. By now, this sort of barnyard imbroglio was familiar to Rose and me. Even a year earlier, I would have been paralyzed. Now I was totally confident, arrogant on my dog's behalf, with no doubt she'd bring order while I stood around and cleared my throat.

It was, as always, great fun to watch Rose sort out a mess. As usual, she stopped, took in the scene, made decisions through some process I would never quite grasp, then went to work.

She gathered up the farmer's sheep, then moved them in with the newcomers. She eyeballed the ram through his enclosure, unnerving him with that piercing "make my day" stare. Soon, urging the newly reconfigured flock back to me, she had things organized.

I love Rose, but in a different way than I love Orson. This isn't the love you feel for a needy creature, but the bond you have with a partner and friend you can absolutely trust. We'd been through so much together, Rose and I; I depended on her.

In ten minutes, the barnyard was quiet, order restored, and Rose back in my pickup, glowering through the window at the ram. I was receiving plaudits, having, as usual, done nothing much but drive her from one farm to another.

That's Rose, that's who she is.

The same week, I was scheduled to visit an assisted-living facility in nearby Saratoga Springs, to give a talk about dogs. I brought along Clem, now eight months old. As we entered the well-tended building, she trotted alongside me, off-leash, darted over to greet the receptionist, helped herself to some of the water gurgling from a fountain in the lobby.

We took the elevator upstairs—border collies dislike elevators, but Clementine barely seemed to notice that the little room was moving—and walked into a large room filled with perhaps a hundred people. Watching their faces as they spotted Clementine, I saw that the room was filled with dog lovers. Seeing her, patting and stroking her, meant a great deal to them. Some people recalled their own dogs; a few took pictures; I noticed a couple of residents in tears, overjoyed at the sight of her and the memories she evoked of their lives with dogs.

No politician ever worked a room more skillfully. Clem shuttled up and down the center aisle, accepting pats, offering licks. Although she still sometimes had the obnoxious Lab habit of jumping up on people she liked, she jumped on nobody in this place, apparently somehow sensing that these folks were too frail. Soon she found a woman in the fourth row who'd owned yellow Labs for years, and plopped at her feet for scratching.

Within a few minutes, I saw her lying on her back next to her new friend, snoring.

Partway through my talk, Clem woke up, made her leisurely way to find me, and lay down by the lectern to watch the crowd and rest. What an easy creature she was, so at home in the world.

I tossed a treat down from time to time to reinforce her calm. After the talk, she greeted people as they came up to take pictures or say hello. A line formed so that I could sign books; she camped by the table, wagging warmly at whoever came by.

Afterward, we took the elevator back downstairs and went out through the lobby, pausing only long enough for her to bid the receptionist farewell. Outside, she paused at the street—we'd been working hard at this every day on the farm. I stopped at a nearby field so that she could relieve herself. Then she hopped into the truck and dozed all the way home, snoring loudly much of the way.

I was just as proud of her as I was of Rose. She was on her way to being a dog that could go anywhere, read a crowd, be calm while things around her were noisy and confusing. She was going to be an ambassador for dogs, I hoped, a dog whose work was to be a living testament to choosing a dog well and training her successfully.

I'm far from finished with this work; it has just begun. And I have no illusions about owning perfect dogs. I have none and don't expect to have any. Clem doesn't need that kind of pressure, and in any case, no such dogs exist.

But this night was important. I trusted this dog to move about the world in a way the border collies really couldn't. Orson was too excitable, Rose too sensitive. But that's Clem.

What an interesting group we were becoming.

FOR ME, THIS IS THE GLORY OF DOGS.

Within my little universe are three creatures of distinctly different personalities. I have the most intense dog and the least. I have a dog so filled with confusing instincts he can still blast through a closed window and one whose instincts are so focused she can organize a barnyard in minutes. My newest dog, still taking shape, can sit among strangers in an unfamiliar facility for two hours, treating fragile people gently, fitting in as naturally as if she'd grown up among them.

Yet while I believe training never ends, I am also constantly reminded of its limits, of dogs' individual personalities, wills, and idiosyncrasies. I'm aware of the many demands on my time, patience, and energy, and of the many other factors in our world—from sickness to passing snowmobiles—that I can't control, but that shape their lives.

Still, I am responsible for them. Because they can't speak, I feel called to speak for them. They reflect not only their own powerful animal spirits but mine, my fatigue and impatience, but also my love and respect, my wish to do and be better. In that sense, we are fused, a reflection of one another. Dogs mirror the people we are and the people we want to be.

To me, there has always been something darkly beautiful about loving a dog. Dark because they don't live as long as we do, because they're so completely dependent on us, so vulnerable to abuse and misunderstanding, so hard to part from.

Choosing, training, and living with dogs is not, ultimately, only a pragmatic process but a spiritual one. How much are we willing to step out of ourselves? How hard are we willing to work to show these simple but wonderful creatures how to share our lives? How much will our patience be tested and to what degree can we rise above that impatience, find the better parts of ourselves, and have the dogs we want, with the lives they deserve?

THOMAS MERTON, THE LATE TRAPPIST MONK AND HONORED WRITER, AND a significant influence on my life, wrote that it is impossible for a human being to live without some sort of faith. Getting a dog is an act of faith for me. I am accountable for the creature I bring under my roof. I assume the awesome but inspiring responsibility of guiding this animal so that it can live in our world. Acquiring a dog is awfully easy; teaching one well is hard. But the pairing of a human and a dog is a journey of two souls, a powerful act of connection in a culture where connection is often difficult. What makes our relationship unique in all the animal world is the degree to which our two species are willing, eager, to attach to each other.

There is no single best way to pair up with a dog, or to train, love, or live with one. As Merton wrote in another context, this journey is in many ways a solitary one, like walking alone in the woods after the sun has set. We can bring along a flashlight to see a few feet ahead, but the hard truth is that we mostly feel our way in the dark.

"It is by the light of reason that we interpret the signposts," wrote Merton, "and make out the landmarks along the way." My dogs and I make our way together as best we can, day after day, and there's something ritualistic, familiar, and deeply comforting in the process. In the quiet of my farm, on a summer day of intoxicating beauty or in the deep silence of a blizzard, I feel our connection very powerfully.

And there is sadness, always, just over the horizon. We are headed together on an excursion that will bring the loss of one or another of us. When I look at my dogs, I'm often conscious that none of them is likely to outlive me. All of us will come to that awful and beautiful place where our journey ends, and we will have to take our separate paths.

What a sad time that will be. These dogs and I have persevered together through so much.

I can't imagine a life without them, but standing in that assisted-living facility with Clem, looking at the longing and loving faces of the elderly people in the crowd, I could see the future. This was a room filled with dog lovers who had no dogs.

GOOD DOGS

Like almost anyone who loves dogs, I dread and fear that day, but I also accept its inevitability. It is as integral a part of living with a dog as getting a lick first thing in the morning. Seeing what's ahead deepens my resolve to spend our time together well, to earn the trust these dogs have given me, to help as best I can to share with others the many, many things they've taught me.

MY EXPERIENCE WITH TRAINING AND OTHER DOG-RELATED BOOKS HAS been spotty. I've found many good and helpful ones, yet the relationship between people and their dogs is so individual and idiosyncratic that I can't really claim that one book will supply the answers. More than almost anything, dog lovers want the perfect book to go with the perfect dog; I am asked constantly for recommendations. Alas, what works in a behaviorist's office doesn't always work in our backyards.

Yet a number of books contain interesting and useful ideas and information. I agree with some and disagree with others, but I think these few may help you learn about dogs, consider different points of view, make up your own mind, decide what's best for you and your dog.

Several books on the list will challenge you to consider yourself and your own behavior as well as your dog's. That's good advice when it comes to living with dogs. In the same way that every dog isn't for everybody, every book isn't for everybody. Universal theories and techniques don't always apply. Trainers and behaviorists and vets and breeders disagree all the time, about a host of things.

Having said that, I'm glad I read these books. In no particular order:

The Other End of the Leash: Why We Do What We Do Around Dogs, by Patricia B. McConnell, Ph.D. Ballantine Books.

Genetics and the Social Behavior of the Dog, by John Paul Scott and John L. Fuller. University of Chicago Press.

The Culture Clash, by Jean Donaldson. James and Kenneth Publishers.

The Art of Raising a Puppy, by the Monks of New Skete. Little, Brown and Co.

How to Be Your Dog's Best Friend, by the Monks of New Skete. Little, Brown and Co.

How Dogs Learn, by Mary R. Burch, Ph.D., and Jon S. Bailey, Ph.D. Howell Book House, Wiley Publishing.

The Handbook of Applied Dog Behavior and Training, Volume One: Adaptation and Learning, by Steven R. Lindsay. Iowa State University Press.

The Handbook of Applied Dog Behavior and Training, Volume Two: Etiology and Assessment of Behavior Problems, by Steven R. Lindsay. Iowa State University Press.

Feeling Outnumbered?: How to Manage and Enjoy Your Multi-Dog Household, by Karen B. London, Ph.D., and Patricia B. McConnell, Ph.D. Dog's Best Friend, Ltd.

The Perfect Match: A Dog Buyer's Guide, by Chris Walkowicz. Howell Book House, Wiley Publishing.

The Dog Department: James Thurber on Hounds, Scotties and Talking Poodles, edited by Michael Rosen. HarperCollins Publishers.

How Dogs Think: Understanding the Canine Mind, by Stanley Coren. Free Press.

Animals and Human Society: Changing Perspectives, edited by Aubrey Manning and James Serpell. Routledge.

The Domestic Dog: Its Evolution, Behaviour and Interactions with People, edited by James Serpell. Cambridge University Press.

Man Meets Dog, by Konrad Lorenz. Routledge Classics.

The Power of Positive Dog Training, by Pat Miller. Howell Book House, Wiley Publishing.

Pack of Two: The Intricate Bond Between People and Dogs, by Caroline Knapp. Delta.

Between Pets and People: The Importance of Animal Companionship, by Alan Beck and Aaron Katcher. Purdue University Press.

ACKNOWLEDGMENTS

I DON'T REALLY KNOW HOW TO PROPERLY ACKNOWLEDGE THE LOVE, support, and sacrifices of my wife, Paula Span. She remains unequivocally my best move in life. My life with dogs has taken us to strange places, and some of them are places only I and my dogs really wanted to go. She's come along anyway.

Thanks also to my daughter, Emma Span, whose meaning in my life is also beyond measure.

My agent, Richard Abate, has provided support and direction for my creative life. Every writer should be so lucky.

My editor, Bruce Tracy, has worked with me for nearly a decade. His instincts have shaped my work and saved me from many missteps. This is the kind of relationship that once defined publishing, to the great benefit of writers like me, and I deeply appreciate it.

Brian McLendon, my close friend, has believed in my work and fought hard for it long after others would have (and had) given up. As my publicist, he is very much responsible for the generous attention my books have received.

At Bedlam Farm, life would be unimaginable without my friend Anthony Armstrong. His friendship, courage, love, creativity, and hard work have shaped this place and made my sojourn here possible. Friendship is always a miracle, especially among men, and my friendship with Anthony is one of the great gifts of my recent years. Thanks, also, to his wife and my friend, Holly, for putting up with both of us, and to their daughter, Ida Jane.

I deeply appreciate Ray and Joanne Smith, whose journey is an inspiration on so many levels. They're always there when I need them, with love, understanding, and hard-earned wisdom.

I am grateful for the friendship of Meg and Rob Southerland and their children, Elizabeth and Hunter. It's been an honor to get to know Harold McEachron of MacClan Farms. I thank the staff at Gardenworks for providing a home away from home. I am lucky to have a friend like Becky MacLachlan.

I'm especially appreciative of Stanley Mickiewicz, a warm and gifted man whose many skills and great love of animals (and computers) have helped me through many ups and downs. There is almost nothing this man can't do, and do cheerfully and well.

I thank Jordan Lowry, for his friendship, decency, and extraordinary mucking and firewood-stacking skills. Also for his example of courage and grace in weathering hard times.

I thank the folks at Big Green Farm, especially Jane and Peter and Dean Hanks, for their support and encouragement. Pete is a gifted photographer as well as a dairy farmer. His lovely pictures, which grace this book, have brought my experiences here to life. I appreciate them, as have the many people around the country who've seen and admired them.

I am fortunate for the friendship, love, and humor of Sheila Blais and Nancy Mansson. And I thank Pat Freund for introducing me to the loving and wonderful world of donkeys.

No life with dogs is possible without good vets, and I have three great ones in Mary Menard, Whitney Pressler, and Jen Steeves, along with the hardworking and efficient staff of the Borador Animal Hospital in Salem, New York. The donkeys and the sheep owe much to the staff of the Granville Veterinary Service, especially veterinarians Kirk Ayling and Amanda Alderink. The two have spent many a cold, dark, and rainy time at Bedlam Farm in the service of my animals. I am grateful to some great dogs other than my own: Arthur, Sophie, Woody, Fly, Jack, Topsy, Toby, and the late Julius and Stanley, who opened my heart to the real meaning of loving dogs.

I'm grateful to the farmers, workers, and residents of Hebron, New York, who have been so generous in their advice, help, and friendship. I particularly thank Don and Alice Coldwell, who embody the notion of good neighbors and community. I am grateful for the hardworking plow and snow crews of Floyd Pratt's Hebron Highway Department who have kept Bedlam Farm functioning through two nasty winters. Life would be bleaker here without Marie Mulligan and Jennifer Hernandez and the Bedlam Corners Variety Store. And I acknowledge Jacob Worthington, always a friend.

I've worked with several fine trainers in recent years, but I acknowledge a particular debt to Carolyn Wilki of the Raspberry Ridge Sheep Farm in Bangor, Pennsylvania, who opened my eyes to the importance of training dogs well. I'm grateful daily to two fine breeders, Deanne Veselka of Wildblue Border Collies and Pam Leslie of Hillside Labradors.

I also owe a great deal to Tagalie Heister and Dr. Deborah Katz of the University of Kentucky, whose research and work on animal attachment have helped me greatly. And to animal ethicist James Serpell of the University of Pennsylvania veterinary school, whose writings on domestic dogs and the human-animal bond have enhanced my understanding and greatly influenced my thinking. And I appreciate the fine editing of David Plotz at Slate.com, where some of the ideas and anecdotes in this book first appeared.

Finally, I thank the thousands of vets, trainers, breeders, and dog lovers whom I have met, and who have e-mailed and written me from all over the country, sharing their wisdom, stories, and love of dogs. A number of their stories have been included here; usually I have changed their names and certain identifying details to protect their privacy.

We are a tribe, and if many of us struggle to connect to people in the real world, we have found common ground in the love of dogs.

About the Author

Jon Katz has written fourteen books—six novels and eight works of nonfiction—including *A Dog Year*, *The New Work of Dogs*, and *The Dogs of Bedlam Farm*. A two-time finalist for the National Magazine Award, he has written for *The New York Times*, *The Wall Street Journal*, *Rolling Stone*, and the *AKC Gazette*. A member of the Association of Pet Dog Trainers, he writes a column about dogs for the online magazine *Slate* and is cohost of *Dog Talk*, a monthly call-in show on Northeast Public Radio. Katz lives on Bedlam Farm in upstate New York and in northern New Jersey with his wife, Paula Span, who is a *Washington Post* contributing writer and a teacher at Columbia University, and their dogs. He can be e-mailed at jdkat3@aol.com.

ABOUT THE TYPE

This book is set in Fournier, a typeface named for Pierre Simon Fournier, the youngest son of a French printing family. He started out engraving woodblocks and large capitals, then moved on to fonts of type. In 1736 he began his own foundry and made several important contributions in the field of type design; he is said to have cut 147 alphabets of his own creation. Fournier is probably best remembered as the designer of St. Augustine Ordinaire, a face that served as the model for Monotype's Fournier, which was released in 1925.